THE BASICS

Proofreading
A Programmed Approach

Dona Orr

Boise State University
Boise, Idaho

Carol W. Henson

Clayton State College
Morrow, Georgia

H. Frances Daniels

East Carolina University
Greenville, North Carolina

SOUTH-WESTERN
CENGAGE Learning

Australia • Brazil • Japan • Korea • Mexico • Singapore • Spain • United Kingdom • United States

SOUTH-WESTERN
CENGAGE Learning

The Basics of Proofreading: A Programmed Approach, Fourth Edition
Dona Orr, Carol W. Henson, and H. Frances Daniels

VP/Editorial Director: Jack W. Calhoun

VP/Executive Publisher: Dave Shaut

Team Leader: Karen Schmohe

Acquisitions Editor: Joseph Vocca

Production Manager: Patricia Matthews Boies

Production Editor: Tim Bailey

Consulting Editor: Marianne Miller

Editorial Assistant: Stephanie L. White

Contributing Writer: Julie Roehl Coffin Educational Consultant Columbus, Ohio

Executive Marketing Manager: Carol Volz

Channel Manager: Chris McNamee

Marketing Coordinator: Lori Pegg

Production Assistant: Nancy Stamper

Compositor: Lachina Publishing Services, Cleveland, Ohio

Art Director: Tippy McIntosh

Cover Designer: Lou Ann Thesing

Manufacturing Coordinator: Kevin Kluck

Senior First Print Buyer: Doug Wilke

Credits: Cartoons on pages 7, 27, 55, 117, 160, 185, and 231 © 2001 Ted Goff. Photo on page 64 © copyright PhotoDisc, Inc. 1997-2001

For product information and technology assistance, contact us at **Cengage Learning Customer & Sales Support, 1-800-354-9706**.

For permission to use material from this text or product, submit all requests online at **www.cengage.com/permissions**. Further permissions questions can be emailed to **permissionrequest@cengage.com**.

U.S. Student Edition Package: Student Edition + CD:
ISBN-13: 978-0-538-72452-4
ISBN-10: 0-538-72452-8

U.S. Student Edition (core text only):
ISBN-13: 978-0-538-72374-9
ISBN-10: 0-538-72374-2

CD:
ISBN-13: 978-0-538-72376-3
ISBN-10: 0-538-72376-9

South-Western Cengage Learning
5191 Natorp Boulevard
Mason, OH 45040
USA

Cengage Learning products are represented in Canada by Nelson Education Ltd.

For your course and learning solutions, visit **www.cengage.com**

Printed in the United States of America
6 7 8 15 14 13

YOUR COURSE PLANNING JUST GOT EASIER!

The Basics Series is like nothing you have seen on the market today. Focused on "just the basics," each text delivers a concise, yet thorough presentation of the topic using clear-cut, relevant examples and exercises to reinforce learning.

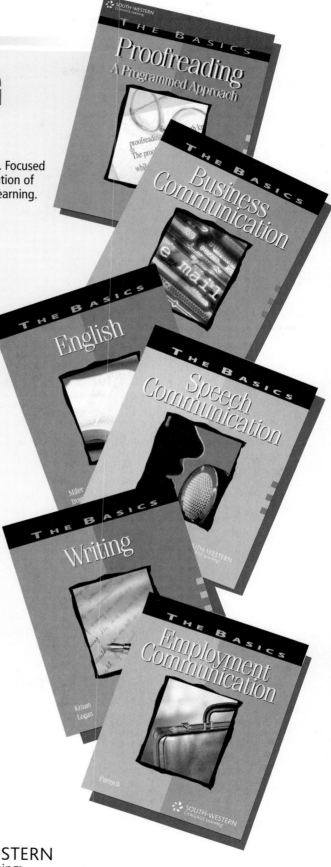

Proofreading: A Programmed Approach, 4e
by Orr, Daniels, and Henson
Student Text   0-538-72374-2
Text/CD Package   0-538-72452-8
Template CD-ROM   0-538-72376-9
<u>words@work</u> Individual User   0-538-69049-6
  CD-ROM Package

Business Communication, 2e
by Merrier
Text   0-538-72295-9

English, 2e
by Miller and Brantley
Text   0-538-72299-1

Speech Communication, 2e
by Timm
Text   0-538-72297-5

Writing, 2e
by Krizan and Logan
Text   0-538-72301-7

Employment Communication, 1e
by Parzych
Text   0-538-69028-3

Instructor support material available for all titles.

SOUTH-WESTERN
CENGAGE Learning™

Join us on the Internet at www.cengage.com/southwestern

CONTENTS

PREFACE

Business ranks communication skills high on the list of desirable qualities needed for success on the job. A person who is an effective communicator must possess good proofreading ability. *The Basics of Proofreading: A Programmed Approach*, 4th edition, provides business-related exercises that can improve proofreading ability for business or personal use.

The Basics of Proofreading may be used in a traditional classroom setting, for one-on-one tutoring, or for individualized instruction.

ORGANIZATION

The Basics of Proofreading provides a comprehensive review of rules for effective written communication. Each chapter concentrates on a specific type of error. Rules and proofreading exercises are presented in order of increasing difficulty, from simple keyboarding errors to errors in grammar, punctuation, format, and sentence construction, to editing the content of messages. Frequently misspelled words are applied in end-of-chapter exercises. Tips for strengthening proofreading skills also appear at the end of most chapters.

- Chapters 1, 2, 3, and 4 introduce you to proofreading and proofreading symbols. You learn to identify and correct keyboarding errors, abbreviation errors, and word division errors.

- Chapters 5 and 6 present rules for number expression and formats of business messages. You learn to identify and correct errors in number expression and formatting errors in letters, memorandums, e-mails, and reports.

- Chapters 7, 8, and 9 present grammar rules of agreement and words that are often confused. You learn to identify and correct errors in subject-verb agreement and in pronoun agreement. You learn the correct use of words that are often confused as well as how to choose the correct word for the context.

- Chapters 10, 11, and 12 cover the mechanics of punctuation and capitalization. You learn to identify and correct terminal and internal punctuation errors, and you apply capitalization rules.

- Chapters 13, 14, and 15 discuss editing for content, conciseness, and clarity. You learn editing practices to create direct and forceful business messages.

SPECIAL FEATURES

The Basics of Proofreading: A Programmed Approach is more than a textbook. It is a practical, results-oriented tool with the following features designed to help you develop proofreading skills:

- *Checkpoints* throughout the text challenge you to know what items to include in a message as well as why and how to include them.

- *Checkpoint solutions,* provided in the chapter margins, let you verify your understanding of one section before you begin another section.

- *Examples* clarify and reinforce chapter concepts.

- *Margin notes* help you recall key concepts taught in the chapter.

- *Anecdotes, quotations, and cartoons* add realism and humor to your study of proofreading.

- *Chapter summaries and proofreading tips* reinforce the principles covered in the chapter.

- *Spelling applications* are presented in each chapter. The spelling words are also used in the end-of-chapter applications for further reinforcement.

- *Proofreading applications,* consisting of four paragraphs or three mini-documents, apply all of the rules in the chapter.

- *Progressive proofreading jobs,* consisting of three or four realistic business documents, apply the rules covered in the chapter and selected rules from previous chapters. Solutions to these jobs are provided at the end of the text.

- *Computerized proofreading* applications provide practice proofreading, editing, formatting, and printing word-processed documents. Documents for these applications are provided separately on the template CD-ROM. Solutions to the applications that appear in the text are provided at the end of the text with the other chapter solutions. Solutions to the optional Computerized Proofreading activities appear in the Instructor's Manual.

ICONS

The Basics of Proofreading: A Programmed Approach uses icons to quickly identify some of its special features.

 The team icon identifies opportunities to work with others and sharpen your teamwork skills.

 The workplace connections icon identifies workplace success tips that reinforce the foundation skills and personal qualities employers look for when hiring.

 The Internet/e-mail icon marks activities where you may practice your online computer skills.

 The *words@work* icon alerts you to specific lessons and exercises from the *words@work* CD-ROM that correlate with each chapter. *Words@work* can be ordered separately from South-Western Cengage Learning.

TEMPLATE CD–ROM

To develop online proofreading and editing skills, document files for the Computerized Proofreading Applications are available for Windows and Mac Office 97. The template CD-ROM must be used in conjunction with these commercial word processing programs. The template CD-ROM (ISBN: 0-538-72376-9) is available separately from South-Western Cengage Learning.

THE SERIES

The Basics of Proofreading: A Programmed Approach may be used as a stand-alone resource or in conjunction with The Basics Series, a series of text-books that helps you master the communication skills needed in the workplace. The other books in the series are *The Basics of Business Communication, The Basics of English, The Basics of Writing, The Basics of Employment Communication,* and *The Basics of Speech Communication.*

ACKNOWLEDGMENTS

Thanks are extended to the following individuals for reviewing the manuscript and for offering suggestions:

Beverly Baker Crespo, Mt. San Antonio College, Walnut, CA
Evelyn L. Hall, Vance-Granville Community College, Henderson, NC
Barb Jensen, Madison Area Technical College, Portage, WI
Julie A. LaFuria, South Hills School of Business & Technology, Philipsburg, PA
Judy R. Rethmeier, Front Range Community College, Fort Collins, CO

PROOFREADING FOR QUALITY CONTROL

"As writers, we are all judged by the words we put on the page. We all want to be considered competent and careful, and writing errors work against that impression." These words, from the authors of *The New St. Martin's Handbook*, summarize the "problem," as it were. We *are* judged by what we put on paper. So what is the solution to that problem? The solution is to become adept at ensuring that what we put on the page or on the screen is our best work. To become a good proofreader is a writer's best insurance policy.

WHAT ARE PROOFREADING AND EDITING?

Proofreading is the art of finding and correcting errors in written communication. Proofreading demands concentration, patience, and attention to detail. It requires reading the document for the deliberate purpose of finding errors. The proofreader may be the originator (the creator of the document), a keyboarding specialist, a word processor, an administrative assistant, or a person designated as a proofreader.

Proofreaders use special symbols called **proofreading symbols** to indicate errors. Because proofreading symbols both identify the error and indicate how the error should be corrected, they should be used by everyone who works with the printed document. Proofreading symbols save the originator the time of writing lengthy instructions; and they enable anyone who is processing the document (keying, proofing, or editing it) to recognize the correction immediately.

To become proficient in proofreading, you must be able to recognize errors in format, content, mechanics, and references.

Document format influences the overall appearance of the document. The format should be attractive, be easy to follow, and conform to business standards. Margins, spacing, and placement and alignment of document parts all affect format.

> ### LEARNING OBJECTIVES
>
> - Define proofreading and editing.
> - Explain the importance of proofreading.
> - Explain the various methods of proofreading.

> ### WORKPLACE CONNECTIONS
>
> Most companies have established formats for letters, memos, and reports. Employees are responsible for being aware of and following those formats.

Content errors occur in facts and meaning. When proofreading for content, you should ask yourself, "Does this copy make sense? Do I understand the message?" Sentence structure, word choice, and punctuation all affect the meaning.

Proofreading for mechanical errors requires diligence in locating keyboarding errors and skill in recognizing errors in spelling, abbreviations, grammar, capitalization, punctuation, number expression, and word usage.

Proofreaders should check references for names, addresses, dates and times, figures and math, and any other unusual or technical reference as a final separate step.

In addition to being correct, an effective message should be concise and easy to understand. **Editing** is the process of making the text as clear as possible. This can include locating clichés, overused words and expressions, use of passive voice, and redundant phrases that cause the message to be wordy or unclear. Editing involves changing words or sentences or even rewriting pieces of the text.

Editing should be complete before proofreading begins.

IMPORTANCE OF PROOFREADING AND EDITING

Proofreading and editing are extremely important to anyone whose daily activities involve working with written communication. Students, managers, professionals, executives, and office personnel all strive for excellence in their communication. Why? Because a written message represents the person or firm who sends it. A document that is easy to understand, attractive, and correct creates a good impression.

A carefully prepared document makes a good impression.

Conversely, carelessness can cause a person's or a firm's reputation to suffer. The originator of a written communication that includes even one of the format, content, mechanics, or reference errors discussed in this chapter may be viewed as careless—or worse, unintelligent or uneducated. Taking the time to proofread and edit your written work will ensure that your meaning will not be lost in the message due to errors that could have been avoided.

Today's business world operates at high speed. Communications are created, produced, and transmitted by computer faster than ever before, often without the benefit of proofreading from a printed, or hard, copy. Salespeople transmit information from the field, professionals create and combine written documents, and managers forward drafts to support staff for polishing or rearranging. You may be involved in one or more of these steps. If these communications are to have value, they must be correct.

Electronic communications must be written, edited, and proofread just as carefully as paper documents.

Although the originator of the message has the ultimate responsibility for the correctness of the document, in reality, this responsibility is shared. Originators are responsible for the content of the document. Keyboarders and proofreaders strive to perfect the mechanics and appearance of a communication as well as to detect errors in content and reference.

PROOFREADING TECHNIQUES

Proofreading a document usually takes less time than rekeying it. Therefore, take the time to become a good proofreader.

Because most documents are created on computers, an originator can take a first step toward accuracy by operating the spell check function available on most word processing programs. This is not a proofreading step; this step merely saves time for the proofreader by locating common errors such as incorrect spelling and repeated words. Some word processing programs also contain a grammar check and a thesaurus. These tools can be very useful in editing, and they will be discussed in greater measure later in the text.

To achieve a high degree of accuracy, a good proofreader will use a **three-step process for proofreading** that includes reviewing the copy at least once for format, reading for content and mechanical errors, and checking references, if necessary. Checking references needs to be done when the document contains statistical information, amounts of money, or technical terms or information.

Consider the following methods of proofreading to improve your proofreading skill.

Comparative Proofreading

Comparative proofreading involves comparing the final document to the original document to be sure that the information has been keyed correctly and that copy has not been omitted. A proofreader will always use this method when a document has been revised from a draft or when there is a **source document,** which is a document containing factual material (for example, a report, a database printout, or even a business card). This method is especially important when proofreading statistical copy or tables.

To use the comparative method, place a printed copy of the final document next to the original document and compare word for word and line for line. Use a card or your index finger to point to each word. Check for each proofreading symbol on a draft to be sure the final copy was revised accordingly.

Team Proofreading

If the copy to be proofread is long, complicated, or especially important, the team method is an effective way of proofreading. Using this method, one person reads from the original copy and the other person checks the final copy. Because the time of two people is involved, team proofreading is a more costly method.

Running a spell check on your word processor does not replace proofreading.

Proofreading is a three-step process.

To compare a final document with an original document, place the two copies side by side and follow along word for word.

Team proofreading is especially useful if a document contains tables or lists of figures.

Computer Screen Proofreading

@ % & ! @

From a student paper . . .
The man walked up the stares, threw the door, and down the hall.

Proofreading from a computer screen is especially demanding but is becoming more common because of the emphasis on e-mail. Follow these tips to ensure accuracy:

1. Always begin by using the spell check function. A spell check function compares each word in the document to the software's dictionary and points out discrepancies. Although a spell check will highlight spelling errors, such as *thier* or *accomodate*, it will not recognize usage errors, such as *there advise* (their advice).

2. Proofread the document on the screen for errors such as incorrect words (*as* for *is*), omitted words, or words used improperly. Check especially for extra words that may not have been deleted when text was edited.

3. Check line endings for large gaps or for words that have been incorrectly divided. Also check for proper alignment of paragraphs and to make sure the correct number of blank lines have been placed between paragraphs and sections.

4. If possible and/or practical, print the document.

5. Proofread the printed copy using the three-step process of reviewing format, reading for content and mechanics, and checking references.

6. If you find additional errors, revise the document again.

CHAPTER SUMMARY

♦ Develop a critical attitude toward all written communication.

♦ Understand the difference between proofreading and editing.

♦ Apply principles of proofreading to ensure accuracy and to create attractive documents for business.

♦ Learn various proofreading techniques to apply to proofreading situations.

♦ Develop the habit of proofreading and the necessary skills to proofread against a hard copy and on a computer screen.

♦ Practice proofreading as a three-step process of reviewing format, reading for content and mechanics, and checking references.

♦ Remember that proofreading requires concentration and practice.

KEYBOARDING ERRORS

Communicating effectively in writing is a skill cited by employers as "vital" to an employee's success. Knowing what to say and how to say it is one thing. Putting it in writing is another. Whether the final product is an e-mail message or a company brochure, the proofreader must ensure that the work is error-free. Even "small" errors caused by keyboarding mistakes can mislead or cause confusion. Think of proofreading as a long look in the mirror after you dress in the morning. Is anything missing? Is anything in the wrong place? Do not continue with the day until everything is in order.

KEYBOARDING ERRORS OF OMISSIONS, ADDITIONS, AND MISSTROKES

Every word in the English language can be distorted by a keyboarding error, or **typo.** A typo results when a keyboard operator sees the correct form in the copy but keys it incorrectly. A misspelled word in the original copy is not a typo. Regardless of whether errors are caused by keyboarding or spelling, the proofreader has the responsibility of finding the errors.

Keyboarding errors are usually one-letter or one-digit errors. They are often in the form of omissions, additions, or misstrokes. Entire words or sentences may also be omitted, added, or replaced. Sometimes a spell check function will catch these errors; but as you will see, sometimes it will not. Chapter 2 will give you practice in identifying each of these types of errors.

2-1 A letter or character left out of a word is an omission. Sometimes a space or entire words, phrases, or lines may be missed while keying the text. Use these proofreading symbols to mark errors of omission:

∧ Insert copy.	Katie Simpson was ∧ late for the meeting.
# ∧ Insert space.	Ms. Shackleford talked to ∧# Katie about punctuality.

LEARNING OBJECTIVES

- Recognize keyboarding errors such as omissions, additions, or misstrokes.
- Identify errors in figures, enumerations, and dates.
- Identify errors in transposition.
- Use appropriate proofreading symbols to indicate changes in text.
- Spell correctly a list of commonly misspelled words.

The proofreader's job is to find errors.

Use the appropriate proofreading symbols to mark errors of omission in the following paragraph:

Proofreading is one of the most valuable skills you can acquire. Like keyboarding, however, proofreading requires patience and practice. It also requires intense concentration, attention to detail, and mastery of English skills.

2-2 Check for words, phrases, lines, or spaces that may have been repeated when the text was keyed. Look closely at the beginnings and ends of lines for repetitions of short words of two to four characters, such as *the, and, your,* and *if.* Use these proofreading symbols to mark errors of addition:

⌒ Close up space.   I can not go to school today.

ℓ Delete copy.   There is just one error in this ~~this~~ sentence.

Use the appropriate proofreading symbols to mark errors of omission and addition in the following paragraph:

Using a spell check word processing function is just the ~~the~~ beginning of the proofreading process. Do n't be fooled into thinking it is the last step; it is merely the first step.

By reading aloud, a proofreader is more likely to catch errors such as extra letters and repeated words.

2-3 Keyboarding errors frequently involve errors of omission and errors of addition of single letters, digits, words, or spaces. A missing letter or an extra letter may result in a word that *looks* correct but is not the correct word. In order to locate such errors, read each symbol or word carefully. Note the difference the omission or addition of one letter makes in these words:

bridge	bride	county	country
debit	debt	envelop	envelope
exist	exit	intestate	interstate
your	you	the	them, then, they

Use the following proofreading symbols to mark errors of omission and addition of single characters:

∧ Insert a character.   I believe that is a debt card.

ℓ Delete a character.   Your can use the card like cash.

ℓ Delete a character;   I had two debit card transactions
  close up space.   on my last statement.

2-1

however, proofreading

and

detail, mastery of

Use the appropriate proofreading symbols to mark errors of omission and addition in the following paragraph:

With word processing software, they task of changing and correcting copy has become much easier; but the responsibility for proofreading coy accurately has be come much more important. So many far-reaching decisions are made one the basis of written communication. Dire consequences can result if the information on which a decision is is made is inaccurate.

2-4 Another common error is keying incorrectly, or making a mis-stroke. Careful proofreading is required in order to find misstrokes in short words, such as those listed below:

■   of, on, or   not, now   than, that, then

Use the following symbol to mark misstrokes:

/ Change a character.   Because of your help, we will not complete the project on time.

2-2

just the the beginning

Do n't be fooled

it the last step;

Use the appropriate proofreading symbols to mark errors of misstroke in the following paragraph:

At times is is a good idea to print a document and proofread the hard copy carefully. This is especially true when the document as complex and lengthy. A proofreader should mark any errors with the proper proofreading symbols. Than the document processor can read and interpret those symbols and make the necessary changes to the document before it is printed if final form.

© 1997 Ted Goff

2-3

they task of

proofreading coy

has be come

one the basis

decision is is made

KEYBOARDING ERRORS IN FIGURES, ENUMERATIONS, AND DATES

Accuracy of figures is critical because important decisions are frequently based on figures. Amounts of money, dates, percentages, social security numbers, and telephone numbers are just a few examples of important numbers. Errors in such numbers could result in serious consequences.

Never assume that a number is correct. Always check the original document or a source document to be sure that a number has been copied correctly. Verify extensions and totals. Proofread numbers digit by digit.

2-5 When proofreading copy containing figures, always compare the keyed copy to the source document. Another good idea is to use a card or a ruler to read line by line through numerical data.

CHECKPOINT 2-5

Mark any errors in the printed list by comparing it to the correct hand-written copy.

Invoices unpaid as of April 30:

1.	Invoice 3478	$28.20
2.	Invoice 3693	$363.20
3.	Invoice 3649	$82.02
4.	Invoice 3700	$19.20
5.	Invoice 3854	$467.86
6.	Invoice 3911	$82.02

Invoices unpaid as of April 30:

1.	Invoice 3478	$28.20
2.	Invoice 3693	$363.20
3.	Invoice 3648	$82.22
4.	Invoice 3900	$19.10
5.	Invoice 3884	$467.66
6.	Invoice 3910	$82.02

2-4

At times it is

as complex

Than the

in final form.

2-6 Errors frequently occur in dates and in the sequence of enumerations (listed items), especially when items are added to or deleted from the list or the list is rearranged. Check to be sure dates and enumerated items are in the correct sequence.

CHECKPOINT 2-6

Use the appropriate proofreading symbols to mark any errors in the following paragraph:

The oldest federal constitution in existence was framed in Philadelphia in May 1787 by a convention of delegates from 13 of the 12 original states. (Rhode Island failed to send a delegate.) The states ratified the constitution in the following order:

1.	Delaware	December 7, 1787
2.	New Jersey	December 18, 1787
3.	Pennsylvania	December 12, 1787
4.	Georgia	January 2, 1788
5.	Connecticut	January 9, 1788
5.	Massachusetts	February 6, 1788
6.	Maryland	April 28, 1788

TRANSPOSITION ERRORS

One of the most common keyboarding errors is the transposition error. Letters, numbers, words, or sentences keyed in the wrong sequence are called **transpositions.** Use the following symbol to mark transposition errors:

∿ Transpose letters, numbers, or words.

These letters must be transposed.

There were 31 original colonies.

The speaker began to rapidly talk.

2-5

3. Invoice 3643 $82.22

4. Invoice 3700 $19.70

5. Invoice 3854 $467.86

6. Invoice 3910 $82.02

2-7 Short words (*hte*), word endings (*medcial*), and vowels (*thier*) are especially susceptible to transposition. These words are often caught during a routine spell check on your word processor. However, other transpositions can be difficult to detect when proofreading since a transposition error can result in a word that is familiar but does not make sense when used in place of the original term. Observe how the transposition errors are marked in these sentences:

Geometry is the study of points, lines, angels, surfaces, and solids.

Larry received a letter form Fujio.

Karate, judo, and jujitsu are examples of marital arts.

CHECKPOINT 2-7

Proofread the following paragraph for transposition errors. Use the transposition symbol to mark your corrections.

Continued sue of electronic workstations can induce eyestrain, stress, and mucsular pain. Consideration must be to given purchasing adjustable furniture and to providing workstations with movable keyboards and adjustable displays. Employee productivity, health, nad job satisfaction are at stake.

ROUGH DRAFT APPLICATIONS

The originator may use certain proofreading symbols to revise text. Keyboard operators should learn to recognize and understand the following symbols in order to key and proofread text accurately:

Move copy as indicated.

Paul designed the new office with several ergonomic features in Kenwood Plaza.

stet or . . .   Ignore correction; let it stand.

$25 for the preparation of 100 letters

Change copy as indicated.

advance notice *prior* before to the public sale

2-8 Note the use of these symbols in the following paragraph and the manner in which the revisions were made in the second paragraph.

2-7

Correspondence can be expensive ~~even without counting the originator's time~~ *stet*. Fast Copy Service charged us $25 for the preparation of 100 letters and envelopes. Additionally, a part-time employee was paid $8 an hour for folding the letters and stuffing the envelopes. They charged us $18.25 for the stationery and the envelopes. By the time we had paid $34 for postage, *this* ~~one~~ mailing had cost us $85.25.

isue
muscular pain.
be to given
bad job

Correspondence can be expensive even without counting the originator's time. Fast Copy Service charged us $25 for the preparation of 100 letters and envelopes. They charged us $18.25 for the stationery and the envelopes. Additionally, a part-time employee was paid $8 an hour for folding the letters and stuffing the envelopes. By the time we had paid $34 for postage, this mailing had cost us $85.25.

CHECKPOINT 2-8

Did the typist make all the necessary changes?

Yes

Spelling—it is basic. For the proofreader—it is critical. If you have trouble spelling, remember these tips:

1. Develop the *habit* of always spelling correctly.
2. Check a dictionary whenever you are not positive a word is spelled correctly.
3. Pronounce words slowly to be sure you are not missing any syllables. (The word is *mathematics*, not *mathmatics*; *February*, not *Febuary*.)

2-9 Compare the words in Column A with the corresponding words in Column B. Use the appropriate proofreading symbols to correct the misspelled words. If both columns are correct, write **C** to the left of the number.

2-8

Yes

		Column A	Column B
	1.	annalize	analyze
C	2.	brochure	brochure
	3.	committment	commitment
C	4.	congratulations	congratulations
	5.	consensus	concensus
C	6.	familiar	familiar
	7.	integrall	integral
	8.	knowledgable	knowledgeable
	9.	persuade	pursuade
	10.	procedure	precedure

CHAPTER SUMMARY

Proofread carefully for the following kinds of keyboarding errors:

♦ Omission of letters or characters in words

♦ Omission of a space or words, phrases, or lines of text

♦ Repetition of short words (such as *the, and, you,* and *if*) at the beginnings and ends of lines

♦ Omissions or additions of single letters, digits, words, or spaces

♦ Misstrokes, particularly at the ends of words

♦ Errors involving numerical data

♦ Sequences of dates and enumerations

♦ Transpositions of letters, numbers, words, or sentences

Study the following proofreading tips, and apply them as you proofread:

♦ When proofreading the work of others, do not assume the original draft is error-free. Originators often concentrate more on the content of the document than they do on its mechanics.

♦ Compare the final keyed copy word for word with the draft copy to ensure no words or lines were omitted and no proofreading symbols (such as move or delete copy) were overlooked.

♦ As a separate step, verify the final portion of copy that contains figures or enumerations, comparing the figures to the source document.

words@work Open *words@work.* Click on the Grammar and Usage tab; then click on Lessons. Use the lesson on Editing, Proofreading, and Spelling and the appropriate *words@work* exercises to reinforce what you learned about the use of proofreading symbols in this chapter.

PROOFREADING APPLICATIONS

1. an~~n~~alize *y*
2. C
3. commit~~t~~ment *o*
4. C
5. con~~c~~ensus *s*
6. C
7. integra~~l~~ *or*
8. knowledgable *e*
9. p~~u~~rsuade *e*
10. pr~~e~~cedure *o*

Proofread the following exercises for keyboarding and spelling errors. To aid you, the number of errors is indicated in parentheses at the end of Exercises P-1 and P-2. You must find the errors on your own in Exercise P-3.

P–1 Is the ability to sell a knack that one is born with, or it is a skill that is learned as a result ~~as a result~~ of committment and practice?Steven Taback, president of Taback Associates, says, "Selling is basically a series of strategies that turn leads into prospects and prospects in to customers." That may sound easy, but selling effectively is a matter of learning these strategies and than having the confidence to put them to use.

(6 errors)

P-1

1. it is
2. as a result ~~as a result~~
3. commit~~t~~ment
4. practice?Steven
5. in to customers."
6. and th~~a~~n having *e*

P–2 People are persuaded to buy a product because the feel a real or perceived need for it. This need is often linked to ~~to~~ achievement, recognition, or money. To pursuade, therefore, the seller must analyze the buyer to become knowledgable or familiar with person's primary need. For example, is the person concerned about prestige, comfort, convenience, or savings? Having identified the buyer's primary, the seller can convert the features of the product into benefits fore the buyer.

(7 errors)

P-3 Proofread the printed memo by comparing it to the original handwritten copy. Assume that the handwritten copy is correct.

TO: Western Division Sales Staff

FROM: Ann Barnes, Sales Manager

DATE: January 6, 20--

SUBJECT: February 14 Lecture

The third lecture in our Fitness, Health, and Nutrition series will be held on Tuesday, Febuary 14, at 2 p.m. in the Noble conference room. Dr. Donald B. Fowlkes will be the speaker. Mr. Fowlkes is a nationally-known speak He is and expert on the topic of stress and, in particular, how stress affects sales professionals. The title of his lecture is "Managing Stress for the Sales Professional." I look forward to seeing all of you at this informative session. Dr. Fowlkes will include a question-and-answer session at the end at the end of his discussion.

P-2
1. because the
2. linked to to
3. To pursuade,
4. knowledgable
5. with person's
6. primary, the
7. benefits fore the

Memo to the Western Division Sales Staff, January 6

The third lecture in our Fitness, Health, and Nutrition series will be held on Tuesday, February 14, at 2 p.m. in the Noble conference room. Dr. Donald B. Fowlkes will be the speaker. Dr. Fowlkes is a nationally known speaker. He is an expert on the topic of stress and, in particular, how stress affects the lives of sales professionals. The title of his lecture is "Managing Stress for the Sales Professional." Dr. Fowlkes will include a question-and-answer session at the end of his discussion. I look forward to seeing all of you at this informative session.

Anne Barnes, Sales Manager

P-3
1. Ann Barnes,
2. Tuesday, Febuary
3. Mr. Fowlkes is
4. nationally known speaker
5. He is and expert
6. stress affects the lives of sales
7. move copy (last two sentences)
8. at the end at the end of his discussion.

Job 1 Use the appropriate proofreading symbols to mark errors of omission, addition, or misstroke in the following letter.

Minneapolis Financial Corp.
928 Irving Avenue S
Minneapolis, MN 55403-7640
Phone (800) 555-0100
Fax (612) 555-0101
minneapolisfinancial.com

January 16, 20--

Dear Friend and Financial Member

We would like to take this opportunity to thank you for your business last year. We were pleased your chose our company to provide solid financial services and advice to you. Our goal is to make our members completely satisfied with the services and products they receive from Minneapolis Corp.

We are looking forward to a continued relationship with you in the coming year. The new changes in tax laws will affect how we manage our financial products. Our financial consultants are fully trained in the new laws and are ready to meet with you you individually or speak with you by phone to answer your questions and annalyze your financial needs.

Again this spring we will be offering several "Spring into Action" seminars in the Minneapollis area to help you better understand the products that could be of benefit to you. You will soon receive a brochur with an early noticed and invitation to attend. Only after our valued members have the first opportunity to register will we publicize the seminars and open then to the public. We hope you will be able to join us.

To make contacting our financial consultants easier, we have expanded our customer service lines. Please call our toll-free number to speak to a financial consult. We are here to serve you any day of the week from 10 p.m. to 8 a.m. You may also contract your financial consultant at any time by e-mail through a link at our web site at any time. As always, our commitment is to you, our valued member.

Sincerely yours

Craig Mason
Vice President, Member Services

Job 2
Proofread the purchase order by comparing it to the partial price list. Verify all prices on the order, the total, and the following information: To **MINNEAPOLIS FINANCIAL CORP., 928 Irving Avenue S, Minneapolis, MN 55403-7640**; Date **12/29/20--**; Purchase Order No. **4PS285710**; Terms **2/10, n/30**; Shipped Via **CNC Lines**; Date Shipped **12/30/20--**.

BRENTWOOD COMPUTER CENTER
213 Rainbow Circle
Camden, NJ 08101-7650

PURCHASE ORDER

MINNEAPOLIS FINANCIAL CORP.
928 Irving Avenue S
Minneapolis, MN 55403-7640

Purchase Order No.: 4PS287510
Date: December 29, 20--
Date Shipped: December 29, 20--
Terms: 2/10, n/30
Shipped Via: CNC Lines

Quantity	Description/Stock No.	Unit Price	Total
3	Conversion Software, ASV1	$ 62.00	$ 186.00
3	Spelling Verification Pkg., 235	175.00	425.00
1	Memory Expansion Board, 183M	345.45	345.45
1	Scanner, KC833	7,500.00	7,500.00
1	Sheet Feeder, 21TC	125.00	125.00
			$8,591.45

PRICE LIST

Stock No.	Description	Unit Price
ASC1	Conversion Software	$ 62.00
TCC	Formatted Standalone Tape Drive	6,260.00
C230	Ink Jet Printer (Color)	1,360.10
LM2616	Laser Printer	3,626.00
183M	Memory Expansion Board	345.65
KC830	Scanner	7,500.00
TC21	Sheet Feeder	125.00
23S	Spelling Verification Package	175.00
XPV	Terminal Font, PCO9G	55.00

Job 3 Proofread the file cards on the following page by comparing them to the information contained in the printout below. Using the appropriate proofreading symbols, mark any errors you find on the cards. Check the identification numbers and the telephone numbers carefully.

NAME/IDENTIFICATION NO.	STREET ADDRESS	CITY, STATE, ZIP	TELEPHONE
MRS DOROTHY BRANDON	102 FLETCHER PLACE	GREENVILLE NC 27834-5645	252-555-0188
255-58-6624			
MS GRACE L MORAN	106 BRINKLEY ROAD	DRY FORK VA 24549-5492	804-555-0145
277-76-8283			
MISS BRENDA D ACEVEZ	PO BOX 3066	DAVENPORT VA 24239-4392	540-555-0150
245-34-5868			
MR JERRIE BIDDINGER	308 CIRCLE DRIVE	CRYSTAL HILL VA 24539-4308	804-555-0134
246-66-7790			
MR JOHN C ASLAKSON	93 QUAIL RIDGE DRIVE	BRISTOL VA 24201-4019	540-555-0102
266-87-9963			
MR PAT STALLINGS	PO BOX 1901	PINETOPS NC 27864-0381	252-555-0169
249-76-8888			
MR HENRY STINDT	ROUTE 2 BOX 301	FRANKLIN VA 23851-7787	757-555-0171
258-68-8987			

Stindt Henry Mr ✓

Mr. Henry Stindt
Route 2, Box 301
Franklin, VA 23851-7787
Phone 757-555-0171
(258-68-8987)

Stallings Pat Mr

Mr. Pat Stallings
P.O. Box 1901
Pinetops, NC 27864-0381
Phone 252-555-0169
(224-76-8888)
49

Moran Grace L Ms

Ms. Grace L. Moran
106 Brinkly Road
Dry Forks, VA 24549-5492
Phone 804-555-0145
(277-76-8823)

Brandon Dorothy Mrs

Mrs. Dorothy Brandon
102 Fletcher Place
Greeneville, NC 27834-5645
Phone 252-555-0188
(255-58-6624)

Biddinger Jerrie Mr

Mr. Jerrie Biddinger
308 Circle Drive
Crystal Hill, VA 24539-4308
Phone 804-555-0134
(246-7790)

Aslakson John C Mr

Mr. John C. Alaskson
93 Quail Ridge Drive
Bristol, VA 24211-4019
Phone 540-555-0102
(266-87-9963)

Acevez Brenda D Miss

Miss Brenda D. Acevez
P.O. Box 3066
Davenport, VA 24239-4392
Phone 555-0150
(245-34-5868)

COMPUTERIZED PROOFREADING

Job 4 Proofread and edit a page from an employee manual.

1. Load the file C02JOB4 from the template CD-ROM. The file was keyed from the following handwritten draft. The page is from an employee manual.

2. Proofread the page on the CD-ROM against the rough draft below. Make sure any errors in the handwritten copy have been corrected. Spell check the document. Check all figures carefully.

3. Set 1″ side margins. Save the page as C02JOB4R.

4. Print the page.

5. Proofread the printed document. If you find additional mistakes, revise, save, and reprint the page.

Minneapolis Financial Corp. 401(k) Plan

The following is an example of the benefits that may be achieved for the plan year for a single employee with a salary of $20,000 (based on estimated 20 — tax rates).

Contributions	Amount
Employee salary deferral (5%)	$1,000
Employer matching contribution (25% of first 4% deferred)	200
Employer basic contribution (3%)	600
Total benefits	$1,800

	Tax Savings
Federal taxes (19% of salary deferral)	$190
State taxes (4%)	40
Tax savings to employee	$230
Net out-of-pocket cost	$770 *

* for a $1,000 salary deferral

The use of abbreviations is on the rise. This is especially true within certain industries. Workers who are immersed in their own "language" of abbreviations cope quite well. Those of us who do not know the language can easily get lost.

Abbreviations are supposed to make things easier for us. We use them when space is tight. We also use them to avoid spelling out words or phrases that would be awkward or cumbersome, such as *Doctor of Philosophy* for *Ph.D.* Keep in mind that abbreviations are useful only when your audience recognizes and understands them.

ABBREVIATIONS

Abbreviations are shortened forms of words or phrases used to save time and space. Although abbreviations are not suitable for all business communication, they are generally used in business forms, catalogs, tables, notes, and bibliographies. Use abbreviations sparingly when a more formal style is desired, as in correspondence or reports. Abbreviations that are pronounced by the initials are called **initialisms,** such as *CD* for compact disc. Abbreviations that are pronounced as words are called **acronyms,** such as *ZIP,* as in ZIP Code for Zone Improvement Plan.

Debate still exists as to whether periods should be used in various abbreviations. The trend is toward eliminating periods, especially when the elements are capitalized (NATO, IBM). Do not eliminate periods in abbreviations that could be mistaken for words in themselves, such as *c.o.d.* Although you will find variations in the use of periods, spacing, and capitalization of abbreviations, be consistent within a document. Additionally, how an abbreviation is pronounced determines whether to precede it with the word *a* or *an.*

If a reader may not be familiar with an abbreviation, create a **defined term** in a document by spelling out the abbreviation the first time it is used followed by the abbreviation in parentheses.

Space once after the final period of an abbreviation. Do not space after a period within an abbreviation (*a.m.*), and do not repeat the period if the abbreviation falls at the end of a sentence (*Call me at 6 p.m.*). In addition, be careful to use correct capitalization for abbreviations; initialisms and acronyms generally are written in all capital letters.

> ## LEARNING OBJECTIVES
>
> - Apply rules of abbreviation correctly.
> - Use appropriate proofreading symbols to indicate changes in text.
> - Spell correctly a list of commonly misspelled words.

> Use abbreviations, initialisms, and acronyms consistently within a document.

When you note errors in the form or use of abbreviations, use the following proofreading symbols to mark your corrections:

⟨sp⟩ Spell out.

⟨sp⟩ (Adm.) Walker will join us for dinner at 7 p.m.

⊙ Insert a period.

Ms⊙ Jarvis will be present for the briefing.

Delete the period; close up space.

Is there an F/D/R/ Memorial?

3-1 Personal names.

Spell out first names unless you have a source document that indicates a person's preference for the abbreviated style. When using abbreviations in names, each initial is followed by a period and a space. When using initials only, you may omit the periods and spaces. Do not set off the terms *Jr.*, *Sr.*, *2d*, or *III* with a comma unless you know it is the person's preference.

WORKPLACE CONNECTIONS

Using names, titles, and forms of address correctly shows respect for authority as well as for colleagues, clients, and other workplace contacts.

William (*not* Wm.) Taft	George (*not* Geo.) Prechtel
F. Scott Fitzgerald	W. E. B. DuBois
Franklin D. Roosevelt *or*	FDR
Desmond Calhoun Sr.	Michael D. Hause, II (if preferred)

3-2 Titles with names.

Always abbreviate these courtesy titles when they are used with full names or last names only.

Personal titles are always abbreviated.

Mr.	*or*	Messrs. (plural form of Mr.)
Mrs.	*or*	Mmes. (plural form of Mrs.)
Ms.	*or*	Mses or Mss. (plural forms of Ms.)
Dr.	*or*	Drs. (plural form of Dr.)

Note: The title *Miss* (and plural form *Misses*) is not an abbreviation. Other titles that appear before a name should be spelled out. Titles appearing before a name, as well as titles after a name in an inside address, are capitalized.

Governor Dirk Kempthorne

Professor Laurel Traynowicz

Mrs. Jody Feamer, vice president, will host the conference.

Mrs. Jody Feamer, Vice President
CNP Trucking Company
681 Van Ness Street
San Francisco, CA 94109-7681

Abbreviate academic degrees and professional designations after names. Also, abbreviate academic degrees that stand alone. Each abbreviated letter of an academic degree is followed by a period; professional designations may or may not contain periods. Do not use the personal titles *Dr.*, *Mr.*, *Mrs.*, *Ms.*, or *Miss* before a name that is followed by a designation. However, you may use another title before a name if that title does not reflect the degree or designation that follows.

Abbreviations for academic degrees *do* contain periods. Many professional designations do *not* contain periods.

> Vera McCrink, Ed.D.   her B.A. degree
>
> Larry Waldorf, Ph.D. (*not* Dr. Larry Waldorf, Ph.D.)
>
> Mr. Antonio Pappas, CPS

CHECKPOINT 3-1, 3-2

Use the appropriate proofreading symbols to mark abbreviation errors in the following paragraph:

President Fred R. Eakin Jr. announced a $1.3 million gift to the university from the estate of the late Prof. Thom. Waters. Prof. Waters' daughter, Dr. Molly R. Aim, Ph.D., presented the check to Pres. Eakin at a news conference.

3–3 **Agency and government names.** The names of well-known government agencies, business organizations, associations, unions, and other groups are often abbreviated. These abbreviations are usually written in all capital letters without periods.

3-1, 3-2

Prof. Thom Waters.

Prof. Waters' daughter,

~~Dr.~~ Molly R. Aim, Ph.D.

or

Dr. Molly R. Aim, ~~Ph.D.~~

Pres. Eakin

> AAA   CBS   NAACP   C-SPAN
>
> AFL-CIO   FBI   NFL   IRS

Company names often contain abbreviations such as *Co.*, *Corp.*, *Inc.*, or *Ltd.*; these terms may or may not follow a comma after the company's name. Check a source document for the company's preference.

> Computers-R-Us, Ltd.   Ace Widget Mfrs.

Names of countries, governments, and geographic locations are generally spelled out in text. If abbreviated, the initials are followed with periods. Spell or abbreviate the name *United States* according to its usage. When used as part of an agency name or as an adjective, abbreviate the name to *U.S.* (except in formal usage) or include it in an initialism. When used as a noun, spell out *United States*.

> P.R.C. (People's Republic of China)
>
> U.K. (United Kingdom)
>
> U.S. Department of Agriculture   *or*   USDA
>
> The U.S. government (*used as an adjective*) supports tourism in the United States (*used as a noun*).

Use the appropriate proofreading symbols to mark abbreviation errors in the following paragraph:

We saw a news report on CNN that stated American Service Parts, Inc., has recently given a million dollar donation to the N.A.A.C.P. The report stated the money is earmarked for scholarships for students studying manufacturing technology at any two- or four-year college in the U.S., Great Britain, or the P.R.C.

3-3
N.A.A.C.P.
in the U.S.,
or the P.R.C.

3-4 Time designations. Common time designations, such as *A.D.*, *B.C.*, *a.m.*, and *p.m.*, are usually abbreviated. Standard time zones and daylight saving time zones are also abbreviated with all capital letters and no periods.

> EST (eastern standard time)
>
> PDT (pacific daylight time)

Days of the week and months of the year should not be abbreviated except in tables, when space is limited, or in business forms.

> Wednesday, December 12   *or*   Wed., Dec. 12

3-5 Addresses and place names. Street addresses are spelled out in text and inside addresses. Compass directions before the street name are spelled out, but those appearing after the street name are abbreviated. Generally, do not abbreviate words in place names such as *Fort*, *Mount*, or *Point*; however, do abbreviate *Saint* in U.S. place names.

> 2115 Hudson Avenue
>
> 826 North Parkway Boulevard
>
> 4600 South Hamilton Street, NW
>
> Mount Ranier is near Seattle, not St. Louis.

Spell out words in street addresses in text and in inside addresses. In lists, tables, or envelopes, you may use abbreviations.

For inside addresses, you may use the two-letter state abbreviation. In all other instances, either spell out the state name or use the standard abbreviation. A list of the state, district, and territory abbreviations appears in the Appendix. Always check these abbreviations carefully in letter addresses and on envelopes.

Use the appropriate proofreading symbols to mark abbreviation errors in the following letter:

Aug. 12, 20--

Ms. Teresa Harbacheck
3851 S. Oak St.
Rapid City, S.D. 57702-5006

Dear Ms. Harbacheck

We have rescheduled your interview for Wed., Sept. 14, at 2 p.m. E.S.T. by conference call. All other information about the interview, as stated in our correspondence to you dated July 28, remains the same. We look forward to speaking with you.

Sincerely yours

3-6 **Weights and measurements.** Weights and measurements are spelled out in text but may be abbreviated in technical writing and on business forms. Abbreviated units of measure do not contain periods unless not using a period may cause confusion. Additionally, the singular and plural forms are written the same way.

In Text	Abbreviated
8 1/2 by 11 inches	8 1/2 × 11 in *or* 8½" × 11"
9- by 12-foot room	9 × 12 ft room *or* 9' × 12' room
20 pounds of nails	20 lb of nails

3-7 **Shortened word forms.** Some commonly used business terms are shortened word forms that appear to be abbreviations. Learn to recognize these terms and the words they stand for, but do not use a period as you would with a regular abbreviation.

memo (memorandum)   fax (facsimile)

exam (examination)   typo (typographical error)

cell phone (cellular phone)   condo (condominium)

3-8 **Symbols.** In general, spell out symbols in text, such as the word *percent*. When using symbols in tables or forms, be sure to space correctly. Leave a space before and after these symbols: **@, &,** and **=.** However, do not leave spaces when **&** appears in an abbreviation with all caps, such as *AT&T.* Do not leave a space between figures and these symbols: **%, °, ¢,** and **#**; for example, *6%, 98°, 10¢, 12#.*

3-4, 3-5

Aug. 12, 20--

3851 S. Oak St

Rapid City, S.D.

Wed., Sept. 14,

2 p.m. E.S.T.

Spell out words such as *percent* and *pounds* in text rather than using abbreviations or symbols.

Use the appropriate proofreading symbols to mark abbreviation errors in the following paragraph:

To: Ashley Barrett

From: Jane Smyth

Date: April 4, 20--

Subject: Urgent Paper Order

Please order 100 reams of 20-lb 8 1/2- by 14-in. copy paper and 10 reams of 30-pound 8 1/2- by 14-inch cover stock. The prefab lab needs the paper right away, so send the order by facsimile or electronic mail. Give the supplier all the info it needs to have the order shipped by overnight delivery, and ask for our usual 15% discount. Thanks.

#@%&!@#

E-mail, with its tendency toward informality, is spawning the use of initialisms. Their misuse, though, is evident in this e-mail message. Can you translate?

BTW the EOM report shows us four days ahead of schedule. IMO we'll lose that time in the next phase. OTOH Cal West says his team is ready, so maybe I'm wrong. I'll let you know about ordering those supplies ASAP.

3-6—3-8

100 reams of 20 lb

8 1/2- by 14 in. copy

fax
~~facsimile~~ or

~~electronic~~ e-mail.

15% discount

3-9   Punctuation, spacing, and capitalization with abbreviations.

As this chapter has demonstrated, some abbreviations contain periods and some do not. Most abbreviations made up of lowercase letters contain periods and no spaces.

> a.m.   p.m.   f.o.b.   i.e.   e.g.   a.k.a.

When an abbreviation consists of two or more words and one of the words contains more than a single-character abbreviation, leave a space between them.

> N. Dak.   Lt. Gov.   cu cm

As previously stated, if an abbreviation falls at the end of a sentence, do not repeat the period if the sentence ends in a period. If the sentence ends with a termination punctuation mark other than a period, place that mark after the period used in the abbreviation.

> The conference call has been set for 3 a.m.
>
> Did you mean to set the conference call for 3 p.m.?

Abbreviations usually carry the same capitalization style as the words for which they stand. When in doubt, be sure to check a dictionary.

Chapter 3: Abbreviation Errors

3-10 Compare the words in Column A with the corresponding words in Column B. Use the appropriate proofreading symbols to correct the misspelled words. If both columns are correct, write **C** to the left of the number.

		Column A	Column B
	1.	accidentally	accidently
C	2.	annual	annual
	3.	compatable	compatible
	4.	competitive	competative
	5.	developement	development
	6.	grammar	grammer
C	7.	representative	representative
	8.	sponsered	sponsored
	9.	surprise	surprize
C	10.	therefore	therefore

© 1999 Ted Goff

YOUR PRINT JOB CONTAINS 562 SPELLING ERRORS AND IS REALLY BORING. PRINT ANYWAY?

CHAPTER SUMMARY

Check closely to be sure your documents follow these abbreviation rules:

♦ Spell out personal names, or follow a person's individual preference.

♦ Abbreviate courtesy titles, academic degrees, or professional designations when used with individual names; spell out other titles.

♦ Abbreviate well-known government agencies, business organizations, associations, and unions; abbreviate the titles that often follow company names, such as *Inc.*

♦ Abbreviate time designations and time zones.

♦ Spell out street addresses and compass directions before a street name; abbreviate compass directions that follow a street name.

♦ Spell out weights and measures in text.

♦ Use shortened word forms correctly.

♦ Spell out symbols in text.

♦ Follow correct punctuation, spacing, and capitalization rules with abbreviations.

Study the following proofreading tips, and apply them as you proofread:

♦ Create defined terms in documents by spelling out the abbreviation the first time it is used followed by the abbreviation in parentheses.

♦ Whenever possible, find a source document for individual and company names that shows not only the correct spelling but also any preference for abbreviations and/or commas.

♦ Although two forms of an abbreviation may be correct, use only one throughout the same document.

♦ Check the spellings of cities and the abbreviations for states in all addresses.

words@work Open *words@work*. Go to the Index tab, and click on *abbreviations*. Review the two-page lesson on abbreviations.

PROOFREADING APPLICATIONS

Individually or with a classmate, proofread the following correspondence and itinerary using the appropriate proofreading symbols to mark errors you find in spelling and abbreviations. To aid you in proofreading, the number of errors to be found is indicated in parentheses for Exercises P-1 and P-2; however, you must find the errors on your own in P-3.

P-1

January 28, 20--

Mrs. Gretchen K. Sorensen
Customer Service Mgr.
ICM, Inc.
1020 E. First Street
Butte, MT 59702-4125

Dear Mrs. Sorensen

Would you like to have one of your representatives present your acctg. software to the eight members of our software purchasing committee? Either Feb. 28 or March 14 will fit our schedule.

Please let me know if either of these dates is compatable with your schedule.

Sincerely yours

(6 errors)

P-2

TO: Department Heads

FROM: Andrea Zoeller

DATE: February 12, 20--

SUBJECT: ICM Software Demonstration

A I.C.M. software demonstration is scheduled for Tues., March 14, at 9 a.m. in Conference Rm. B-101 by our representative Geo. Armstrong Sr. He will demonstrate four software packages under developement for our company.

Please review the specs for the software your department needs before you attend this demonstration. Mr. Armstrong should be able to address your questions or concerns.

(7 errors)

3-10
1. accidently — *al*
2. C
3. compatable — *i*
4. competative — *i*
5. developement — *g*
6. grammer — *a*
7. C
8. sponsered — *o*
9. surprize — *s*
10. C

P-1
1. Mrs. Gretchen
2. Customer Service Mgr. — *sp*
3. 1020 E. First Street — *sp*
4. your acctg. software — *sp*
5. Either Feb. 28 or — *sp*
6. compatable — *i*

P-2

1-2. A I.C.M. software

3. Tues., March 14,

4. Conference Rm.

 B-101

5. Geo. Armstrong Sr.

6. under

 development

7. Mr. Armstrong

 should

WORKPLACE CONNECTIONS

Accurate, clear communication is critical in the workplace, especially when dealing with schedules, such as travel itineraries and meeting agendas.

P-3

1. 6 a.m. (M.S.T.)

2-3. 10:15 am. (C.S.T.)

4. Appt. with Candace

5. in Exec. Suite 10,

6. Arr. Helena

 Municipal

ITINERARY
for
Van K. McLaurin II

Helena – Chicago   April 27, 20--

6 a.m. (M.S.T.)   Depart Helena Municipal Airport
Western Airlines Flight 428

10:15 am. (C.S.T.)   Arrive O'Hare Airport, Chicago

12 noon   Lunch with Tony Dattilo, sales manager, in Alfredo's Restaurant at the airport

2 p.m.   Appt. with Candace McKenzie, president, Pacific Foods, in Exec. Suite 10, Western Airlines Terminal

3 p.m.   Tour of Pacific Foods facilities, located at 7204 South Kennedy Avenue

6:15 p.m.   Depart O'Hare
Western Airlines Flight 187

8:30 p.m.   Arr. Helena Municipal Airport

PROGRESSIVE PROOFREADING

You are an office assistant in a software training school. One of your responsibilities is to proofread the materials that are produced to ensure that they are accurate. Four jobs have been given to you for proofreading. Using the proofreading symbols that you have learned, mark all errors.

Software Success Learning Center

INCORPORATING TECHNOLOGY INTO THE CLASSROOM SUMMER SESSIONS FOR K-12 EDUCATORS

Software Success Learning Center (SSLC) is offering summer sessions that present the latest information and ideas about technology to educators. Conveniently held during June, July, and Aug., our classes are offered in three-week sessions designed to meet your scheduling and instructional needs. All SSLC courses are offered in our computer labs where hands-on training takes place.

Courses	Sessions Offered
Fundamentals of Classroom Tech.	1B, 1C, and 2A
Incorporating Word Processing into Classroom Curriculum	1B, 2A, 2C, and 3A
Using Writing and Grammer Software	2A and 3C
The Internet for K-12 Educ.	1C, 2C, and 3C
Development of Online Projects for Secondary Students	2A & 2B
Beginning Web Pages for Educators	2B
Beginning Desktop Publishing for Educators	1A, 2A, and 2B
Advanced Desktop Publishing for Educators	2B, 3A, 3B, and 3C

	Schedule of Sessions			
1	First three-week session	June 4-22	Mon.-Friday	A	9 a.m. – noon
2	Second three-week session	July 9-27	Mon.-Friday	B	1 p.m. – 4 p.m.
3	Third three-week session	Aug. 6-24	Mon.-Friday	C	6 p.m. – 9 p.m.

Faculty

Prof. Paul Uhr Senior, M.B.A.
Miss Lillie Taylor, CPS, Office Manager, Quadrangle Products, Inc.
Dr. William R. Joyner, Ph.D., Information Sciences Dept., State College of Tech.
Ms. Wanda Masterson, MOUS Certified Instructor

Registration is limited to 25 per classroom; enrollment is accepted until classes are full. All classes are $199 each; register for two or more classes and receive a 10% discount on each class.

Job 2 Printed on the next page is a partial list of previous customers who will be sent the flyer about the summer sessions. Check for keying errors in the printed list by comparing it carefully with the handwritten list below. Check the printed addresses carefully for proper use of abbreviations. Do not assume the abbreviations are listed correctly on the handwritten list.

Customer Names and Addresses

1. Ms. Carmen Alvarez
    4012 Exeter Drive, NE
    Rocky Mount, NC 27801-4439

2. Mr. Davidson Tyler
    1518 Bennett St.
    Washington, NC 27889-6902

3. Mrs. Charles Varlashkin
    P.O. Box 30561
    New Bern, NC 28560-5713

4. Mr. D.L. Pate Sr.
    217-B North Meade Street
    Greenville, NC 27834-4209

5. Dr. Jacqueline Harris
    470 Shoreline Ave.
    Elizabeth City, NC 27909-8261

6. Mr. Christoper Churchill
    1036 Dogwood Trail
    Greenville, NC 27835-3479

7. Mr. Kevin Curran
    8941 Graystone Lane
    Pinetops, NC 27864-2297

8. Miss Susan Haines
    235 Windsor Blvd.
    Greenville, NC 27834-6140

9. Mr. Jim Gothard
    602 Fairview Drive
    Wilson, NC 27893-4230

10. Miss Kara Herndon
    2018 Garrett Avenue
    Farmville, NC 27828-9817

11. Mrs. Valerie Beckman
    301-C Westbrook Apartments
    105 S. 11th Street
    Goldsboro, NC 27530-6346

12. Mr. Seth Jackson
    1442 18th Street, S.E.
    Jacksonville, N.C. 28540-7294

	Name	Address	City	St	ZIP
1	Ms. Carmen Alvarez	4012 Exeter Drive, N.E.	Rocky Mount	NC	27801-4439
2	Mr. David Tyler	1518 Bennett Street	Washington	NC	27889-6902
3	Mrs. Charles Varlashkin	P.O. Box 30651	New Bern	NC	28560-5713
4	Mr. D.L. Pate Sr.	217-B North Meade Street	Greenville	NC	27834-4209
5	Dr. Jacqueline Harris	470 Shoreline Drive	Elizabeth City	NC	27909-8261
6	Mr. Christopher Churchill	1036 Dogwood Trial	Greenville	NC	27835-3479
7	Mr. Kevin Curran	8941 Graystone Lane	Pinetops	NC	27864-2297
8	Miss Susan Haines	253 Windsor Blvd.	Greenville	NC	27834-6140
9	Mr. Jim Gothard	602 Fairview Drive	Wilson	NC	27893-4230
10	Miss Kara Herndon	2018 Garrett Avenue	Farmville	NC	27828-9817
11	Ms. Valerie Beckman	301-C Westbook Apartments			
		105 South 11th Street	Goldsboro	NC	27530-6346
12	Seth Jackson	1442 18th Street, SE	Jacksonville	NC	28540-7294
13					
14					
15					
16					
17					
18					
19					
20					

1 Name   LIST   \<F1=HELP>

Press ALT to choose commands or F2 to edit.

Job 3 Proofread the announcement on the next page by comparing it with the rough draft below. Remember, errors may occur on the original document. Mark your corrections on the keyed copy.

INTERNET USERS' GROUP

Organizational Meeting

You are invited to attend the initial meeting of a new group of our clients—Internet users who want to meet and share knowledge of research and other Internet use practices. The Internet User's Group will be held in the Prince Rm. of the Tryon Hotel on Feb. 20 at 7:30 PM.

Anyone using or interested in using the Internet for research, for information searches, or for fun is encouraged to join. Therefor, please pass this announcement along to your friends. Dr. Rachel A. Shaw, Ph.D., professor of Internet research at Texas A&M Univ., will be the guest speaker at this organizational meeting.

The Internet User Group will meet monthly to discuss research-related topics. Guest speakers from industry will share how they are using their computers *the Internet* to achieve results. New browsers and valuable Internet sites will be demonstrated and discussed. Group members will be happy with the support and education they receive, including our plan to have an annual conference sponsored by competative software developers.

The goals of the Internet Users' Group are to provide a network so that all members will be able to use the Internet most effectively and to keep *software* developers aware of consumer needs.

Members attending the first organizational mtg. will determine the best time and location for the monthly meetings and will appoint representitives to board positions.

INTERNET USERS' GROUP

Organizational Meeting

You are invited to attend the initial meeting of a new group of our clients—Internet users who want to meet and share knowledge of research and other use practices. The Internet Users' Group will be held in the Prince Rm. of the Tryon Hotel on Feb. 20 at 7:30 PM. Dr. Rachel A. Shaw, Ph.D., professor of Internet research at Texas A&M Univ., will be the guest speaker at this organizational meeting.

Anyone using or interested in using the Internet for research, for information searches, or for fun is encouraged to join. Therefore, please pass this announcement along to your friends.

The Internet User Group will meet monthly to discuss research-related topics. Guest speakers from industry will share how they are using the Internet to achieve results. New browsers and valuable Internet sites will be demonstrated and discussed. Group members will be happy with the support and education they receive, including our plan to have an annual conference sponsered by competative software developers.

The goals of the Internet Users' Group are to provide a network so that all members will be able to use the Internet most effectively and to keep software developers aware of consumer needs.

Members attending the first organizational meeting will determine the best time and location for the monthly meetings and will appoint representitives to board positions.

COMPUTERIZED PROOFREADING

Job 4 Proofread and format an interoffice memorandum.

1. Proofread the rough draft of the memorandum, and correct any errors that you find.

2. Load the file C03JOB4 from the template CD-ROM.

3. Revise the memorandum on the CD-ROM according to the rough draft. Make all needed corrections. Spell check the document.

4. Format the memorandum using a 1 1/2" top margin and 1" side margins.

5. Save the memorandum as C03JOB4R.

6. Print the memo.

7. Proofread the printed memo. If you find any mistakes, revise, save, and reprint it.

Software Success Learning Center

INTEROFFICE MEMORANDUM

TO: Department Managers and Supervisors

FROM: Garry Morrison, Gen. Manager

DATE: September 26, 20--

SUBJECT: Expense Reduction

Please analize your *tentative* budget carefully; then let me have your strategies for reducing our costs.

review the budget, As you will see *that* our utilities expense is almost double what it was four years ago. Advt. expense has increased about 30 percent. Taxes are up more than 20 percent. The cost of ins. rises every year. If we are to remain competitive in the busi. enviroment, we must reduce our expenses.

~~Please let me have your suggestions~~ ASAP but no later that October 10.

My goal is to incorporate your ideas into the management plan for the November 7 anual meeting.

dw

WORD DIVISION ERRORS

Word processors do so much work for us that we often fail to appreciate them. When was the last time you had to think about where to break a line of type? One could argue that we need not learn how to divide words at the ends of lines. Well, if that is true, then we need not learn to add or subtract because calculators can do it for us. On the other hand, the accuracy and effectiveness of final products depend on a writer's own good sense in making knowledge-able decisions based on accepted conventions and rules.

GUIDELINES FOR CORRECT WORD DIVISION

Words are sometimes divided at the ends of lines to give a document an attractive, well-balanced appearance. The right margin should be as even as possible, yet word divisions can be unattractive and may interrupt readers. When word divisions are unavoidable, be sure to follow word division rules and be careful to insert the hyphen correctly.

The best word division practices are not to divide words on two consecutive lines, words on the first or last lines of a paragraph, or the last word on a page. Words may be divided only between syllables, and pronunciation rather than roots or derivations is the key to division. You should use a word division manual or dictionary to determine correct syllabication; however, a knowledge of the rules presented in this chapter will prevent extensive searching in reference materials, reduce word division errors, and save valuable keyboarding time.

Word division has become easier as a result of the automatic hyphenation feature in most word processing software. With the automatic hyphenation feature turned on, the software consults its dictionary and determines word division by inserting a soft hyphen. A **soft hyphen** disappears if the text is changed, and the word no longer appears at the end of a line. A good proofreader must be aware of excessive hyphenation and words that could be divided in places better than the software has chosen.

Some words contain internal hyphens; these are **regular hyphens.** When these words fall at the ends of lines, word processing software divides the words at the regular hyphens. Some words and numbers

LEARNING OBJECTIVES

- Identify words that are divided incorrectly.
- Recognize items that should not be divided.
- Use appropriate proofreading symbols to indicate changes in text.
- Spell correctly a list of commonly misspelled words.

To insert a **hard hyphen** using Word, depress CONTROL-SHIFT-HYPHEN; using WordPerfect, depress CONTROL-HYPHEN.

To insert a **hard space** using Word, depress CONTROL-SHIFT-SPACE BAR; using WordPerfect, depress CONTROL-SPACE BAR.

contain internal hyphens and should not be divided. These words and numbers need **hard hyphens** so they will not wrap, or turn over. For instance, the word *part-time* contains a regular hyphen and can be divided at the hyphen; a phone number should contain a hard hyphen and should not be divided at the hyphen. Additionally, some word pairs and word and number pairs should not be separated; for example, months and days (*May 5*), titles and names (*Mrs. Ito*), and nouns with numbers (*page 14*). These pairs need to have **hard spaces** between them so they will not divide at the ends of lines.

When you note errors in word division, use the following proofreading symbols to mark your corrections:

=/	Insert a hyphen.	We must read and study an up-to/date textbook to learn the skill of editing and proofreading business documents.
	Correct a word division at the end of a line.	Reading helps, but we must app-ly all the rules we have learned.
		Reading helps, but we must app-apply all the rules we have learned.

4–1 Divide words only between syllables; a one-syllable word cannot be divided.

▪ height   ac- com- mo- date   for- eign

CHECKPOINT 4-1

Insert a hyphen to indicate where the following words can be divided. Place a check mark beside a word that cannot be divided.

a. volunteer   c. dispose   e. stretched ✓

b. placed ✓   d. accusation   f. straight ✓

4–2 At least two characters *and* a hyphen must appear on the upper line, and at least three characters (one of which may be a punctuation mark) must appear on the lower line.

▪ re- cently   print- ers   *but* about, eighty

CHECKPOINT 4-2

Insert a hyphen to indicate the preferred division. Place a check mark beside a word that cannot be divided.

a. pointed ✓   c. elusive   e. wealthy ✓

b. inform   d. already   f. excess

4-3 Divide a compound word between the elements of the compound. If the compound word contains a hyphen, divide only after the hyphen.

■   sales- person   self- esteem   over- payment

CHECKPOINT 4-3

Insert a hyphen to indicate the preferred division. If the word should be divided at the existing hyphen, indicate a break point with a forward slash. Place a check mark beside a word that cannot be divided.

a. time-share   c. go/-between   e. eye-witness

b. master-piece   d. trouble-shoot   f. full-/time

4-4 When a single-letter syllable occurs within a word, divide *after* the single letter. However, divide *before* a single-letter syllable that immediately precedes a terminating two-letter syllable (such as *clar- ify*) or one of these syllables: *-ble*, *-bly*, *-cle*, *-cal*, and *-ly*.

■   stipu- late   pene- trate   *but* bus- ily

CHECKPOINT 4-4

Insert a hyphen to indicate the preferred division. Place a check mark beside a word that cannot be divided.

a. pos-i/tive   c. bene-ficial   e. neg-ative

b. congrat-u/late   d. imper-ative   f. for-cibly

4-5 When two single-vowel syllables occur together in a word, divide between them.

■   gradu- ation   physi- ological   medi- ation

CHECKPOINT 4-5

Insert a hyphen to indicate the preferred division. Place a check mark beside a word that cannot be divided.

a. anx-i/ety   c. humili-ation   e. evalu-ation

b. insinu-ation   d. val-u/able   f. patri-otic

4–6 Divide a word *after* a prefix or *before* a suffix, rather than within the prefix or suffix or within the root word. However, avoid word divisions that may confuse the reader. If a word contains both a prefix and a suffix, divide the word at a point that makes the most sense.

intro- duce   re- invest   helpless- ness (*not* help- lessness)

CHECKPOINT 4-6

Insert a hyphen to indicate the preferred division. Place a check mark beside a word that cannot be divided.

a. preparedness

b. interrogate

c. cooperate

d. substandard

e. reallocate

f. anticlimax

4–1

a. vol un teer

b. placed ✓

c. dis pose

d. ac cu sa tion

e. stretched ✓

f. straight ✓

4–7 You may usually divide a word between double consonants. However, if a root word ends in double consonants and has a suffix ending, divide *after* the double consonants, provided the suffix creates an extra syllable.

hur- ried   enroll- ment   sell- ers   *but* pressed

When the addition of a suffix to a word results in double consonants, divide *between* the double consonants, provided the suffix creates an extra syllable.

permit- ting   question- naire   stir- ring

CHECKPOINT 4-7

Insert a hyphen to indicate the preferred division. Place a check mark beside a word that cannot be divided.

a. bulletin

b. referral

c. recommend

d. necessary

e. fulfillment

f. planned ✓

4–2

a. pointed ✓

b. in form

c. elu sive

d al ready

e. wealthy ✓

f. ex cess

4–8 Sentences containing dashes or ellipsis marks may be broken between words within dashes or after a dash or ellipsis marks.

Upper Line	Lower Line
Three people—Ted,	Ellen, and Morgan—were chosen.
I urged—only once—	for you to listen.
or I urged—	only once—for you to listen.
not I urged	—only once—for you to listen.
"Employees were . . .	happy with the pay increases."

WHEN TO AVOID WORD DIVISION

4-9 Avoid dividing words with fewer than six letters regardless of the syllables.

> handy   admit   renew   exit   doing

4-10 Do not divide abbreviations, acronyms, contractions, or numbers. An extremely long number may be divided after an internal hyphen or comma if necessary.

> c.o.d.   UNICEF   haven't   (208) 555-0116

Upper Line	Lower Line
VIN 534290-	234038-293XX34

4-11 Avoid dividing URL (Uniform Resource Locator) and e-mail addresses. If word division is necessary, you may divide a URL or an e-mail address *after* a single slash (/) or double slashes (//) or *before* a dot (.), a hyphen (-), or the @ sign. Never insert a hyphen in these addresses to show word division.

Upper Line	Lower Line
http://www.nasa.gov/	cool.html
http://	www.pbs.org
or http://www	.pbs.org
cmewrite@campus	.central.com
or cmewrite	@campus.central.com

4-12 Avoid separating parts of dates, proper names, titles with names, and addresses. If word division is necessary, you may divide according to the following styles. Use a hard space between word pairs that should not be divided.

Upper Line	Lower Line
May 15,	1948
Tuesday,	March 10
Booker T.	Washington
Miss Lucinda	Garcia
Francine S.	Oberrecht, Esq.
1490 Third	Street

4-3
a. time|share
b. master|piece
c. go-|between
d. trouble|shoot
e. eye|witness
f. full-|time

4-4
a. pos|itive
b. congrat|ulate
c. bene|ficial
d. imper|ative
e. neg|ative
f. forc|ibly

4-5
a. anx|ety
b. insin|uation
c. humil|ation
d. val|uable
e. eval|uation
f. patri|otic

4-6
a. prepared|ness
b. in|terrogate
c. co|operate
d. sub|standard
e. re|allocate
f. ant|climax

4-7

a bul|letin

b. refer|ral

c. recom|mend

d. neces|sary

e. fulfill|ment

f. planned ✓

> **"** To err is human, but when the eraser wears out ahead of the pencil, you're overdoing it. **"**
>
> —Josh Jenkins

4-13 Some word groups, such as nouns and numbers in pairs, are read together as a unit and should not be divided. Use a hard space between these words to avoid word division at the ends of lines.

| page 103 | Flight 121 | 6:15 p.m. | $12 million |

SPELLING APPLICATIONS

4-14 Compare the words in Column A with the corresponding words in Column B. Use the appropriate proofreading symbols to correct the misspelled words. If both columns are correct, write **C** to the left of the number.

	Column A	**Column B**
1.	beginning	begining
2.	calendar	calender
3.	dependable	dependible
4.	enthuziasm	enthusiasm
5.	height	heigth
6.	merchandize	merchandise
7.	nickle	nickel
8.	ninth	nineth
C 9.	schedule	schedule
10.	similiar	similar

4-14

1. begining

2. calender

3. dependible

4. enthuziasm

5. heigth

6. merchandize

7. nickle

8. nineth

9. C

10. similiar

CHAPTER SUMMARY

Check closely to be sure your document follows these word division rules:

♦ Divide only between syllables; a one-syllable word cannot be divided.

♦ Leave at least two characters and a hyphen on the upper line; leave at least three characters on the lower line.

♦ Divide compound words between the elements of the compound or after a hyphen in a compound.

♦ Generally, divide words that contain single-letter syllables after the single-letter syllable.

♦ Divide between two single-vowel syllables when they occur together in a word.

♦ Generally, divide a word after a prefix or before a suffix, being careful to not confuse the reader.

♦ Generally, divide a word between double consonants.

♦ Break sentences after a dash or ellipses marks or between words within dashes.

♦ Avoid dividing words containing fewer than six letters.

♦ Do not divide abbreviations, acronyms, contractions, numbers, and URL and e-mail addresses.

♦ Avoid dividing parts of dates, proper names, titles with names, addresses, and other word groups that read as a unit.

Study the following proofreading tips, and apply them as you proofread:

♦ Pronounce words carefully to determine syllabication.

chil- dren *not* child- ren   knowl- edge *not* know- ledge

♦ Be alert for words that change syllabication as pronunciation changes.

min- ute (*n.*) 60 seconds   mi- nute (*adj.*) tiny
pres- ent (*n.*) gift; not absent   pre- sent (*v.*) hand over
proj- ect (*n.*) undertaking   pro- ject (*v.*) throw forward
rec- ord (*n.*) written account   re- cord (*v.*) write down

♦ Check a word division manual or a dictionary whenever you are in doubt about how to divide a word.

♦ Be aware that dictionaries do not always have the same syllabication. For example, the word *dictionary* is divided in one dictionary as *dic- tion- ar- y* but in another dictionary as *dic- tio- nar- y*. Use the same dictionary throughout a project.

P-1

1. blind- ly
2. C
3. C
4. e- nough
5. presi- dent-elect
6. understate- ment
7. C
8. allowa- ble
9. C

P-2

1. extra- neous
2. o'- clock
3. spel- ling
4. aud- it
5. C
6. would- n't
7. C
8. read- dress
9. situa- ted

P-3

1. si- m- lar
2. C
3. . . . June 10, 2005 . . .
4. clie- nts
5. cat- egories
6. . . . joe@ @hotmail.com . . .
7. cr- eed
8. C
9. C

Proofread the following groups of words using the appropriate proofreading symbols to mark errors you find in word division. Write **C** if a word is divided correctly. To aid you in proofreading, the number of errors to be found is indicated in parentheses for Exercises P-1 and P-2; however, you must find the errors on your own in P-3.

P-1

1. blind- ly
2. paper- weight
3. continu- ation
4. e- nough
5. presi- dent-elect
6. understate- ment
7. height
8. allowa- ble
9. order- ing

(5 errors)

P-2

1. extra- neous
2. o'- clock
3. spel- ling
4. aud- it
5. http://bsu.edu
6. would- n't
7. width
8. read- dress
9. situa- ted

(7 errors)

P-3

1. si- milar
2. progres- sive
3. . . . June 10, 2005 . . .
4. clie- nts
5. cat- egories
6. . . . joe@ hotmail.com . . .
7. cr- eed
8. 42 miles
9. . . . Dr. T. L. Osborn . . .

PROGRESSIVE PROOFREADING

You are working five hours a week as an office volunteer for Partners, Inc., a local charitable organization. Proofread the documents carefully for keyboarding, abbreviation, word division, and spelling errors. Using the proofreading symbols that you have learned, mark all errors. Remember that the original drafts may also contain errors.

Job 1

Proofread these form paragraphs, which will be used in correspondence with supporters of Partners, Inc.

1. You have been an enthusiastic and dependible supporting member of Partners, Inc., for five years.

2. You have backed Partners with enthusiasm for a number of years—thank you!— and we want you to know your support has not gone unnoticed.

3. Because you have so generously contributed your time and other resources to Partners, the Advisory Board members invite you to be our guest at our annual ga-la dinner on March 30 at the City Center at 6:30 p.m. You may bring a guest.

4. We are already at the heigth of planning the annual Partners' Auction. This year the auction will be held on Feb. 15. As in the past, all proceeds will go to help the yo-uth of our community. May we count on your continued support?

5. If your answer is YES, and we hope it will be, please notify us by January 20 using the enclosed reply card. You may also phone in to tell us of your support at 555-0123 during normal working hours.

6. As we prepare for this year's auction scheduled for February 15, may we once a-gain count on your support? If your answer is YES, and we hope it will be, please let us know the items or service that you will provide for the action by January 20.

7. If you will be able to attend, please return the enclosed reservation form by March 16 so that we can reserve a place for you.

8. Please be sure to mark your calender for the big event—this is the one fundrais-ing event you won't want to miss!

9. For further information about Partners, Inc., look us up on the Web at http://www.partners4u.org.

10. Enclosure

Partners, Inc.

January 10, 20—

Ms. Joan Daniels, Mgr.
WEXZ Newstalk 1530
517 North Nineth Street
Denver, CO 80204-7825

Dear Ms. Daniels

PUBLIC ANNOUNCEMENT

For the past four years, your station has very generously advertised the Partners' Auction
as a public service announcement. The Partners' Action is held annually to raise money to
support projects for the youth in our community. Can we count on on your continued enthusiasm and support this year?

If your response is YES, and we hope it will be, please read the enclosed news release on
your Community Calender program. We would like the announcement to begin on January
20 and have it run through February 5.

Sincerely yours

Joseph A. Ramirez
Executive Assistant

gg

Enclosure

Chapter 4: Word Division Errors

Partners, Inc.

NEWS RELEASE

January 10, 20--
To release January 20, 20--

FIFTH ANNUAL PARTNERS' AUCTION

The Fifth Annual Partners' Auction will be telecast on W.R.A.L.-TV from noon to midnight on Sat., February 5. Local merchants and business have generously donated approximately fifteen hundred gifts, including merchandize, trips, and services. Viewers can bid on any of then by calling one of the numbers that will be listed on the television screen. The retail value of each item will be given, an each item will be sold to the highest bidder. Most of the items can be viewed prior to the auction by visiting Partner's web site at www.partners-4u.org.

All people working with the auction donate their time with enthusiasm. That way every nickle, dime, and dollar goes directly to aid the youth of the community. Because of community involvement, last year's action raised over $1.2 million. Remember, show your support for youth projects by marking your calendars to support Partners' Auction on Feb. 5.

Job 4   Proofread the letter on the next page by comparing it to the rough draft below. Remember, errors may occur on the draft. Mark your corrections on the keyed copy on the next page.

January 14, 20—

Mr. E.C. Troiano
AMS Electronics
5245 Trade St.
Denver, CO 80214-8275

Dear Mr. Troiano

Mark your calendar for the Fifth Annual Partners' Action to be held on Saturday, February 5, in Scott Pavilion. The auction is sponsored by area businesses for the benefit of Partners, Inc., an organization devoted to helping the youth of the community. ~~Since you are aware of the importance of~~ the auction *is* as a means of raising funds for the (org.), ~~you will want to attend.~~ *As a loyal supporter of Partners, you know how vital*

WRAL-TV will telecast the auction from noon to midnight. As each item is put up for bid, it will be displayed on television and its \value retail\ will be given. You can place your bid for any item by calling *the* ~~phone numbers~~ listed on the (t.v.) screen. *Should* ~~Remember, too, that if~~ your bid ~~is~~ *be for* more than the the retail value of the item, the difference between the two ~~amounts~~ is ~~tax~~ deductible on your taxes.

We hope that you will ~~make a definite decision to~~ participate in Partners' biggest fund-raiser of the year. When Partners benefits, the entire community—not just one group—benefits.

Sincerely yours   *Because the auction is staffed with vol, all proceeds go directly to Partners.*

Joseph Ramirez
Executive Assistant

Partners, Inc.

January 14, 20--

Mr. E. C. Troiano
AMS Electronics
5245 Trade St.
Denver, CO 80214-8275

Dear Mr. Troiano

Mark your calendar for the Fifth Annual Partners' Auction to be held on Saturday, February 5, in Scott Pavilion. The auction is sponsored by area businesses for the benefit of Partners, Inc., an organization devoted to helping the youth of the community. As a loyal supporter of Partners, you know how vital the auction is as a means of raising funds for the organization.

WRAL-TV will telecast the auction from noon to midnight. As each item is put up for bid, it will be displayed on television and its retail value will be given. You can place your bid for any item by calling the phone numbers listed on the television screen. Should your bid be for more than the retail value of the item, the difference between the two is deductible on your taxes.

Because the auction is staffed with volunteers, all proceeds go directly to Partners. We hope that you will participate in Partners' biggest fund-raiser of the year. When Partners benefits, the entire community—not just one group—benefits.

Sincerely yours

Joseph Ramirez
Executive Assistant

1110 Logan Street · Denver, CO 80203-9176 · Phone (303) 555-0123 · Fax (303) 555-0124 · www.partners4u.org

COMPUTERIZED PROOFREADING

Job 5   Proofread and format a business letter.

1. Load the file C04JOB5 from the template CD-ROM.

2. Proofread the letter on the CD-ROM; proofread it against form paragraphs 1, 3, 7, 9, and 10 from Job 1. Also, proofread the inside address against the address list below.

3. Make all corrections. Spell check the document.

4. Format the letter using a 2″ top margin and 1 1/2″ side margins. Save the letter using the file name C04JOB5R.

5. Print the letter.

6. Proofread the printed document. If you find additional mistakes, revise, save, and reprint the letter.

Partners, Inc.

Donor Name	Company	Address	City	ZIP Code
Ms. Joan Daniels, Mgr.	WEXZ Newstalk 1530	517 N. Ninth St.	Denver	80204-7825
Mr. E.C. Troiano	AMS Electronics	5245 Trade St.	Denver	80214-8275
Mr. Peter Wallace, Sales Mgr.	General TV and Appliance, Inc.	1927 Greeley Blvd.	Denver	80208-1927

5 CHAPTER

When does a spell check function do you absolutely no good? The answer is when numbers are involved. Never is proofreading more critical than when numbers are involved because no one but you can check whether the numbers have been keyed or expressed correctly. No one but you can double-check the calculations to make sure they are correct. Overlooking numbers in a document is easy to do because you have nothing to "read," as it were. You should *say* the numbers as you proofread. Saying the numbers forces you to slow down and actually look at what is on the paper or screen in front of you.

GUIDELINES FOR CORRECT NUMERICAL EXPRESSION

An important aspect of developing proofreading skills is learning to detect errors in the expression of numbers. Numbers appear in documents in either figure style or word style, and which style to use is often the writer's choice. A fundamental difference between figure style and word style is the emphasis that is placed on a number when it is a figure instead of a word. The writer decides whether or not an emphasis on the number is appropriate.

Because figures are quickly and easily perceived, numbers used in technical writing and business communications are usually expressed in figures. On the other hand, numbers used in formal documents, such as social invitations, are spelled out. Style manuals often present conflicting rules regarding number expression, but learning and following the basic rules presented here will benefit you as a proofreader. The examples used in this chapter apply to the expression of numbers in business documents unless otherwise noted.

Use the following proofreading symbols to mark errors in the expression of numbers and in the calculation of numerical items:

⟳ *sp*	Spell out.	We enrolled ⟲10 *sp* students in the class.
/ or ___	Change copy as indicated.	Before lunch Jolbert wrote 14 e-mails and answered ~~two~~² letters. I read only ~~1/2~~ half of the contract.

> **LEARNING OBJECTIVES**
>
> - Identify errors in the expression of numbers.
> - Identify keyboarding errors in numerical calculations.
> - Use appropriate proofreading symbols to indicate changes in text.
> - Spell correctly a list of commonly misspelled words.

> Because most of us do not key numerals very frequently, they are a common source of keyboarding errors.

BASIC RULES

5-1 As a general rule, write the numbers 1 through 10 in words; write numbers greater than 10 in figures.

> Plan to take about five people with you on the field trip.
>
> It takes 12 years to qualify for membership.

When keying figures, use the numeric "one" and "zero" keys for the numerals *1* and *0*. Never use a lowercase *l (ell)* for a one or a capital *o (O)* for a zero.

5-2 If a sentence contains a series of related numbers, any of which is greater than ten, use figures for consistency. However, the expression of numbers that are not related to other numbers in the same sentence should be evaluated separately.

> For the picnic, the two departments bought 24 pounds of chopped beef, 8 dozen rolls, 36 quarts of lemonade, and 96 turnovers.
>
> The River Tours Company registered 37 women, 28 men, and 5 children for the three trips offered.

5-3 Use figures for all numbers, even 1 through 10, if the number must stand out for technical or emphatic reference. This is *figure* style.

> The note is payable on a 5-year plan.
>
> By 2 p.m. the truck will be loaded with 3 tons of gravel.

When proofreading a document that is heavy with numeric data, use team proofreading to ensure accuracy.

Use words for all numbers, even greater than ten, if the number is an approximation or does *not* need to stand out for technical or emphatic reference and can be expressed in one or two words. This is *word* style.

> About three thousand people attended the rally.
>
> Approximately fifty men entered the contest.

5-4 Express round numbers (such as 1500) in hundreds rather than thousands. Express round numbers (or round numbers followed by a simple fraction or decimal) of millions or higher in figures followed by the word *million* or *billion*.

> We ordered fifteen hundred balloons for the party.
>
> The population of Chicago is more than 3.5 million.

A figure such as 17,000,000 is more easily misread or misconstrued than the expression *17 million*.

5-5 Spell out a number that begins a sentence. However, if the number requires more than two words when spelled out, rearrange the sentence so that it does not begin with a number.

> Twenty-five people have enrolled.
>
> *not* 165 parking spaces were assigned to new employees.
>
> *but* New employees were assigned 165 parking spaces.

All compound numbers from twenty-one through ninety-nine should be hyphenated when spelled out.

Proofread the following sentences for errors in the expression of numbers. If a sentence is correct, write *C* to the right of the sentence.

C

a. Thirty-five people telephoned their regrets.

b. I ordered 12 boxes of paper, ~~two~~ 8 dozen printer cartridges, and ~~three~~ 3 boxes of disks.

c. Do you think ~~ten~~ 10 billion pinto beans are in that warehouse?

d. ~~Two hundred twenty-seven~~ The test had 227 questions were on the test.

e. We received almost ~~200~~ two hundred inquiries about the ad.

SPECIFIC RULES

Specific situations require additional guidelines to clarify the message. Consider the rules covered in this section.

5-6 Adjacent numbers. When two numbers are used together and one is part of a compound modifier, spell out only one of the two— preferably the number that can be expressed as the smallest word.

> Calvin loaded two 40-pound cartons onto the truck.

> Martha bought 20 three-cent stamps.

If both adjacent numbers are either figures or words, use a comma to separate them.

> At Station 976, 36 more problems have been identified.

> Working past six, two of our auditors missed the train.

5-7 Ordinals. Spell out ordinal numbers (first, second, third, and so on) that can be written as one or two words; use figures for larger ordinals. (Consider a hyphenated number, such as thirty-fifth, as one word.)

> Is this the seventh meeting we have attended this week?

> This is the 110th day of the strike.

5-8 Addresses. Spell out street names from one through ten and the house number *one*. Street names of ten and under are always expressed as ordinals (Third Street, Fifth Avenue). Street names above ten may be expressed in figures as cardinal numbers (15 Street) or as ordinal numbers (15th Street).

> 1609 Fifth Avenue   One Park Avenue
>
> 2 East 11th Street
> *or* 2 East 11 Street

WORKPLACE CONNECTIONS

With regard to customer service, getting a customer's name and address correct is critical. Double-check names and addresses on all correspondence.

5-9 **Ages.** In nontechnical, informal material, spell out ages ten and under; use words or figures for ages 11 and up. Use figures for ages expressed in years and months. Use figures for references to age in business documents.

> When will Moe turn four? When will Chris be 21?
>
> Sara turned sixteen in April.
> *or* Sara turned 16 in April.
>
> Hunter is 3 years and 9 months old.
>
> Mary Ann Walker, age 42, was promoted to Senior Counsel.

5-10 **Numbers with nouns.** Use figures to express numbers preceded by nouns.

> Please refer to page 16 in Chapter 2 when you do your research.
>
> The meeting will be held in Suite 112; all Level 1 and 2 managers are encouraged to attend.

CHECKPOINT 5-6—5-10

Proofread the following sentences for errors in the expression of numbers. If a sentence is correct, write *C* to the right of the sentence.

a. The school is located at Eight West 23 Street, not West 24 Street.

b. See page seven in the book and page 257 in the appendix for the references.

c. We need five one-year employees and 20 two-year employees for the committee.

d. Eduardo has moved from One Meade Street to 1270 Seventh Avenue.

e. Mrs. Alfonso, sixty-six, has been with the company since it opened for business.

f. Proper use of abbreviations is discussed in Lesson 3, which begins on page 10.

g. This is the 15th phone call I have returned to him this week.

5-11 **Fractions.** Generally, spell out and use a hyphen with a fraction when it occurs without a whole number. Use figures to express a fraction that is not easily read as a word or a fraction that is part of a mixed number (a whole number plus a fraction).

> Only two-thirds of the members were present.
>
> Please order one-half dozen pies for the social hour.
>
> The measurement was off by a scant 5/32 inch.
>
> In just this week we used 4 1/2 reams of paper.

5-12   Time. Spell out time when stated in numbers alone or before *o'clock*. Use figures for time when *a.m.*, *p.m.*, *noon*, and *midnight* are used. Zeros are not necessary for on-the-hour times of day, even when used in sentences with mixed hour times.

> I will meet you for the conference call at eleven.

> The reception will begin at six o'clock.

> Henrietta has a meeting at 10 a.m. and another at 2:30 p.m.

> The announcement will be made at 12 noon and 5 p.m.

5-13   Dates. Use figures after a month to express the day and year. Set the year off by commas if the day directly precedes the year; otherwise, do not use commas.

> The events of March 31, 1979, will be long remembered.

> The events of March 1979 will be long remembered.

Express the day in ordinal figures when it precedes the month or the month is omitted. (In formal messages ordinal words may be used.) Because it is shorter, the preferred abbreviation of the ordinals containing second and third is *d* alone, not *nd* or *rd* (2d, 3d, 42d, 93d).

> Payment was due on the 4th, but it has not been made.

> He will arrive on the 2d of July and depart on the 3d.
> *or* He will arrive on July 2 and depart on July 3.

© 2001 Ted Goff

"My answer is .5 yes."

5-14 **Periods of time.** Express technical references to periods of time in figures to emphasize the significance of the number, such as with credit terms. Spell out nontechnical references to time, unless the number requires more than two words.

> Our workweek is being changed from a 40-hour week to a 42-hour week.
>
> The loan is for 48 months at 12 percent interest.
>
> The office will be closed for the next fifteen days.

To proofread technical material that contains many figures, make one pass to verify the figures against the source document. Make another pass to verify the accuracy of the calculations.

5-15 **Dimensions, measurements, and weights.** Use figures in expressing dimensions, measurements, and weights. You may use words to express an isolated, nontechnical measurement or weight.

> The room was 9 feet by 12 feet.
>
> The bucket of sand weighed 21 pounds 5 ounces. (technical reference)
>
> The bag felt ten pounds heavier when I carried it home. (nontechnical reference)

CHECKPOINT 5-11–5-15

Proofread the following sentences for errors in the expression of numbers. If a sentence is correct, write *C* to the right of the sentence.

a. Lunch will be served at noon on November 3d to welcome all new employees.

b. The staff worked from 8 a.m. to 5:45 p.m. to finish the project.

c. All merchandise has been marked 1/3 off the regular price.

d. To convert miles to kilometers, multiply the number of miles by one and three fifths.

e. Ronson's sale will begin on September 29th at 10:00 a.m.

f. I need four and a half feet of weather stripping for the door.

g. Mr. Moser asked for a six-month payout of the loan proceeds.

5-16 **Money.** Use figures to express amounts of money. Decimals and zeros are not used after even amounts except when they occur in a column with amounts that contain cents. Then add a decimal and two zeros to all whole dollar amounts to maintain a uniform appearance.

> Bruce earned $60 in tips.
>
> Please pay $120 now and $61.50 for the next two months.
>
> *but* $120.00
>   <u> 61.50</u>
> $181.50

If the amount is less than a dollar, spell out the word *cents*. However, if other amounts in the same sentence require a dollar sign, be consistent.

> Lea's statement showed an error of 25 cents. (*not $.25*)

> An error of $.25 should not delay Lea's past-due payment of $210.

In legal or formal documents, express amounts of money or important figures in capitalized words followed by figures. Be sure the words and figures are an exact representation of each other; that is, the expression of dollars and cents is the same in words as it is in figures.

> Walter Casady agrees to pay Cynthia Castillo Fifteen Hundred Dollars ($1,500) without interest.

> *or* Walter Casady agrees to pay Cynthia Castillo Fifteen Hundred and no/100 Dollars ($1,500.00) without interest.

Isolated, nonemphatic references to money and indefinite amounts of money should be in word form.

> Our office manager gives hundred-dollar bills for bonuses.

> Heidi furnished her new office for just a few thousand dollars.

Use a dollar sign with a figure and the word *million* or *billion* to represent large amounts of money. Repeat the word if the amount is used in a series.

> Our new office complex will cost over $12.5 million to complete.

> The original project cost was between $10 million and $12 million.

5-17 Percents and decimals.
Use figures to express percents and decimals. To prevent misreading a decimal, use a zero before the decimal point for amounts less than one.

> Lars obtained a loan at a rate of 9 percent.

> The accuracy percentage for documents produced in the word processing center was 0.95 for the first 500 and 0.93 for the remainder.

5-18 Numbers with abbreviations or symbols.
Always use figures to express numbers with abbreviations or symbols. These will normally be used in tables, charts, or other nontext material. (In text, abbreviations and symbols would generally be spelled out.) Repeat the symbols in a range of numbers.

> | | | |
> |---|---|---|
> | No. 345 | 36% | I-95 |
> | 9' × 12' | 65°-75° | $10-$15 |

5-11—5-15

a. November 3d
b. C
c. marked 1/3 off
d. by one and three fifths.
e. September 29th at 10:00 a.m.
f. four and a half feet
g. six-month

WORKPLACE CONNECTIONS

Manipulating figures, interpreting financial information, and presenting financial information are responsibilities of many jobs. You do not have to be an accountant to find yourself communicating about budgets, revenues, expenses, and other business-related financial matters.

5-19 **Serial numbers.** Serial numbers are usually written without commas, but other marks of punctuation and/or spaces are sometimes used.

Invoice 38162

Model G-4356

Identification No. 2238-586-6600

License No. 5014 587 035

5-20 **Telephone and fax numbers.** Telephone and fax numbers may follow one of several styles, including word form (which corresponds to the numbers). Unless the number is written in words, divide the number by area code, the first three numbers, and the remaining numbers. Key a space after an end parenthesis with an area code, but do not use parentheses for area codes if the phone number is already enclosed in parentheses within the text.

(800) 555-0166   *or*   800-555-0166   *or*   800.555.0166

1-800-PICK-UPS   1-800-GOFEDEX

Please call toll-free information (800-555-0166) to get the number.

CHECKPOINT 5-16–5-20

Proofread the following sentences for errors in the expression of numbers. If a sentence is correct, write *C* to the right of the sentence.

a. Rent will be due on the fifth day of each month in the amount of Seven Hundred Twenty-five Dollars ($725.00).

b. A 25% discount is given on rooms reserved 30 days in advance.

c. Kwame just learned that he won a jackpot of one and a half million dollars.

d. I bought 200 markers on sale for $24.99, which is 88 cents less than the regular price.

e. Call their office ((800) 555-0192) to see if Invoice 1,124 was paid by the deadline.

SPECIAL RULES

This section provides special rules concerning number usage and proofreading expressions of numbers.

5-21 When a number consists of four or more digits, use commas to separate thousands, hundreds of thousands, and so on. The comma may be left off a four-digit number when other numbers in the document are not higher, thus requiring a comma.

5,400 *or* 5400   320,267   43,824,321

5-22 Numbers appearing in a sequence should be joined by a hyphen (with no spaces before or after) or by the words *to*, *through*, or *and*. Use a word instead of a hyphen if the numbers are introduced by the words *from* or *between*.

> 1999-2005   pages 35-42   lines 6 through 10
>
> from 1990 to 1995   between 1776 and 1976

When using shortened forms of numbers in a series, be sure to make the meaning clear.

> $9 to $10,000 (a range of nine dollars to ten thousand dollars)
>
> $9,000 to $10,000 (a range of nine thousand dollars to ten thousand dollars)

5-23 Verify the correctness of all numbers. Check all calculations for accuracy. Check all days and dates with a calendar and all times with a source document to ensure accuracy.

> The book cost $3.50 and the card cost $.75, making the total $4.25. (Check math calculation.)
>
> The next committee meeting is scheduled for Friday, May 14, 20--, at 10:30 a.m. (Verify day, date, and time.)

SPELLING APPLICATIONS

5-24 Compare the words in Column A with the corresponding words in Column B. Use the appropriate proofreading symbols to correct the misspelled words. If both columns are correct, write **C** to the left of the number.

	Column A	Column B
1.	absence	absense
2.	accummulate	accumulate
3.	consious	conscious
4.	convenients	convenience
5.	extension	extention
6.	foreign	foriegn
7.	fourty	forty
8.	licencse	license
9.	morgage	mortgage
10.	waive	waive

5-16—5-20
a. Seven Hundred Twenty-five Dollars ($725.00).
b. a 25% discount
c. one and a half million dollars
d. 88 cents
e. ((800) 555-0192) Invoice 1,124

CHAPTER SUMMARY

Proofread carefully to be sure your documents follow the following number expression rules:

♦ Generally, use words for numbers 1 through 10; use figures for numbers greater than 10.

♦ Use figure style for numbers with technical significance or for emphasis.

♦ Use word style for approximate numbers or for numbers with no technical significance.

♦ Spell out numbers that begin sentences.

♦ Spell out the number of the smallest word when two numbers are used together and one is part of a compound modifier.

♦ Spell out ordinals that can be written as one or two words.

♦ Spell out ordinals for street names one through ten; use figures for street names above ten.

♦ Use figures to express numbers preceded by nouns.

♦ Spell out and use a hyphen with isolated fractions; use figures for mixed numbers.

♦ Spell out time when numbers are used alone or before *o'clock*; use figures when *a.m., p.m., noon,* and *midnight* are used.

♦ Use figures to express dates; use ordinals for days that precede the month or when the month is omitted.

♦ Express periods of time in words or figures, depending on the technical significance.

♦ Generally, use figures to express dimensions, measurements, weights, money, percents, decimals, serial numbers, and telephone/fax numbers.

♦ Use figures to express numbers with abbreviations or symbols.

Study these tips, and apply them as you proofread:

♦ If numbers have been transferred from another document, verify that they have been copied correctly.

♦ Check all enumerations, such as numbered lists, and all mathematical calculations for accuracy.

♦ When figures are in columns, align decimals. Proofread columns of numbers across rather than down the columns. Use a straightedge to guide your eye across the page.

words@work Open *words@work*. Click on the Grammar and Usage tab. Click on Lessons; then click on Numbers. Review the summary of number expressions; then complete the lesson exercises.

Individually or with a classmate, proofread the following interoffice memorandums using the appropriate proofreading symbols to mark errors you find in the expression of numbers and spelling. Remember, at times a writer has a choice between figure style and word style. To aid you in proofreading, the number of errors to be found is indicated in parentheses at the end of the first two exercises.

P-1

INTEROFFICE MEMORANDUM

TO: Adam
FROM: Mary Catherine
DATE: May 6, 20--
SUBJECT: Prospective Clients

Today I talked with Mr. and Mrs. Dominic Morales. They are interested in selling their house located at 3285 4th Street. The house has 3 bedrooms and 2 baths and 1680 square feet of floor space. The Moraleses have spent more than $5500 in the past two and 1/2 years for repainting and for installing new carpet. The lot, which is just under 3/4 acre, is about average for the neighborhood.

Would you like to talk with them to try to secure their business? Their home phone number is 555-0153; their cell phone number is 555/0131.

(5-7 errors)

P-2

INTEROFFICE MEMORANDUM

TO: Mary Catherine
FROM: Adam
DATE.   May 6, 20--
SUBJECT: Morales' Appointment

I have scheduled an appointment with Mr. and Mrs. Morales for 3 o'clock tomorrow afternoon. I plan to use these 4 points as to why they should choose our agency and me to sell their house:

1. Our company is affiliated with a national relocation service.
2. It has consistently commanded 24% of the local market.
3. All of our agents are experienced and licensed.
4. I personally have accumulated 82 sales and listings over the past 2 years.

Thanks for referring them to me. I'll let you know how our meeting goes.

(6 errors)

P-3   INTEROFFICE MEMORANDUM

TO: Mary Catherine
FROM: Adam
DATE: May 7, 20--
SUBJECT: Morales' Contract

My meeting with the Moraleses went well, and on the nineth *9th* we will meet again to sign a listing contract for the sale of their home.

During the meeting we discussed several options, including these ③: *sp*

1. With a sizeable down payment and adequate income, the Moraleses may consider carrying a morgage note with a fixed interest rate over the life of the loan.

2. A professional home inspection should not be waived.

3. Using the concept of pricing items at 99 cents rather than $1.00, we discussed pricing their home at $129,900 rather than at $130,000.

The Moraleses are also looking for land to buy to build a new home, and I have offered to assist them. Mr. Morales is retiring in 2 years; *sp* he and his wife wish to live out of town but within a 30-minute drive to the city. If you hear of approximately ten to 20 acres with improvements that is zoned for residential, please let me know. The Moraleses want to stay within the price range of $75 to $95,000 for the land.

PROGRESSIVE PROOFREADING

You are employed as office manager for the Phelps Real Estate Agency. In your basket today are four items to be proofread. Check for spelling, keyboarding, abbreviation, word division, and number expression errors.

PHELPS REAL ESTATE AGENCY

1125 Umstead Drive   Indianapolis, IN 46204-6142
Phone (317) 555-0142   Fax (317) 555-0182

January 20, 20--

Ms. Patsy Strum
901 Kildaire Farm Road
Indianapolis, IN 46205-9241

Dear Ms. Strum

Good news! The house you are interested in on Thirty-third Street has been reduced $5,000. The price is now within the range you mentioned to me on the 4th. May I urge you to act quickly.

Because of the favorable mortgage rates that are now available, you can own this 2200-square-foot house and still have mortgage payments of less than $900.00 per month. For a limited time the Indianapolis Federal Savings and Loan Association will approve your application for an adjustable rate loan within ten working days. If it is not approved, you will not be charged the 1 % discount rate.

Please call me at the office (555-0142) or on my cell phone (555-0110) to set up an appointment. My office hours are from 9:00 to 5 p.m. Mon. through Sat., but as you know, I would be happy to meet with you at your convenients.

Sincerely

Terry B. Andrus
Agent

df

Job 2
Proofread the ad at the bottom of this page using the fact sheet below. In addition to looking for the usual proofreading errors, be sure to verify the accuracy of the information in the ad.

RESIDENTIAL FACT AND FEATURE SHEET

Property: 4231 Charles Street

Price: $122,900

Location: Greenwood

Home Features:

Style: single-level, single-family

Total Square Feet: 1,723

Exterior Finish: wood shingle

Age (years): building (71) roof (2)

Heat/AC: heat pump

Garage: 19 feet by 14 feet, detached

Appliances: stove, dishwasher, refrigerator, and gas logs

Bathroom(s): two (2)

Bedroom(s): three (3)

Special Features: formal living room with fireplace

one bedroom with built-in bookcases, could be used as a den

large eat-in kitchen

beautiful front porch and curb appeal

backyard deck 12 feet by 27 feet, plus hot tub area 12 feet by 12 feet

Lot Features:

Lot Size: 125 feet by 275 feet

Landscaping: yes; semiwooded backyard

Site Features: nice family neighborhood, playground located nearby

For further information call Chris at 555-0170.

GREENWOOD SUBDIVISION. Spacious and convenient single-level for economy-consious owner. While its main features are 3 bedrooms and a formal living room with fireplace, it also has a nearby park/playground, a semiwooded backyard, a 12 × 27 foot deck, and a 12 × 27 foot hot tub area. Check out the curb appeal!

For more details, call Chris at 555-01700.

PHELPS REAL ESTATE AGENCY

1125 Umstead Drive   Indianapolis, IN 46204-6142
Phone (317) 555-0142   Fax (317) 555-0182

January 25, 20--

Mr. Nicholas Toracelli
Delhi Association of Realtors
325 Alabama Street
Indianapolis, IN 46204-6154

Dear Mr. Toracelli

I have a new listing in the Greenwood sub division that I would like to place on the week-ly realtors' tour. The facts you need for the tour are as follows:

     a.   Address: 4231 Charles Street
     b.   Price: $129,900
     c.   Bedrooms/Baths: 3/2
     d.   Square Feet: approx. 71 years
     e.   Age: 1,723
     f.   Lot Size: 125 feet by 75 feet

This home sounds average by description, but it is actually a beautiful home that has been immaculately maintained. It is well worth the competative asking price. I would like as many realtors as possible to tour it.

Please let me know when you can acommodate my request to place this home on the tour shedule. The only day not available on my calender is the fourth of February. If you have any questions, you can reach me on my cell phone (555-0170).

Sincerely

Chris Rice
Agent

df

Job 4 Proofread these minutes very carefully. Assume the numbers are accurate; however, they may not be expressed correctly.

Delhi Association of Realtors
325 Alabama Street
Indianapolis, IN 46204-6154
(317) 555-0196

MINUTES OF MEETING
DELHI ASSOCIATION OF REALTORS

<u>Place of Meeting</u>	The Delhi Assoc. of Realtors held its monthly meeting on Tuesday, January 18, 20--, at The Heritage Restaurant. The social hour began at 6:00 o'clock, and dinner was served at 7. Seventy-eight of the 85 members were present in addition to four guests.
<u>Call to Order</u>	Immediately following dinner, J.R. Hawkins, president, called the meeting to order and welcomed the members and guests. She noted that the January attendance was 10% above the December attendance.
<u>Approval of Minutes</u>	The minutes were presented by Secretary Tom Phelps. James Miller noted that the state convention would be held on the nineth of March instead of on April 10, as stated in the minutes. The correction was made, and the minutes were approved.
<u>Treasurer's Report</u>	In the absense of Sabrina Peoples, Tom Phelps gave the treasurer's report. The Association has a balance of $1,210 in the treasury, and bills amounting to $76.10 ($35.10 to Rouse Printing Company and $41.00 to The Heritage Restaurant) are outstanding. An extention of 15 days has been granted to members who have not paid their dues.

2

Market Review

Rodney Blankenship was called on to give a summary of the developments that have taken place in the local real estate market. Phelps Real Estate Company has been selected as exclusive marketing agent for Breckenridge subdivision on Leesville Rd. The 79-lot single-family subdivision is a Drexter development. Northwoods Village, a 228-unit luxury apartment community developed by Dallas C. Pickford & Associates, will open on the 1st of August. The community is located at Ten Northwoods Village Drive, one-half mile south of Interstate 40.

Speaker

Following the business session, President Hawkins introduced ~~Mrs.~~ Sally Dunbarton, president of Dunbarton Associates, as speaker for the meeting. Mrs. Dunbarton discussed the potential effects of recent tax legislation on the real estate market. She predicted that the prime rate will drop another 1/2 point before it hits bottom. In the local area an additional 12 - 15 apartment buildings should be on the market within the next 6 months.

Adjournment

Following the presentation, Tom Phelps drew the lucky number to determine who would win the centerpiece. ~~320~~ was the lucky number, *Was 320* and the winner was Midori Genda.

The meeting was adjourned at 9:15 a.m. Members were reminded that ~~that~~ the next meeting would be on the 3d Tuesday of February.

Respectfully submitted,

Tom Phelps, Secretary

COMPUTERIZED PROOFREADING

Job 5 Proofread and format a journal article.

1 Load the file C05JOB5 from the template CD-ROM.

2. Proofread the article on the CD-ROM, making all needed corrections. Spell check the document.

3. Format the article as follows:
   a. Use a top margin of 1 1/2" for the first page and 1" for page 2. Set 1" side margins.
   b. Double-space the article and indent paragraphs.
   c. Key a page number at the top right-hand margin of page 2.
   d. Center the title of the article.

4. Save the article as C05JOB5R.

5. Print one copy of the article.

6. Proofread the printed document. If you find any mistakes, revise, save, and reprint the document.

6 CHAPTER

We should not judge a book by its cover, but we do it anyway. We should judge coworkers on the quality of their ideas, not on how they present them—right? However, the business world does not always work that way. We all have to be idea people, and we all have to be communicators extraordinaire. Being able to produce written business documents that conform to expected business standards is one way to present your great ideas without creating barriers to communication.

IMPORTANCE OF FORMAT

Every time you produce a written document, whether it is a memo, a letter, or a lengthy report, your readers judge you. They may not even know you, but they judge you nonetheless. The appearance of your document creates an impression that may be favorable or unfavorable. The neatness of the document, the quality of the print and stationery, and the format of the document all combine to create the overall appearance. Chapter 6 provides an overview of basic format standards for letters, interoffice memorandums, e-mail messages, and reports.

Format is perhaps the most complex factor in the appearance of a business document. The format of a document includes margin settings; vertical spacing; and placement of document components such as headings, text, dateline, and inside address.

To be a good proofreader, you must be knowledgeable about document format rules and apply them consistently. Checking for format errors is the first step in the three-step process of proofreading—before proofreading for content and mechanical errors and checking for references, if necessary. When proofreading for format errors, focus only on format issues. Do not try to look for spelling or keyboarding errors at the same time. You will be more successful if you consider the "big picture"—the overall appearance—separately from other proofreading details.

When you find errors in formatting, use the proofreading symbols illustrated on the next page to mark your corrections.

> ### LEARNING OBJECTIVES
>
> - Recognize and correct format errors in letters, interoffice memorandums, e-mail messages, and reports.
> - Use appropriate proofreading symbols to indicate changes in text.
> - Spell correctly a list of commonly misspelled words.

> Proofread for format errors as a first and separate step of the proofreading process.

SS **Single-space.**	**Change case to lowercase.**
SS This is a new day and age for our company and our stockholders.	/ MR. Eda introduced the Speaker.
	Mr. Eda introduced the SPEAKER.

DS **Double-space.**	**Change case to a capital letter.**
DS This is a new day and age for our company and our stockholders.	Call jojo barker at 1-800-HOT-dogs to place an order.

QS **Quadruple-space.**	_____ **Set underscore;** ital **set italics.**
QS Sincerely yours, Wendy Lopez	Flexible Scheduling ital All employees are required to set regular working hours within the parameters of the company's flexible scheduling.

⌗ **Start a new paragraph;** No ⌗ **do not start a new paragraph.**	**Delete underscore; delete italics.**
The minutes were accepted⌗Ms. Lloyd raised the issue of next month's fundraiser. No ⌗ The group will focus on three issues.	Flexible Scheduling No ital All employees are required to set (regular) working hours within the parameters of the company's flexible scheduling.

‖ **Align copy.**	⊐⊏ **Center text.**
‖ 1. Survey employees. 2. Assess needs versus costs. ‖ 3. Research real costs.	⊐Annual Company Picnic⊏ You and a guest are cordially invited to attend this year's annual picnic.

⊐ **Move right;** ⊏ **move left;** ⨉⊐ **move a specified amount of space.**	+lℓ⚹→ **Insert a line;** −lℓ⚹→ **delete a line.**
Item Status Number 1 Stable 67X-9025 2 ⊏Charging 67X-2560 3 Stable 68Y-1410 .5″ Please check the status on Item 2 to see how the charging process is proceeding.	TO: New Hires FROM: Personnel Department DATE: July 2, 20-- −lℓ⚹→ +lℓ⚹→ SUBJECT: Insurance Options All employees hired after January 1 of this year are eligible for participation.

> Review these marks carefully, and note how they are used in the rough draft shown in Figure 6-1. Then note the changes that have been made in the finished letter.

Figure 6-1 Rough Draft

Finished Letter

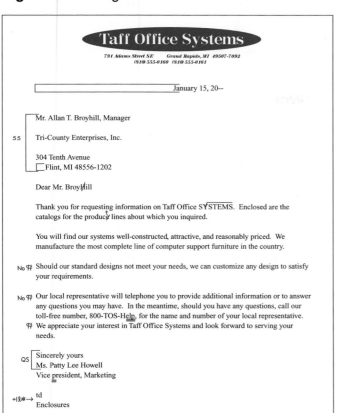

LETTER FORMAT

To locate format errors in business letters, a proofreader must be familiar with the correct sequence and placement of letter parts. Refer to Figure 6-2 as you read about the letter parts. Placement of the letter parts and punctuation may vary with the style of letter used. These specific points will be discussed in the subsequent section on business letter styles.

WORKPLACE CONNECTIONS

Every employee's responsibility is to know and use the company's preferred document styles.

Date

To allow space for the company letterhead, the date should be placed between 2 and 3 inches from the top of the page, depending on the length of the letter. Many businesses, however, use a standard or set placement for the date regardless of the letter length. Usually, allow at least a double space below the last line of the letterhead for the date.

6-1

Yes

Figure 6-2   Model Business Letter

In a single-spaced document, when guidelines specify a double space (DS), press the Enter key twice to leave *one* blank line between lines. For a triple space (TS), press the Enter key three times to leave *two* blank lines between lines. For a quadruple space (QS), press the Enter key four times to leave *three* blank lines between lines.

Sunrise Publications, Inc.
630 Chestnut Street
Manchester, NH 03101-4168
Phone: 603-555-0188 Fax: 603-555-0148
sunrisepub@email.com

June 16, 20--

Miss Belinda Rubenstein
P.O. Box 4128
Camden, NJ 08101-9800

Dear Miss Rubenstein

SUNRISE BOOK CLUB MEMBERSHIP

Thank you for your recent membership in the Sunrise Book Club. The four complimentary books you selected as part of your membership should arrive within two weeks.

Each month you will receive the *Sunrise News*, which reviews more than one hundred books in each issue. You can buy as many or as few books as you like. If you find, as we certainly think you will, that you like the same books we do, ignore your monthly notice; we will send you the Sunrise Selection of the Month and bill you later. You may, however, choose an alternate selection or no book at all.

Your first *Sunrise News* should reach you within two weeks. Enclosed is a flyer describing the exciting new selections from which to choose. Best wishes for hours of enjoyable reading ahead.

Sincerely

Frank McCarthy
Customer Relations Manager

pt

Enclosure

c Sam Joiner

Because you are a valued new member of the Sunrise Book Club, you are eligible to receive a free tote bag with your first order.

If a letter is prepared on plain stationery rather than on letterhead, the writer's return address is placed immediately above the dateline.

Letter Address

The letter address contains the recipient's complete name and address.

The letter address, or inside address, gives complete addressing information about the person to whom the letter is directed. It contains the recipient's name, job title (when appropriate), and complete address. If the letter is addressed to a company, an attention line to a person or a department may be included as the second line of the letter address. The letter address begins on the fourth line, or a quadruple space (QS), below the dateline. A proofreader should always check the spelling and accuracy of the names and addresses against a source document to be sure they are correct.

If the addressee is an individual, a personal title (such as Mr., Miss, Ms., or Dr.) should precede the name. If the letter is addressed to a woman whose personal title is not known, use *Ms.* If the gender of the addressee is unknown and cannot be determined by the first name (e.g., Lee, Kelly, Terry), omit the personal title and use the complete name in the salutation. Official titles, such as *Chair* or *Director of Human Resources*, follow a person's name and require initial capital letters.

Salutation

The salutation, or greeting, should match the name in the letter address. The salutation appears a double space below the letter address. The examples below show the proper salutations to be used in different situations. Note the initial capital letters.

Addressed to a company:	Fisher-Price Securities 31 St. James Avenue Boston, MA 02116-4255 DS Ladies and Gentlemen
Addressed to a company using an attention line:	Fisher-Price Securities Attention Marketing Department 31 St. James Avenue Boston, MA 02116-4255 DS Ladies and Gentlemen
Addressed to a job title:	Advertising Manager Fisher-Price Securities 31 St. James Avenue Boston, MA 02116-4255 DS Dear Sir or Madam
or	Dear Advertising Manager
Addressed to an individual whose gender is not known:	Alex Speight Fisher-Price Securities 31 St. James Avenue Boston, MA 02116-4255 DS Dear Alex Speight

For specific forms of address and salutations for special circumstances, always refer to an up-to-date reference manual. These salutations may involve people of religious, governmental, military, or dignitary status.

The information in the letter address must match the address on the envelope exactly. Because of automated scanning equipment, the U.S. Postal Service prefers (but does not require) envelope destination addresses to be keyed in all capital letters with no punctuation.

Subject and Reference Lines

A letter may or may not have a subject line, which identifies the topic of the letter. A subject line should be keyed a double space *below* the salutation in all capital letters.

> HOLIDAY TEMPORARY WORKERS

A reference notation is used to identify names or numbers that need to be listed as a reference point for the letter. A reference section usually appears a double space below the inside address and *above* the salutation. If more than one line is used in the reference notation, align the text for a neat appearance.

> RE: Insured   Dan Summers
>   Date of Loss   06/23/01
>   Claim No.   A53-678-062398

Body

The body, or message, begins a double space below the salutation or subject line. The body is single-spaced with a double space between paragraphs. Paragraphs may be indented only if the letter style is modified block.

If the body of the letter is two or more pages, key a header on the successive pages that includes the names of the addressee(s), the page number, and the date. Be sure to include two blank lines between the header and the text of the letter. The header can be keyed on one line, or all three elements can be left aligned.

> Mr. Ira F. Will   2   December 10, 20--
>
> *or*   Mr. Ira F. Will
>   Page 2
>   December 10, 20--

<aside>
Most word processing software includes a feature that automatically changes the page numbers in a header. Be sure not to include the header on the first page of a letter.
</aside>

Complimentary Close

The complimentary close provides a cordial farewell. It is keyed a double space below the body of the letter. Only the first word of a complimentary close has an initial capital letter.

Company Name and Sender's Name and Title

When letterhead stationery is used, the company name is rarely included in the closing lines. If the company name is used, it should be keyed a double space below the complimentary close in all capital letters.

<aside>
Some options for a complimentary close include the following:
Sincerely
Sincerely yours
Cordially
Respectfully
Respectfully yours
</aside>

The sender's name should be entered on the fourth line below the complimentary close or the company name, if included. If required, the sender's official title follows the sender's name. A short title (such as *Director*) is placed on the same line, with a comma separating the name and title. A long title (such as *Director of Internal Affairs*) goes on the line below the sender's name.

Reference Initials

Reference initials identify the person who keyed the business letter, if different from the author, and sometimes the person who wrote or dictated the letter. These initials appear at the left margin a double space below the sender's keyed name and title.

Enclosure Notation

The enclosure notation is used when one or more documents accompany the letter. The word *Enclosure* (or some form of the word) appears at the left margin a double space below the preceding element. Always include an enclosure notation if the letter mentions an enclosure.

Delivery Notations

Letters can be sent in a number of ways, and the method of delivery is information that should be stated on the hard copy, or file copy, of the letter. If a letter is sent by regular mail, no special notation is needed. When a letter is sent by another method, make a note of the delivery method below the last line of type (either the reference initials or the enclosure notation). Delivery methods that should be noted include hand delivery, certified mail, fax (including the fax number), and special carriers (such as UPS and FedEx).

Copy Notations

Copy notations indicate other people who will receive a copy of the letter. A regular copy notation appears in lowercase letters at the left margin as *c* followed by the name(s) of the person(s) receiving a copy. The copy notation should appear a double space below the previous notation, whether reference initials or an enclosure notation.

At times a copy of a letter will be sent to someone by blind copy. This means the receiver whose name is listed on the letter address does not know the copy is being sent to someone else. The blind copy notation appears in lowercase letters at the left margin as *bc* followed by the name(s) of the person(s) receiving the blind copy. However, this notation appears only on the blind copy and the file copy, *not* on the original copy of the letter.

Quick Reference for Parts of a Letter

(Optional elements appear in parentheses. The salutation and complimentary close are omitted in the simplified style.)

- Letterhead/return address
- Date
- Letter address
- (Reference information)
- Salutation
- (Subject line)
- Body
- Second page header, if needed
- Complimentary close
- (Company name)
- Sender's name (and title)
- (Reference initials)
- (Enclosure notations)
- (Delivery notations)
- (Copy notations)
- (Postscript)

If more than one enclosure is included with a letter, you may want to indicate the number in the enclosure notation; for example, Enclosures 2 or 2 Enclosures.

Postscript

Occasionally writers use a postscript to emphasize information in a letter or to add an additional thought that does not flow with the content of the letter. The postscript is keyed a double space below the last notation on the letter. Omit the postscript abbreviation *P.S.*

CHECKPOINT 6-2

Proofread the following letter parts for format errors, using appropriate proofreading symbols to mark errors. Refer to page 262 for solutions.

a. Ms. Katrina Ann Dewar
8577 Estate Drive
West Palm Beach, FL 33411-9753

SALES PROMOTION

Dear Madam *Ms. Dewar*

b. Please let me know when we can get together to discuss the property.

Very Sincerely Yours,

Miss Donna Raynor

Enclosure

ah

c. Sincerely

Bradford Liang, Manager

dt

c Celina Walston
Hand Delivered

d. Sincerely Yours

GLOBAL TRAVEL COMPANY

Mallory Duke

We will put your name in the hat for our monthly drawing.

Enclosures

e. January 2, 20--

Mr. Dean Sorensen, President
AcuSale Resources Inc.
One Broadway Avenue
Detroit, MI 48215-1842

f. I am enclosing your copies of the contract with this letter.

Yours truly,

Marlene Sanchez-Dwyer
Director

rlm *Enclosures*
c Peter Forsythe

g. Acme Box Company
Attention Customer Service
P.O. Box 1610
Burleson, TX 76028

Dear Mr. Driver *Ladies & Gentlemen*

h. Offers like these do not happen

every day, so please let us hear

from you soon.

Cordially,

Marsha Stallones
Sales and Marketing director

BUSINESS LETTER STYLES

Punctuation and placement of some letter parts vary with the letter style the writer chooses. Most business letters are formatted in block style, modified block style, or simplified style.

Refer to Figure 6-3, which provides models of these three letter styles. In block style all elements are set at the left margin. In modified block style the date and complimentary close are keyed beginning at a left tab set at the centerpoint. Note that modified block is the only letter style that offers the option of indented paragraphs. In simplified block style the salutation as well as the complimentary close are omitted while all remaining elements are set at the left margin.

Writers have two options of punctuation styles as well, open or mixed. With open punctuation no punctuation appears after the salutation or the complimentary close. Mixed punctuation uses a colon after the salutation and a comma after the complimentary close.

> After choosing a letter style, be consistent and follow the guidelines for that particular letter style. Also, be consistent with the punctuation of your choice, either open or mixed.

Figure 6-3   Block Style with Open Punctuation

1225 Harrison Avenue Columbus, OH 43201-1225 Phone: 614.555.0173 Fax: 614.555.0193

March 17, 20--

Mrs. Cara Kay Ramos
2502 Buckingham Road
Rochester, NY 14617-9213

Dear Mrs. Romas

TRAVEL OPPORTUNITIES

In a recent survey conducted by the National Association of Travel Agents, 74 percent of those surveyed ranked a cruise as the most enjoyable vacation they have ever had. Survey participants listed exotic scenery, good food, and friendly people as elements that contributed to the enjoyment of their cruises.

We are pleased that other people feel this way too. At Perry Travel Agency we have long believed that a cruise is the best way to enjoy the beauty of nature, to relax, and to make new friends.

Perry Travel Agency specializes in cruises. Our cruises provide not only exotic scenery, good food, and friendly people, but also the opportunity for adventures. You will not have to spend long hours on the road or waste time waiting in lines to have fun and enjoy the sights. Book a cruise with Perry, and we will conjure up your dream vacation now!

If you have always dreamed of a fabulous vacation, today is the day to plan your cruise. Examine the enclosed brochure, and begin making plans for your first trip now. Call us at 614.555.0173, or return the attached information sheet. Arranging a cruise with Perry is easy.

Sincerely yours

PERRY TRAVEL AGENCY

Damien C. Perry, Director

lt

Enclosure

Modified Block Style with Mixed Punctuation

1225 Harrison Avenue Columbus, OH 43201-1225 Phone: 614.555.0173 Fax: 614.555.0193

March 17, 20--

Mrs. Cara Kay Ramos
2502 Buckingham Road
Rochester, NY 14617-9213

Dear Mrs. Ramos:

TRAVEL OPPORTUNITIES

In a recent survey conducted by the National Association of Travel Agents, 74 percent of those surveyed ranked a cruise as the most enjoyable vacation they have ever had. Survey participants listed exotic scenery, good food, and friendly people as elements that contributed to the enjoyment of their cruises.

We are pleased that other people feel this way too. At Perry Travel Agency we have long believed that a cruise is the best way to enjoy the beauty of nature, to relax, and to make new friends.

Perry Travel Agency specializes in cruises. Our cruises provide not only exotic scenery, good food, and friendly people, but also the opportunity for adventures. You will not have to spend long hours on the road or waste time waiting in lines to have fun and enjoy the sights. Book a cruise with Perry, and we will conjure up your dream vacation now!

If you have always dreamed of a fabulous vacation, today is the day to plan your cruise. Examine the enclosed brochure, and begin making plans for your first trip now. Call us at 614.555.0173, or return the attached information sheet. Arranging a cruise with Perry is easy.

Sincerely yours,

PERRY TRAVEL AGENCY

Damien C. Perry, Director

lt

Enclosure

Modified Block Style with Open Punctuation and Indented Paragraphs

1225 Harrison Avenue Columbus, OH 43201-1225 Phone: 614.555.0173 Fax: 614.555.0193

March 17, 20--

Mrs. Cara Kay Ramos
2502 Buckingham Road
Rochester, NY 14617-9213

Dear Mrs. Romas

TRAVEL OPPORTUNITIES

In a recent survey conducted by the National Association of Travel Agents, 74 percent of those surveyed ranked a cruise as the most enjoyable vacation they have ever had. Survey participants listed exotic scenery, good food, and friendly people as elements that contributed to the enjoyment of their cruises.

We are pleased that other people feel this way too. At Perry Travel Agency we have long believed that a cruise is the best way to enjoy the beauty of nature, to relax, and to make new friends.

Perry Travel Agency specializes in cruises. Our cruises provide not only exotic scenery, good food, and friendly people, but also the opportunity for adventures. You will not have to spend long hours on the road or waste time waiting in lines to have fun and enjoy the sights. Book a cruise with Perry, and we will conjure up your dream vacation now!

If you have always dreamed of a fabulous vacation, today is the day to plan your cruise. Examine the enclosed brochure, and begin making plans for your first trip now. Call us at 614.555.0173, or return the attached information sheet. Arranging a cruise with Perry is easy.

Sincerely yours

PERRY TRAVEL AGENCY

Damien C. Perry, Director

lt

Enclosure

Simplified Style

1225 Harrison Avenue Columbus, OH 43201-1225 Phone: 614.555.0173 Fax: 614.555.0193

March 17, 20--

Mrs. Cara Kay Ramos
2502 Buckingham Road
Rochester, NY 14617-9213

TRAVEL OPPORTUNITIES

In a recent survey conducted by the National Association of Travel Agents, 74 percent of those surveyed ranked a cruise as the most enjoyable vacation they have ever had. Survey participants listed exotic scenery, good food, and friendly people as elements that contributed to the enjoyment of their cruises.

We are pleased that other people feel this way too. At Perry Travel Agency we have long believed that a cruise is the best way to enjoy the beauty of nature, to relax, and to make new friends.

Perry Travel Agency specializes in cruises. Our cruises provide not only exotic scenery, good food, and friendly people, but also the opportunity for adventures. You will not have to spend long hours on the road or waste time waiting in lines to have fun and enjoy the sights. Book a cruise with Perry, and we will conjure up your dream vacation now!

If you have always dreamed of a fabulous vacation, today is the day to plan your cruise. Examine the enclosed brochure, and begin making plans for your first trip now. Call us at 614.555.0173, or return the attached information sheet. Arranging a cruise with Perry is easy.

DAMIEN C. PERRY, DIRECTOR

lt

Enclosure

CHECKPOINT 6-3

Proofread the letter shown at the right, and mark errors in letter style using appropriate proofreading symbols. (The writer chose block style with open punctuation.) Compare your work with the solution on page 262.

June 16, 20--

Ms. Jennifer Elaine Carson
Route 2, Box 507B
Huntsville, AL 35807-8615

PURCHASE ORDER 471

Dear Ms. Carson

Thank you for your order for six reams of antique white stationery, Stock No. 331. The quality of the stationery you have selected will let your customers know that they are important to you.

Because of the recent shipping strike, we have encountered delays in receiving merchandise from the factory. However, you can expect your order within ten days. We hope this delay will not inconvenience you.

We appreciate the business you have given us in the past, and we look forward to serving you in the future.

Sincerely,

Audrey D. Leapley, Manager
Shipping Department

ec

c R. P. Michaels

LETTER PLACEMENT

The spacing and placement of the various letter parts contribute to the readability of a document as well as to its overall attractiveness. Placing the body of a letter too high or low or too far to the left or right on the paper upsets the balance and detracts from the letter's appearance as well as its message. To create an overall attractive letter appearance, the operator must use appropriate side, top, and bottom margins. These margins depend on the size of stationery used, the letterhead mast, and the length of the letter.

As a proofreader you should be more concerned with the overall balance of a letter than with its exact margins. Regardless of the size of the stationery and the length of the document, the letter should appear balanced on the page. Your goal in proofreading is to train your eye to identify an improperly placed letter. Consider the following letter placement table as a guide:

Default left/right margins for documents prepared in Word are 1.25 inches; in WordPerfect, 1 inch. Of course, you may need to adjust the margins.

In some offices a specific dateline position is used for all letters, regardless of classification.

LETTER PLACEMENT TABLE GUIDE

Letter Classification	Side Margins	Dateline Position* (from 1″ top margin)
Short (1-2 paragraphs)	2″	2″
Average (3-4 paragraphs)	1½″	1¾″
Long (4+ paragraphs)	1″	1¼″
Two-page	1″	1¼″

*When a deep letterhead prevents use of this dateline position, place the date a double space below the last line of the letterhead.

CHECKPOINT 6-4

Study the three letters shown, and indicate which letter has the best placement.

Letter A

Letter B

Letter C

The best placement is demonstrated in Letter ___A___.

MEMORANDUM FORMAT

Interoffice memorandums (memos) are used to send informal messages within an organization. Memos cover one subject or topic that can be discussed in a few paragraphs. As with any business correspondence, accuracy of the message and the proper format are important. Coworkers and managers judge an employee's written products just as critically as do clients and customers.

Standard Memo Format

Most word processing programs have templates that include memo formats. Operators can use these templates as is or modify them.

Memos are usually prepared in a standard format and printed on plain paper or on company letterhead. Standard memos contain the four main headings of TO, FROM, DATE, and SUBJECT. After each heading, information specific to a given memo is keyed. Begin all lines of the heading at the left margin. Key a colon after each heading, and double-space between headings.

> TO: Juan Olmos
>
> FROM: Francis Jameson
>
> DATE: February 14, 20--
>
> SUBJECT: March 1 Seminar

The message of a memo begins a double space below the last line of the heading. The body of the message is single-spaced and double-spaced between paragraphs. If a memo is longer than one page, key a header on successive pages that includes the name of the addressee(s), the date, and the page number. The originator usually signs or initials beside his or her name in the heading. Optional reference initials are keyed a double space below the body.

Figure 6-4   Standard Memo
Printed on Plain Paper

Standard Memo
Printed on Company Letterhead

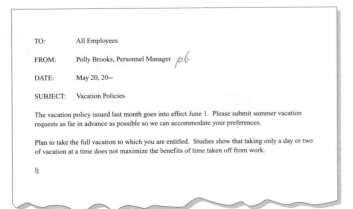

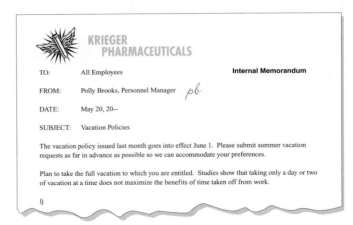

Proofread the following memo, and mark the format errors using appropriate proofreading symbols. Check your solution on page 262.

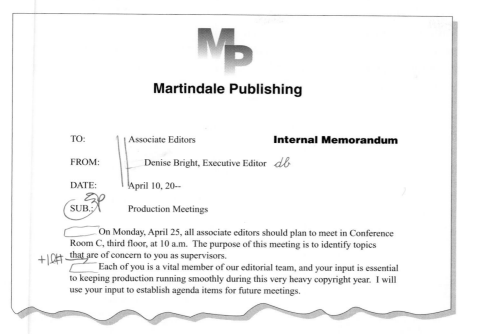

E-MAIL FORMAT

Sending messages by e-mail is fast, convenient, and easy—and is becoming a preferred way to communicate in writing for business use as well as personal use. In the business world computer users send e-mail messages *internally* (instead of memos) to other employees within their own companies and *externally* (instead of business letters) to customers, clients, and vendors.

Even though e-mail messages are easy to prepare, they represent the same significance as memos and business letters and should not be treated casually. In addition, confidentiality of e-mail messages cannot be guaranteed; therefore, communications that must be assured of confidentiality should not be sent as e-mails.

The appearance of an e-mail message is largely dictated by the software program used; but the format will generally look like a memo, containing fields for TO, FROM, DATE, and SUBJECT. The most important line to the recipient is the subject line, which describes the nature, importance, and urgency of the message. Use only a few key words for the subject line; and, like memos, limit an e-mail message to one subject. However, unlike a printed memo or business letter, the recipient will read the message on a computer screen. Therefore, if the message is more than several paragraphs long or is very detailed, a memo or business letter might be a better choice than an e-mail.

Some writers use special abbreviations in their e-mail messages, such as BTW (by the way) and JK (just kidding). Always consider the recipient, and do not use abbreviations in e-mails if you think the recipient might not understand them or if you would not use them in other written business communications.

The memo format carries through to the text itself. Internal e-mails can have a more casual appearance; however, external e-mails should have a more formal business letter appearance. External e-mails should include a salutation and a closing (without the blank lines for a signature), as would appear in a business letter. The inclusion of personal titles for the salutation and the closing, as well as the inclusion of the writer's job title in the closing, should be the same as for a business letter. If you anticipate that an external recipient will need an address, a phone number, or a fax number, provide these in the message or after the closing.

Figure 6-5   Internal E-mail

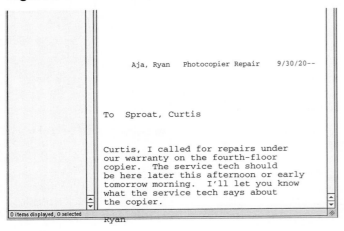

External E-mail

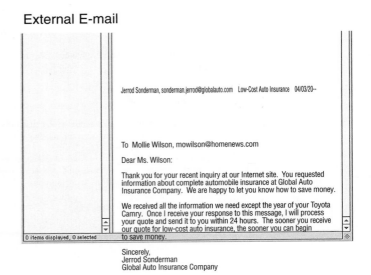

REPORT FORMAT

Business and educational institutions use reports extensively to provide information on specific topics. Reports may be long, formal documents consisting of a number of parts; or they may be short, informal documents consisting of only a heading and the body of the report. Reports may be prepared in letter format, memo format, or report format. Letter and memo formats have already been discussed; the remainder of this chapter will deal with report format.

As with business letters and memos, the text of a report should be positioned in an attractive, easy-to-read format. Reports may be unbound or bound, depending on the size and formality of the report. An unbound report has top, bottom, and side margins of 1 inch. A top margin of 1½ inches is used for the first page. A bound report has top, bottom, and right margins of 1 inch. The left margin is 1½ inches to allow space for binding. Both unbound and bound reports should include page numbers on second and succeeding pages at the top right of the page. A double space follows the page number.

The standard parts of a report include a title page, headings, and references; but other elements may be added as necessary. Refer to Figure 6-6 on page 85 as you read about the format for the main parts of a report.

Title Page

The title page contains four elements, all of them centered on the page. Position the title of the report 3 inches from the top of the paper, the author's name 6 inches from the top, the author's title a double space below his or her name, and the date about 8½ inches from the top.

Headings

The main heading is centered 1½ inches from the top of the first page and is keyed in all capital letters. If two lines are required, the lines may be either single-spaced or double-spaced. If a secondary heading is used, it is centered a double space below the main heading; important words are capitalized.

Side headings indicate subdivisions of the main topic. Side headings are usually keyed in **title case** and may be underlined or bolded. Title case treats the main words in a title with initial capital letters. Double-space before and after a side heading regardless of the spacing used in the body of the report. Paragraph headings indicate subdivisions of side headings. When used, a paragraph heading is placed at the beginning of a paragraph. Only the first word is capitalized, and the heading is underlined and followed by a period. The text of the paragraph begins on the same line as the heading. Paragraph headings are sometimes called run-in headings because they "run in" with the text instead of occupying their own line.

Body

The body, or text, of a report begins a double space below the main heading. The body is either double-spaced with paragraphs indented 0.5 inch or single-spaced with block paragraphs. When text is single-spaced, leave a blank line between each paragraph. Leave at least two lines of a paragraph at the top or bottom of a page so as not to create a widow/orphan. **Widow/orphan** is a term that refers to the first line or last line of a paragraph on a page by itself.

Bibliography or References

When quoting another author or when using another person's ideas, writers must identify their sources. A common method of documentation is to cite the source of the information within the body of the report. This reference includes the author's last name, the year of publication, and the page number. The reference could appear within the text, parenthetically, or as an endnote. Endnotes are keyed in order on a separate page that follows the report.

When checking the appearance of a title page on screen, reduce the page view to 50 percent to see the placement of elements and the balance of the page.

To make headings stand out, writers may choose to use **boldface**, to increase the font size, or to apply a different font color.

The widow/orphan protection on most word processing programs eliminates the occurrence of a single line of a paragraph at the top or bottom of a page.

WORKPLACE CONNECTIONS

Giving credit to others for their ideas is the professional thing to do. This is true whether those ideas belong to a colleague or to the author of an article.

---

within text   According to Macey (1999, 74), employees . . .
parenthetically   According to the research . . . (Macey 1999, p. 74)
endnote   According to expert opinions in this field[1] . . .

Complete information about the sources is found on a reference page at the end of the report. The word *references* or *bibliography* appears at the top of the section and should have the same appearance as the main heading. Each entry in this section consists of the author's name; title of article, book, or interview; date of publication; and page number(s) of the material cited. Report writers may choose from several styles to cite references, but only one style should be used in any report. A proofreader should check a reference manual or an online source for examples of how to cite references in a report according to the writer's chosen style. If the entire reference list will not fit on the last page of the body of the report, all references should be set on a new page.

Optional Elements of Reports

A report may also contain other elements that help the writer convey the message of the report. In addition, elements such as a title fly, a table of contents, and an authorization letter are added when formality is required. A proofreader should refer to a reference or writing manual for further instruction on how to prepare these additional elements of a report:

Quick Reference for Parts of a Report

(Optional elements appear in parentheses.)

- (Title fly)
- Title page
- (Transmittal or authorization letter)
- (Table of contents)
- (List of illustrations)
- (Executive summary)
- Headings
- Body
- (Internal citations)
- (Illustrations)
- (Endnotes)
- References
- (Glossary)
- (Appendix)

Title Fly	Name of the report centered on a separate page; appears as the first page
Transmittal or Authorization	Letter (or memo, if internal) that explains the purpose or the authorization for the report
Table of Contents	List of the headings and the page numbers on which their corresponding sections begin
List of Illustrations	List of illustrations and their corresponding page numbers
Executive Summary	Summary of the contents of the reports, especially any conclusions or recommendations; prepared to save time for a reader
Internal Citations	Individual citations given within the text rather than listed at the end of the report
Illustrations	Figures, tables, graphs, pictures, or any type of nontext illustrations that make the content of the report clear
Endnotes	List of citations given within the text by superscript number; arranged by number on a separate page following the report

Glossary	List of technical or other unusual words used throughout the report that are defined for the reader
Appendix	Separate section of reference material discussed in the report; may be categorized Appendix A, Appendix B, and so on

Figure 6-6   Unbound Report Format

TIPS FOR GETTING ORGANIZED

Do you have trouble getting everything done in the time available? Do you often lose important papers? Do you lose papers on top of your desk? If you are like most people, the answer to some of these questions is a resounding yes! Perhaps a few tips for getting organized would be helpful.

Time Inventory

Record on a time log the amount of time you spend each day in various activities. Do this for a week. Then analyze your time log to discover ways in which you can improve the management of your time. Ask yourself these questions:

1. What is generally my most productive period of the day? Why?

2. What is my least productive period of the day? Why?

3. When do I waste time? On what tasks or activities do I waste time?

4. On what activities could I spend less time and still get the desired results?

5. Do I have all my supplies and materials ready before beginning an activity?

After you have analyzed your time log, focus first on your time wasters.

Identify your time wasters. Some time wasters may be external factors that you cannot easily control, such as telephone interruptions, meetings, and socializing. However, you can control internal factors, such as procrastination and failure to delegate, plan, or set priorities.

Once you identify your time wasters, figure out how to minimize them. You might screen calls to cut down on telephone interruptions. Or you might schedule meetings during your less productive periods of the day, leaving your productive periods for your own use.

Develop a "Things to Do" List

Develop a list of tasks to be completed, placing the most urgent items first. Check your list every day, and revise as needed. Make sure, however, that you are not just shuffling the same items. Strive to cross things off the list. Then add new items to the list, always prioritizing for efficiency.

Maintain a Recording and Filing System

Keep pertinent information in an accessible place. Two such places are an electronic organizer and your personal files.

Electronic organizer. Carry a pocket organizer to keep track of appointments, expenses, addresses, telephone numbers, and reminders.

Filing system. Store important papers in one place--your files. Label folders appropriately; for example, health insurance, benefits, current project, past projects, and so on.

Time is a valuable resource of which few people have enough. The aim of time management is to provide for efficient use of resources, including time, so that individuals are more productive and less stressed.

REFERENCES

Fulton-Calkins, Patsy J., and Joanna D. Hanks. Procedures for the Office Professional, 4e. Cincinnati: South-Western Educational Publishing, 2000.

Odgers, Pattie, and B. Lewis Keeling. Administrative Office Management, 12e. Cincinnati: South-Western Educational Publishing, 2000.

"Time Management Tips." Self-Development Center. 05 Aug. 2000. George Mason University. 18 Oct. 20--. <http://www.gmu.edu/gmu/personal/time.html>.

Reports are generally more lengthy than ordinary letters or memos; therefore, they require more time and effort to proofread. Developing a style sheet will help you treat items consistently. A **style sheet** is a list that shows how special terminology, features, punctuation, capitalization, names, and titles will be handled.

In addition, remember to use the three-step method of proofreading when proofreading reports, as follows:

First, review the report for format. Check all headings and other elements for consistency of presentation. Check page numbers. Review the table of contents to be sure all headings are included.

Second, proofread for content and mechanical errors. If the report has been prepared from a draft copy, proofread the final document against the draft to be sure copy was not omitted and all edits were made.

Third, check each reference for accuracy. If the text refers to an illustration, a figure, or a page within the report, check to be sure the reference is correct. If you are responsible for checking references cited in the report, look up each one to verify it.

Letters, memos, and reports should be attractive displays of organized thought that communicate a writer's intended message. Be sure your documents have the appeal to make a reader want to read them.

SPELLING APPLICATIONS

6-6 Compare the words in Column A with the corresponding words in Column B. Use the appropriate proofreading symbols to correct the misspelled words. If both columns are correct, write **C** to the left of the number.

	Column A	Column B
1.	eliminate	elimniate
2.	employee	employee
3.	judgement	judgment
4.	opportunity	oportunity
5.	optional	opitonal
6.	particularly	particularly
7.	preceed	precede
8.	recommend	reccommend
9.	seperate	separate
10.	useable	usable

CHAPTER SUMMARY

Proofread carefully to be sure your documents follow these format rules:

♦ All business correspondence should conform to a recognized letter style, and format elements should be consistent within that style.

♦ Addresses on envelopes should be keyed in all capital letters with no punctuation.

♦ Salutations must correspond with the name in the letter address.

♦ The most common letter formats are block style, modified block style, and simplified style.

♦ Letters should be placed on a page in a centered or eye-appealing manner.

♦ A standard memo format includes the words *TO, FROM, DATE,* and *SUBJECT.*

♦ E-mail messages should be prepared as carefully as memos and business letters.

♦ Reports may be prepared in letter, memo, or report format; report format may be bound at the left margin.

♦ Reports usually contain the basic elements of title page, headings, body (text), and bibliography or references; but they may also contain additional elements that guide the reader through the contents.

Study these tips, and apply them as you proofread:

♦ Use up-to-date reference and writing manuals to assist you in proofreading for format.

♦ Use the three-step process of proofreading for letters, memos, and reports.

♦ Check references and citations carefully as a separate step.

words@work   Open *words@work*. Click on the Writing tab; then click on Lessons. Read the lessons on Memos and E-mail, Business Letters, and/or Reports and Proposals. Complete the exercises to reinforce your skills in formatting business documents. To view sample business documents, click on the Writing tab; then click on Resources. The Workplace Writing section makes available a number of sample documents.

In Proofreading Applications P-1 through P-4 test your knowledge of the four letter styles presented in this chapter. From the following list identify the required parts used in each letter style.

a. date at left margin

b. date beginning at center

c. letter address

d. salutation

e. text with paragraphs at left margin

f. text with paragraphs indented

g. complimentary close

h. sender's name

P-1 Block   *a c d e g h*

P-2 Modified Block   *b c d e g h*

P-3 Modified Block with Indented Paragraphs   *b c d f g h*

P-4 Simplified   *a c e h*

P-5   Locate information on addressing mail by visiting the U.S. Postal Service web site at http://www.usps.gov/. Perform a keyword search using *addressing and packaging*, or search for Publication 201. Write a two- or three-paragraph memo to your instructor, summarizing your findings.

PROGRESSIVE PROOFREADING

You are employed as an executive assistant to Ms. Elena Suppan, regional manager of Perin Office Systems, Inc. You have just finished keying three documents. In addition to proofreading those documents, you need to proofread documents prepared by a coworker. Check for errors in spelling, keying, abbreviations, word division, number expression, and format.

6-6

1. eliminate
2. employee
3. judgement
4. opportunity
5. optional
6. C
7. precede
8. reccommend
9. seperate
10. useable

P-1

a, c, d, e, g, h

P-2

b, c, d, e, g, h

P-3

b, c, d, f, g, h

P-4

a, c, e, h

PERIN OFFICE SYSTEMS

March 17, 20--

Miss Sandra Mendoza
Phillips and Solomon
31 N. Main St.
Champlain, NY 12919-4300

Dear ~~Mr.~~ Miss Mendoza:

Thank you for the opportunity to demonstrate our new DataPhone telephone system at the TeleCom Exhibition last week. As you make your decision on a new system, keep in mind that DataPhone offers the following features:

1. **Speed dialing.** This feature can bring as many as 25 often-called numbers together in one place on the desktop console. By pressing a preprogrammed button, you can place a call in less than 3 seconds. Speed dialing eliminates searching for phone numbers.

2. **Call pickup.** This feature helps to eliminate unanswered calls by allowing anyone to answer a ringing phone.

3. **Conferencing.** This feature provides an easy, convenient way to bring people together without having to travel or even leave their desks.

3. **Call forwarding.** This feature is particularly useful since it allows calls to be forwarded to another extention. A person who is away from his or her desk or in a meeting is never out of reach.

4. **Speaker.** An optional feature, this is an extremely convenient way to talk hands-free, to take notes, or to operate a computer.

Perin Office Systems provides installation and employee training free of charge to companies that purchase the DataPhone system. Call us today to discuss your phone needs.

Sincerely

Ms. Elena E. Suppan
Regional Manager

ri

3903 Spaulding Drive, Atlanta, GA 30338-3903 · (404) 555-0106 Fax (404) 555-0176 · perin@peachtree.com

PERIN OFFICE SYSTEMS

March 17, 20--

Eastman Brothers, Inc.
Attention Project Committee
7861 Monroe Street
Tallahassee, FL 32301-7654

Ladies and
Gentlemen

PRELIMINARY DESIGN REVIEW

Enclosed is a brief report reviewing the preliminary design factors that
your project committee should consider when planning the 15,000-
square-foot addition to Eastman Brothers' existing facilities.

Stacey Cosentino and her staff will provide complete documentation for
these reccomendations at the initial planning session on April 7. In the
mean time, best wishes as you proceed with your project plans.

Sincerely yours,

Ms. Elena E. Suppan
Reg. Manager

jp

Enclosure

3903 Spaulding Drive, Atlanta, GA 30338-3903 · (404) 555-0106   Fax (404) 555-0176 · perin@peachtree.com

Job 3 Proofread this report to Eastman Brothers. Check correct figures of the floor area with the note supplied by one of the realtors (see note on page 94).

OFFICE DESIGN FACTORS

Eastman Brothers, Inc.

Because office design does affect job performance and job satisfaction, several factors must be considered in the preliminary stages of planning the construction or renovation of any facility. This report discusses these factors and gives recommendations that may decrease absenteeism and increase employees' productivity by as much as 30%.

Work Space

The area where workers spend most of their time is their work space. Factors affecting work-space design are discussed in the following paragraphs.

Enclosures. The open office plan with enclosures, or cubicles, gives workers the privacy they need, supports communication, and improves productivity more than either the fully open or fully closed office plan. To be effective, the partitions surrounding each work area should be higher than standing height on 3 sides.

Floor area. The amount of usable flour space a worker can call his or her own is based on job need and status. According to a survey conducted by Perin Office Systems, the recommended space requirements for various employees are as follows:

Top-level executives	400 square feet
Middle-level executives	300 square feet
Supervisors	200 square feet
Office employees	100 square feet

Layout. The physical arrangement (layout) of furniture and walls greatly affects job performance, comfort, status, and ease of communication. Workers should have two good work surfaces and a single entrance. The layout should be such that another worker's work space is not directly visible from any other worker's work space.

Lighting.

Proper lighting is determined by the quality and quantity of light. Approximately 150 footcandles are recommended for workers who use computers. Most lighting problems are caused by too much light, resulting in glare on documents or reflections on monitors. Although most workers prefer to be be near a window, windows do cause glare.

Ambient light fixtures, which illuminate the entire office area, combined with task lighting, which lights specific work surfaces, create the most effective lighting system.

Noise

Office conversations, ringing telephones, and outside nose account for most office noise. Sound-absorbent materials used throughout the building, acoustical enclosures on printers, and layout are effective means of reducing office noise. Office noise should be less than 65 decibels (Canada Safety Council, 1999).

Energy

Energy needs include lines for power, telephones, and data. To determine these needs, the following questions must be answered: Do you expect high growth in computer usage? Do you expect to rearrange workstations frequently? If so, how often?

Access floors raised of the structural slab provide an excellent solution for distributing heat, air conditioning, and wiring for data and telephone services. These floors have unlimited capacity and may be accessed at any point by service units without calling an electrician. Additionally, quality and speed of transmission will not be affected as your transmission needs gorw.

REFERENCES

Fishman, Charles. "We've Seen the Future of Work, and It Works, But Very Differently."
        Fast Company, Issue 4, August 1996.

"Noise and Acoustics." Office Health and Safety. 14 Jan. 2000. Canada Safety Council.
        26 May 20--. <http://www.safety-council.org/info/OSH/noise.htm>.

From the desk of **JAMIR MOE**   *Date* 3/17

To Elena Suppan

Here are the figures on minimum floor space requirements that Talia compiled, based on the survey she conducted.

Top-level executives	425 sq ft
Middle-level "	350 sq ft
Supervisors	200 sq ft
Office employees	75-100 sq ft

jm

PERIN OFFICE SYSTEMS

March 17, 20--

Please check to be sure that I haven't missed any errors. Mr. Holms prefers the mod. block with indented paragraphs and mixed punct.

Thanks
tr

Mrs. Jessica shimer
2905 Sandcastle Dr.
Tallahassee, FL 32308-9625

Dear Mrs. Shimer:

Thank you for your interest in the Penn Laser Copier, Model 212. Enclosed is a brochure detailing its unique features, particularly its specifications and cost.

The Penn Laser Copier is the most technologically sophisticated copier on the market today. This laser-driven copier uses a scanner to digitize originals. Text (including columns) can be manipulated before printing begins. Because it is digital, the laser copier can transmit images to other printers and produce high-resolution copiers in seconds.

After you have had an opportunity to review this brochure, I will give you a call to provide you with additional product or price information or to set up a demonstration. In the meantime, please call me at the number listed below if you have any questions.

Sincerely Yours,

Robin C. Holms, District Sales Representative

tr

enclosures

COMPUTERIZED PROOFREADING

Job 5 Format and proofread a memo.

1. The technology manager at Perin Office Systems is about to issue a memo to some of her coworkers. First, she wrote the body of the memo by hand, as shown below. Then she keyed the memo.
2. Load C06JOB5 from the template CD-ROM. Format the memo, addressing it to **All Perin Managers** from **Dale Ericson.** Enter the current date, and use **Computer Maintenance** as the subject.
3. Proofread the memo against the handwritten draft below. Check for all types of errors, and correct any errors that you find.
4. Spell check the document.
5. Save the memo using the file name C06JOB5R.
6. Print the memo.
7. Proofread the printed document. If you find any additional errors, revise, save, spell check, and reprint the document.

---

1. Keep equipment away from direct sunlight, heat vents, and open windows. Extreme temperatures can damage chips and other components.

2. Keep food and beverages away from equipment and diskettes.

3. Handle CDs with care. Improper use can impair their performance.

4. Keep paper clips that have been stored in a magnetic container away from diskettes. Keep diskettes away from magnets or any electronic equipment. These item contain magnetic fields that can cause portions of data to be erased.

4. Use anti static mats under your desk area. Static electricity can cause memory loss in your computer.

5. Never oil your printer or any part of your system. Oil will will clog the machine.

6. Check that you have sufficient power to run your equipment.

7. Do not take anything apart, even if, in your judgement, you can fix it. Call Helen Mathys (Ext. 278), and she will contact our svc. representative.

NOTE these procedures for the following chapters:

- Beginning in Chapter 7, specific formatting instructions will not be provided for letters, memos, or reports. If necessary, check the placement table or the models in this chapter.
- The steps of saving, checking spelling, printing, proofreading the printed document, and, if necessary, reprinting the document are standard procedures that you should implement each time you process a job from the template CD-ROM. These instructions will not be repeated.

CHAPTER 7

GRAMMAR ERRORS: SENTENCE STRUCTURE

Subjects and verbs are the workhorses of our language. All it takes is one subject and one verb to make a sentence: *Toby ran.* Without one or the other, a sentence is not complete, no matter how many other words are in the sentence. Given that importance, we, as writers and proofreaders, must ensure that sentences contain subjects and verbs that work together. Ideas expressed by subjects and verbs that agree in number and that make sense can communicate an idea from a sender to a receiver, which is the purpose of writing.

IMPORTANCE OF CORRECT GRAMMAR

The proofreader must be alert for grammatical errors. In addition to clarifying the message, correct grammar conveys a message to the reader about the writer. Correct grammar reflects the writer's ability and attention to detail. The reader will have greater confidence in the writer if the message is grammatically correct. If the grammar is not correct, the reader will react negatively and lose confidence in the writer or the person or company the writer represents.

PARTS OF A SENTENCE

A sentence is a group of words that expresses a complete thought. A sentence requires both a subject and a predicate. The **subject** is the person, place, or thing spoken of in the sentence. The **predicate** indicates what the subject is or does. In addition, a grammatically correct sentence must make sense by expressing a complete idea.

LEARNING OBJECTIVES

- Describe the parts of a complete sentence.
- Create subject and verb agreement.
- Identify and correct sentence structure faults.
- Use appropriate proof-reading symbols to indicate changes in text.
- Spell correctly a list of commonly misspelled words.

7-1 The subject of a sentence will contain a **simple subject,** which is usually a noun or a pronoun. A **noun** is a person, place, thing, or concept (*Barbara, New York, hat, freedom*). A **pronoun** is a word used in the place of a noun (*I, you, he, she, it, we, they*). (In the following sentences S = subject, V = verb, LV = linking verb, C = complement, and O = object.)

> The subject of a sentence is what the sentence is about.

		S V
Noun used as the subject.		Miss Campos signed the contract.
Pronoun used as the subject.		S V He made an offer on the house.

7-2 The predicate of a sentence contains a verb, which may be an action verb or a linking verb. **Action verbs** express action (*eat, sleep, think*). **Linking verbs** link the subject to words that rename or describe the subject. Linking verbs are all the forms of *to be* (*is, am, are, was, were, be, being, been*) and a few other verbs that describe senses (*feels, appears, tastes, seems, sounds, looks, smells*). The words that rename or describe the subject are **complements.** Complements can be nouns, pronouns, or adjectives. A verb may indicate action toward an **object.** The object answers the question *what* or *whom* in the sentence.

> S   V
> Winston works at Global Moving Company.
> (The action verb *works* expresses action by the subject.)
>
> S   V   O
> Winston traded his cubicle for an office.
> (The action verb *traded* expresses action toward the object; the object answers the question *traded what.*)
>
> S   LV   C
> Winston's coworkers were jealous of his window and nice view.
> (The linking verb *were* links the subject to the complement *jealous.*)
>
> S   LV   C
> Sherry felt bad about ordering the wrong stationery.
> (The linking verb *felt* links the subject to the complement *bad.*)

If two or more verbs appear in a verbal phrase, the final verb in the phrase determines whether the verb is an action verb or a linking verb.

> S   V
> The committee is working on the handouts for today's meeting.
> (The verbal phrase *is working* is considered an action verb.)

The predicate of a sentence tells what the subject is or does. The predicate always contains a verb.

An object answers the question *what* or *whom.*

A linking verb requires a complement to make the sentence complete.

A complement renames or describes the subject.

CHECKPOINT 7-1, 7-2

In the following grammatically correct sentences, indicate subjects as either nouns or pronouns by writing *N* or *P* above the subject. Indicate verbs as either action verbs or linking verbs by writing *V* or *LV* above the verb. Indicate complements by writing *C* above the complement. Indicate objects by writing *O* above the object.

a. Mr. Ormand wants the report on his desk by noon.

b. Koshiro will be unable to attend the meeting tomorrow.

c. Three new laser printers have been installed in the office.

d. She will conduct a leadership workshop at the district conference.

e. Many people are working as volunteers in their communities.

f. You may take your vacation the second week in November.

g. Roger's microwave popcorn smells good.

SUBJECT-VERB AGREEMENT

Subjects and verbs must agree in number. The first step is to locate the true subject and the true verb. Then you apply the subject-verb agreement rules presented here.

7-3 A singular subject must have a singular verb, and a plural subject must have a plural verb.

> S   V   S   LV   C
> The author writes clearly. Her two books appear to be best-sellers.
>   (singular subject/verb)   (plural subject/verb)

The personal pronouns *he*, *she*, and *it* require a singular verb; *you*, *I*, *we*, and *they* require a plural verb. The pronoun *you* always requires a plural verb even though it may be used in the singular sense. The pronoun *I* is singular, but it requires a plural verb.

> S V   O   S V   O
> He writes the company's memos. We write the letters.
>
> S V O   S V   O   O
> You write letters also. I write reports and manuals as well.

7-4 A **compound subject** consists of two or more subjects for one verb joined by the word *and*. A compound subject usually requires a plural verb. When using the pronoun *I* as part of a compound subject, always put the other subject first.

> S   S   LV C
> Lyle Mann and Blair Jordan are seniors.
>
> S   S   S LV   C
> Doreen, Raji, and I were classmates in school.

Three exceptions to the above rule are (1) when the compound subject is considered to be one unit; (2) when the compound subject is preceded by *each*, *every*, *many a*, or *many an*; and (3) when the compound subject is made up of two compound pronouns joined by *and*. In these situations use a singular verb.

> S   S   LV   C
> My teacher and advisor, Dr. Underwood, is a baseball fan.
> (The compound subject *teacher and advisor* is one unit.)
>
> S   S   V
> Each teacher and student is expected to attend the assembly.
> (The compound subject *teacher and student* is preceded by *each*.)

7-1, 7-2

a.   N   V
   Mr. Ormand wants
      O
   the report

b.   N   LV
   Koshiro will be
      C
   unable

c.   N
   printers have
      V
   been installed

d.   P   V
   She will conduct
   a leadership
      O
   workshop

e.   N   V
   people are working

f.   P   V
   You may take
      O
   your vacation

g.   N   LV
   popcorn smells
      C
   good.

The grammar checker on your word processing program may be useful for catching errors in subject-verb agreement. Consider the program's recommendations, but base your final decision on the rules presented in this chapter.

S   S   V

Many an honor and award is presented at graduation.
(The compound subject *honor and award* is preceded by *Many an*.)

S   S   V   O

Anybody and everybody who asks receives the discount.
(The compound subject *anybody and everybody* is made up of two compound pronouns joined by *and*.)

7–5 A compound subject joined by *or* or *nor* may require either a singular verb or a plural verb. The verb should agree with the subject nearest the verb. If one of the subjects is singular and one is plural, you may place the plural subject closest to the verb.

For a compound subject joined by *or* or *nor,* the verb must agree with the *nearest* subject.

S   S LV   C

Either you or I am responsible for paying the bills.

S   S LV   C

Neither Jon nor they are qualified for that position.

CHECKPOINT 7-3–7-5

Proofread for errors in subject-verb agreement. If necessary, revise the verb to make the subject and verb agree. If a sentence is correct, write *C* to the right of the sentence.

a. She and her boss appears to be in agreement on the project.

b. Neither the computers nor the printer were working after the power outage.

C c. Amanda Griswold testifies at the sentencing hearing today.

d. The nine videos and four VCRs is checked out until next Monday.

e. The quarterback and captain of the team, Danny Sizemore, have been recruited.

f. Each winner and loser in this game want another chance to play.

g. Neither the children nor their mother is going to Europe this summer.

WORKPLACE
CONNECTIONS

Being clear and concise are two of the most important goals for business writers. If too many words separate a subject from its verb, the writing may be wordy or confusing.

7–6 Locate the true subject of the verb to make the subject and verb agree in number. Sometimes words or word groups separate the subject and verb. These words or word groups may contain nouns, but they are not the true subject. Look for and eliminate prepositional phrases, verbal phrases, and other word groups from consideration as the true subject.

S   LV   C

The author's new book, *Excesses*, is a thriller from start to finish.
(The word *Excesses* separates the subject and verb.)

                              S   LV   C
The bus driver, in addition to the students, was irritable.
(The prepositional phrase *in addition to the students* separates the
subject and verb.)

                    S   V
The employees working on that job have to finish it by July 1.
(The verbal phrase *working on that job* separates the subject
and verb.)

7-3—7-5
a. appears
b. ~~were~~ was
c. C
d. ~~is~~ are
e. ~~have~~ has been recruited.
f. want^s
g. C

7-7 Most of the time subjects appear *before* the verbs in sentences.
This is *normal order*. To locate the true subject of the verb, you may have
to look for the subject *after* the verb. This is *inverted order*. Sentences that
begin with the words *here* and *there* are in inverted order. Questions are in
inverted order. Locate the true subject of the verb to make the subject and
verb agree.

        C LV   S
Here is an example of a report format for you to follow.

        C LV   S
Here are several examples of report formats for you to consider.

LV S   C
Is this the report format you prefer?

In everyday speech,
agreement errors in
sentences that begin
with *here* and *there*
are common. For
example, "Here's the
books you wanted."
Watch for these when
you proofread.

7-8 Collective nouns (*audience, committee, council, faculty, firm, group,
jury, society*) identify groups; they may be used as subjects of verbs. When
the group acts as one unit, use a singular verb; when the group acts as
individual members, use a plural verb.

        S   V
The staff is meeting today to discuss the vacation schedule.

        S   V   O
The staff are rescheduling their vacations to accommodate Jules.

A collective noun
may be singular or
plural depending on
how it is used in the
sentence.

CHECKPOINT 7-6–7-8

**Proofread for errors in subject-verb agreement. If necessary, revise the verb
to make the subject and verb agree. If a sentence is correct, write *C* to the
right of the sentence.**

a. Here are a large bag of glass containers to be recycled. [is]

b. People skills, along with job knowledge, is needed to be successful on the job. [are]

c. Have the jury reached a verdict in the case? [Has]

d. The need for service industry employees are greater today than ten years ago. [is]

e. The production schedule, as well as the specifications, are difficult to meet. [is]

f. Mr. Macrino said the personnel committee decide matters of pay increases. [s]

a. ~~are~~ is

b. ~~is needed~~ are

c. ~~Have~~ Has

d. ~~are~~ is

e. ~~are~~ is

f. decides

7-9 When used as subjects of verbs, treat the words *a number* as a plural subject; treat the words *the number* as a singular subject.

    S   V

A number of people are enrolling in the fitness classes.

    S   V

The number of people is increasing with each session.

7-10 Fractions and portions are sometimes used as subjects of verbs. Look for the nouns to which the fractions or portions refer to determine whether to use singular or plural verbs.

    S   LV   C

Three-fourths of the members are voting delegates.
(The subject *three-fourths* refers to the noun *members*.)

    S   LV C   S LV C

Part of a king's cake is chocolate, and part is vanilla.
(The subjects *part* refer to the noun *cake*.)

7-11 When quantities and measurements are subjects of verbs, determine how they are used in the sentence. If the quantities or measurements indicate a total amount, use a singular verb; if they indicate individual measurements of items that can be counted, use a plural verb.

    S   LV   C

A hundred dollars is too much to pay for that cell phone.
(*A hundred dollars* indicates a total amount.)

    S   V

About twenty are planning to attend our dinner.
(*Twenty* indicates individuals who can be counted.)

For quantities and measurements ask yourself if the words refer to a total amount (singular verb) or to a group of counted items (plural verb).

CHECKPOINT 7-9–7-11

Proofread for errors in subject-verb agreement. If necessary, revise the verb to make the subject and verb agree. If a sentence is correct, write *C* to the right of the sentence.

a. A number of errors are apparent in our calculations. C

b. One-half of the city's teachers ~~is~~ are living in another city.

c. Five dollars ~~are~~ is all you need for lunch.

d. The number of needy people ~~are~~ is too much for our limited resources.

e. Only a portion of the proceeds are going toward the scholarship fund. C

f. Part of the money ~~are~~ is going into David's savings account.

7-12 Subjects of verbs may take the form of **indefinite pronouns**, which are pronouns that are not specific but refer to other nouns. Some indefinite pronouns are always singular, some are always plural, and some are either singular or plural depending on the nouns to which they refer. The following indefinite pronouns are always singular and require a singular verb when used as a subject.

another	every (*see 7-4*)	much	nothing
anybody	everybody	neither	one
anyone	everyone	nobody	somebody
anything	everything	none (formal usage)	someone
each	many a/an (*see 7-4*)	no one	something
either			

    S   V   O
Somebody is bringing a boom box to the party.

    S LV   C
Nothing is as important as finding a solution.

              S LV   C
Of all the ambassadors, none is more impressive than she.
(In this example *none* in formal usage is considered singular.)

Note: Spell *anyone*, *everyone*, and *someone* as two words when they are followed by an *of* phrase. As two words, these are still considered singular subjects.

    S   V
Every one of us competes at the advanced level.

The indefinite pronouns *both*, *few*, *many*, *others*, and *several* are always plural and require a plural verb when used as a subject.

    S   V
Both of the computers are used each hour the lab is open.

    S   V
Several were boxed for storage until needed.

The indefinite pronouns *all*, *any*, *more*, *most*, *none* (general usage), and *some* may be singular or plural depending on the noun to which they refer. Sometimes the noun will be implied, but the subject and verb must still agree.

    S   V
Most of the new students were directed to the auditorium.

    S   V
Most of the Latin program is offered on the Internet.

    S   V   O
None of the casseroles contain meat.
(In this example *none* in general usage is considered plural.)

7-9—7-11
a. C
b. ~~is~~ are
c. ~~are~~ is
d. ~~are~~ is
e. C
f. ~~are~~ is

Business reports, correspondence, and memorandums are considered formal writing.

Indefinite pronouns ending in *-body, -one,* and *-thing* are singular and require a singular verb.

Use this test to "hear" the correct verb when the subject is *all, any, more, most, none,* or *some*. Replace the *of* phrase with either *of it* or *of them*, depending on whether the noun in the phrase is singular or plural. For example, *teachers* is plural, so say "Most of them were assigned . . ." Now you can hear that the verb is correct.

Most plan to attend the soccer match.

(Here the writer intends the word *most* to refer to the plural noun *fans*, as in *Most of the fans plan to attend the soccer match.*)

CHECKPOINT 7-12

Proofread for errors in subject-verb agreement. If necessary, revise the verb to make the subject and verb agree. If a sentence is correct, write *C* to the right of the sentence.

a. Most of the workers in our group agrees that we should file a complaint.

b. None of us are going to lunch before noon.

c. Any one of us are able to take minutes at the meeting.

d. Many a mother and daughter wish to attend the bridal show.

e. Only a few was at the ceremony when Oliver received his award.

f. Somebody or something are affecting the morale in this department.

g. Every person need to save for his or her retirement.

7-12

a. agrees

b. C

c. ~~are~~ *is*

d. wish *es*

e. ~~was~~ *were*

f. ~~are~~ *is*

g. need *s*

#@%&!@#

From a student paper:
A run-on sentence is one that can be a group of words that says something and states nothing.

SENTENCE FAULTS

Sentences cannot be grammatically correct if they contain structure faults. Learn to recognize these sentence faults so your sentences are free of errors.

7-13 A **sentence fragment** lacks either a subject or a verb and does not express a complete thought. Rewrite sentence fragments to change them into complete sentences.

Sentence Fragment: Promoted the clerk and hired a replacement.
Complete Sentence: Jacinta promoted the clerk and hired a replacement.

A **comma splice** contains two complete thoughts incorrectly joined by a comma. A **run-on sentence** contains two complete thoughts but does not contain punctuation to join them. Revise the punctuation to correct a comma splice or a run-on sentence.

Comma Splice: You will learn your new job quickly, Chad is a good trainer.
Run-on Sentence: You will learn your new job quickly Chad is a good trainer.

Revision: You will learn your new job quickly. Chad is a good trainer.

or You will learn your new job quickly; Chad is a good trainer. (Semicolons will be discussed in Chapter 11.)

CHECKPOINT 7-13

Identify each of the following groups of words as either a correct sentence (C), a fragment (F), a comma splice (CS), or a run-on sentence (RO) by writing *C, F, CS,* or *RO* to the right of the sentence. Rewrite fragments and revise punctuation to correct comma splices and run-ons.

a. The project consultant is an expert in urban planning, he will speak to the city council. *CS*

b. Two new computer programs developed by Dena. *F*

c. Hannah became the editor of her hometown newspaper she will enjoy her job. *RO*

d. Julio and Jared will work as census takers beginning next month. *C*

e. Because the word processing center is undergoing renovation. *F*

SPELLING APPLICATIONS

7-14 Compare the words in Column A with the corresponding words in Column B. Use the appropriate proofreading symbols to correct the misspelled words. If both columns are correct, write **C** to the left of the number.

	Column A	Column B
1.	accommodate	accommodate
2.	bulletin	bullatin
3.	consession	concession
4.	eligable	eligible
5.	exaggerate	exagerate
6.	explanation	explaination
7.	pamphlet	pamplet
8.	restaraunt	restaurant
9.	sufficient	sufficient
10.	unanimous	unanimus

7-13

a. CS

b. F

c. RO

d. C

e. F

Sample revisions
(*answers will vary*):

a. . . . planning. He will . . .

b. . . . by Dena were complicated.

c. . . . newspaper. She will . . .

e. . . . renovation, no work can be processed.

CHAPTER SUMMARY

Proofread carefully to be sure your documents follow these sentence structure rules:

◆ A sentence must contain a subject and a predicate, and it must express a complete thought.

◆ Action verbs express action.

◆ Linking verbs connect the subject to a complement. A complement may be a noun, a pronoun, or an adjective.

◆ Subjects and verbs must agree in number. A singular subject requires a singular verb; a plural subject requires a plural verb.

◆ A compound subject joined by *and* usually requires a plural verb; a compound subject joined by *or* or *nor* must agree with the subject closest to the verb.

◆ Intervening words and phrases should be ignored to determine the true subject(s) and verb(s) in both normal and inverted sentences.

◆ As subjects of verbs, *a number* requires a plural verb and *the number* requires a singular verb.

◆ As subjects of verbs, collective nouns, fractions, portions, quantities, and measurements may require either singular or plural verbs, depending on the nouns to which they refer in the sentence.

◆ Some indefinite pronouns are always singular, some are always plural, and some may be either singular or plural depending on the nouns to which they refer in the sentence.

◆ Sentence faults of fragments, comma splices, and run-on sentences must be corrected.

Study these tips, and apply them as you proofread:

◆ Know the structure parts of sentences. A basic sentence must contain a subject and a predicate, and it must express a complete thought. Sentences may also contain complements and objects.

◆ Recognize true subjects, and always make subjects and verbs agree. Use a dictionary to determine singular and plural word forms of both subjects and verbs. Be especially alert to unfamiliar or foreign words used as subjects.

◆ Learn to use the grammar check function of your word processing software to double-check your proofreading for subject-verb agreement. Do not rely on word processing software as the only grammar check.

words@work Open *words@work*. Click on the Grammar and Usage tab. Under Lessons, choose Verbs for a review of basic verb forms and subject-verb agreement. Complete the exercises on verbs.

PROOFREADING APPLICATIONS

Proofread the paragraphs using the appropriate proofreading symbols to mark errors you find in grammar and spelling. To aid you in proofreading, the number of errors is indicated in parentheses for Exercises P-1 through P-3; you must find the errors on your own in P-4.

P-1 The snows of December ^have^ has turned the higher elevations into magnificent ski trails. Our friends Lawanda and Rico tells us that many of the resorts in Alpine Valley are offering special vacation packages to lure skiers. If you would like to have information about these packages, such as dates, pamph~l~ets, and maps, call the National Ski Area Association, to obtain the latest weather bulle~h~tin before heading for the slopes, dial 1-555-SNOW.

(5 errors)

P-2 The majority of ski resorts ~is~ are promoting themselves as four-season vacation spots. Fine accommodations, year-round recreation, attractive amenities (including indoor pools, fitness centers, and saunas), and a variety of rest~a~urants and shops appeal~s~ to people of all ages. Anyone and everyone want to be pampered while on vacation. Resorts find it necessary to make these conce~s~sions to meet the needs of nonskiers and families as well as skiers.

(5 errors)

P-3 Most of the ski resorts ^have^ has profited from installing snowmaking equipment. The equipment guarantee~s~ suf~f~icient quantities of snow from November through April, and the quality of the snow is always good. More people are skiing more often. Consequently, many a resort ha~s~ve expanded its services to include ski schools, service centers, and better acco~m~modations.

(5 errors)

P-2

1. i̶s̶ promoting *(are)*
2. resturants *(a)*
3. appeals⁄ to people ^
4. Anyone and everyone want^s
5. concesions *(s)* ^

P-3

1. resorts h̶a̶s̶ profited *(have)*
2. guarantee^s ^
3. suficient *(f)* ^
4. many a resort h̶a̶v̶e̶ expanded *(has)*
5. accomodations *(m)* ^

P-4

1. v̶a̶r̶i̶e̶s̶ *(vary)*
2. in the United States⁄ B&Bs, ^
3. provides⁄
4. Unanimusly, *(o)* ^
5. recomend *(m)* ^
6. enjoys⁄

P-4 Accommodations at a typical resort varies *(vary)* from rustic lodges to bed-and-breakfasts (B&Bs) to charming inns. The lodges and inns are generally located near the slopes. Relatively new in the United States⁄ B&Bs, a European concept, provides⁄ food and lodging in a private residence. Unanimusly, skiers recomend B&Bs to people who enjoys⁄ a homey atmosphere and a touch of pampering from the host or hostess.

P-5 Test your ability to detect errors in subject-verb agreement by visiting the grammar site at http://webster.commnet.edu/grammar/sv_agr.htm. Take the quizzes, just for fun, to see how well you can "hear" subject-verb *disagreement*.

PROGRESSIVE PROOFREADING

You are the office supervisor for the Louisville Chamber of Commerce. One of your responsibilities is to verify the correctness of all communications produced. Letters in your office are prepared in modified block style with mixed punctuation. Proofread the following items, indicating any corrections that need to be made. Because you are now also proofreading for errors in format, remember to use the three-step approach, which includes proofing the format as a separate step.

Job 1
Proofread this welcome statement, marking any errors you find using the appropriate proofreading symbols.

Louisville Chamber of Commerce

Civic Plaza Building
701 West Jefferson Street
Louisville, KY 40202-4161
502.555.0120
www.louisvillechamber.org

WELCOME, ROSE SOCIETY MEMBERS

A gracious welcome await you and the other 2,500 Rose Society members and guests who will be attending the Society's convention in Louisville. This meeting is the second Society meeting to be held here, the Society first met in Louisville 16 years ago. Both the organization and the city was a bit younger and smaller then.

Louisville, one of Kentucky's fun-filled vacation cities, are located right on the northern edge of Southern hospitality. You'll find Louisville has a lot of things going for it—attractions such as the Kentucky Center for the Arts on the riverfront; turn-of-the-century neighborhoods offering boutiques and restaurants; and Churchill Downs, home of the Ky. Derby. In addition, great food and shopping is around every corner. Everyone who comes to Louisville find something interesting.

Maps and broshures high lighting points of interest is included in your registration packet. We hope that your stay in Louisville will be enjoyable and that you will visit our city again.

Job 2   Using the proofreading symbols you have learned, mark all the errors in this e-mail message.

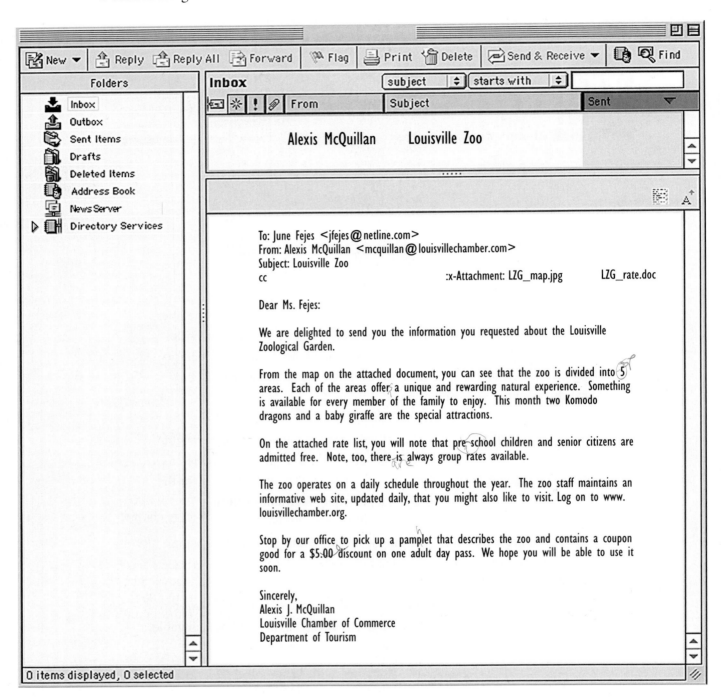

To: June Fejes <jfejes@netline.com>
From: Alexis McQuillan <mcquillan@louisvillechamber.com>
Subject: Louisville Zoo
cc   :x-Attachment: LZG_map.jpg   LZG_rate.doc

Dear Ms. Fejes:

We are delighted to send you the information you requested about the Louisville Zoological Garden.

From the map on the attached document, you can see that the zoo is divided into 5 areas. Each of the areas offer a unique and rewarding natural experience. Something is available for every member of the family to enjoy. This month two Komodo dragons and a baby giraffe are the special attractions.

On the attached rate list, you will note that pre-school children and senior citizens are admitted free. Note, too, there is always group rates available.

The zoo operates on a daily schedule throughout the year. The zoo staff maintains an informative web site, updated daily, that you might also like to visit. Log on to www. louisvillechamber.org.

Stop by our office to pick up a pamplet that describes the zoo and contains a coupon good for a $5.00 discount on one adult day pass. We hope you will be able to use it soon.

Sincerely,
Alexis J. McQuillan
Louisville Chamber of Commerce
Department of Tourism

Louisville Chamber of Commerce

Civic Plaza Building
701 West Jefferson Street
Louisville, KY 40202-4161
502.555.0120
www.louisvillechamber.org

February 10, 20--

Mrs. Alita Guitterez, President
National Sales Company, Inc.
3910 Trade Street
Louisville, KE 40206-5133

Dear Mrs. Guitterez:

Welcome to Louisville! We don't think we exagerate when we say that Louisville is a great place to do business.

As a member of the business community, you are elegible for membership is the Louisville Chamber of Commerce. On the first Tuesday of each month, we have a breakfast meeting to which each new businessman and businesswoman are invited. This meeting provides an opportnuity for us to get to know one another. Each 3d Tuesday we have a dinner and a and a business meeting at the Arbor Inn.

We hope your schedule will permit you to attend the next dinner meeting, which will be at Timmon's Restarant on the 6th at 7:30 a.m. The Hospitality Committee are in in charge of this function if you can attend, please call 555-0120.

To welcome you as a new member of the business community, we plan to include a feature about your company in the next issue of our newsletter. Since you are more knowledgable about your company that we are, we would like you to submit an article of about 500 words giving an explaination of your company's services and/or products. To meet our printing deadline, We need the material by March 25th.

Again, welcome to our city!

Very truly yours

Clyde Shepherd
Director of Public Relations

tr

COMPUTERIZED PROOFREADING

Job 4 Proofread a business letter.

1. Load the file C07JOB4 from the template CD-ROM. This file was keyed from the draft below.

2. Compare the letter on the CD-ROM with the draft. Make sure that any errors in the handwritten copy have been corrected.

3. Using the date noted on the draft, address the letter to **Miss Ruth Niemer, Director, Convention Housing Bureau, U.S. Chamber of Commerce, P.O. Box 54321, Des Moines, IA 50318-4126.** Provide an appropriate salutation and complimentary closing. The letter is being sent by **Allen Keen, Director of Economic Development.**

4. Format the letter in modified block style with mixed punctuation. Save it as C07JOB4R.

5. Produce the document by following the standard procedures.

6/11/--

Don Jenkins, our pres., and I am planning to attend the U.S. Chamber of Commerce Convention in your city, Aug. 20-25.

Since the number of rooms reserved for this convention are limited, we want to make our reservations now. Both of us needs single rooms. We would like to have adjoining rooms, if possible. We would prefer to stay at the convention hotel; however, if it is not available, either the Plaza or the Palmer Hotel are all right.

There are a no. of Louisville Chamber members planning to attend we plan to arrange a breakfast gathering on ~~Tuesday~~ Wednesday morning, the 23rd. Can you forward information from the convention hotel on catering options? I or Mr. Jenkins hopes to begin making those arrangements early next week.

Thank you for your help.

GRAMMAR ERRORS: PRONOUN AGREEMENT AND SELECTION

If you have made an error in pronoun use recently, you are not alone. A survey of college students' papers revealed vague pronoun references as the second most common type of error. (The first was a missing comma after an introductory element.) (Lunsford and Connors 2000) Confusion can occur if the writer has not made clear to the reader to what or to whom the pronoun refers. Consider this example from the minutes of a meeting: "Simone informed Jacki that she must attend next week's conference." Can you tell who is going to the conference? One can only hope that Simone and Jacki know.

GRAMMATICAL ACCURACY

The study of effective communication through the use of accurate grammar continues in this chapter as pronoun-antecedent agreement, pronoun cases, and gender-neutral language are reviewed. Pronouns are an integral component of the English language. As such, writers must master correct pronoun use to be able to communicate ideas and concepts clearly and effectively to a reader.

PRONOUN–ANTECEDENT AGREEMENT

Personal pronouns have various forms to indicate *person*. First person is the person speaking, second person is the person spoken to, and third person is the person or thing spoken about. Pronouns also indicate *number*, which is either singular or plural. They also indicate *gender*, which is either masculine, feminine, or neutral. You applied the concept of pronoun number in Chapter 7 when you proofread for errors in subject-verb agreement. In Chapter 8 you will learn to identify errors in agreement of pronouns and the words to which they refer; you also will learn to find and correct errors in pronoun selection.

If you cannot resolve a question within text, use the following proofreading symbol to query the author:

Query the author.

Rupert asked Khan if he needed to revise the second rough draft by noon.

LEARNING OBJECTIVES

- Identify and correct errors in pronoun-antecedent agreement.
- Identify and correct errors in pronoun case.
- Write sentences with gender-neutral language.
- Use appropriate proofreading symbols to indicate changes in text.
- Spell correctly a list of commonly misspelled words.

8-1 The word the pronoun refers to is an **antecedent.** An antecedent can be a noun, a pronoun, or a noun phrase. You must always make the reference to the antecedent clear to the reader.

> Mr. Maglio told Todd he was going to Europe.
> (Who is going to Europe? To whom does the pronoun *he* refer?)

A pronoun must agree with its antecedent in number and gender. (In the following sentences A = antecedent and P = pronoun.)

>   A   P
> When Karen visited, she surprised us with a gift.
> (The pronoun *she* is singular and feminine to agree with its antecedent *Karen.*)

>   A   A   P
> When Karen and Bernie visited, they surprised us with a gift.
> (The pronoun *they* is plural and neutral to agree with its compound antecedent *Karen and Bernie.*)

If an antecedent is a collective noun, determine whether the noun represents a group acting as a unit or a group acting as individuals. When the group acts as a unit, use a singular pronoun. When the group acts as individuals, use a plural pronoun.

>   A   P
> The committee made its decision.
> (The pronoun *its* is singular to agree with its antecedent *committee*, acting as a group.)

>   A   P
> The committee ordered their lunches using Jose's cell phone.
> (The pronoun *their* is plural to agree with its antecedent *committee*, acting as individuals.)

>   A   P P
> Each member paid for lunch using his or her own money.
> (The pronouns *his* and *her* are singular to agree with their antecedent *each*.)

If an antecedent is an indefinite pronoun, determine whether the indefinite pronoun is singular or plural. Choose the correct pronoun to agree with its antecedent.

>   A   P
> Each of the gardens had its own beauty.
> (The pronoun *its* agrees with its antecedent *each*, referring to *gardens*.)

>   A   P
> We asked several from the class to submit their essays.
> (The pronoun *their* agrees with its antecedent *several*.)

Chapter 8: Grammar Errors: Pronoun Agreement and Selection

Proofread the following sentences for errors in pronoun selection. Identify the antecedent by writing _A_ above it. Then make the pronoun agree with the antecedent. If a sentence is correct, write _C_ to the right of the sentence.

   a. Everybody made ~~their~~ _his or her_ own costume for the Fine Arts Ball.

   b. The committee will select ~~their~~ _its_ chairperson at the March meeting.

   c. Most of the employees spend their time working diligently. _C_

   d. Both Katelyn and Guadalupe will make _their_ ~~her~~ presentations on Friday.

   e. I heard Wade Chanel tell Rick Pinkley that (he) could not drive to work.

PRONOUN CASES

Pronouns are divided into three different categories according to their use in sentences. These categories are **pronoun cases** and include nominative (sometimes referred to as subjective) case, objective case, and possessive case. A personal pronoun changes its case according to how it is being used. Rely on your knowledge of sentence structure to apply correct case for the pronoun being used.

8–2   The nominative, or subjective, case pronouns include _I, you, he, she, it, we,_ and _they._ Use the **nominative case** for a pronoun that is the subject of a verb. (In the following example sentences, S = subject, V = verb, LV = linking verb, and C = complement.)

> S   V
> We are making plans for the off-site training seminar.

> S   V   S   V
> You were informed about the processes she is using.

> S S V
> He and I finished the report.

   Use the nominative case when the pronoun is a subject complement. Pronouns are complements if they refer to the subject and follow a form of the linking verb _to be_ (_am, is, are, was, were, be, being,_ and _been_) or a verb phrase ending in _be, being,_ or _been._

> S LV C   S LV C   S LV C   S LV C
> It is I.   It is she.   It is he.   It was they.

> S LV C
> It was he who found the solution to the problem.

> S   LV   C
> It could have been they who organized the summer festival.

> Nominative case pronouns include _I, you, he, she, it, we,_ and _they._

8–1

          A   his or her
a. Everybody . . . ~~their~~

         A   its
b. committee . . . ~~their~~

         A
c. C (Most . . . their)

         A
d. Katelyn and

         A   their
   Guadalupe . . . ~~her~~

e. Wade Chanel tell

   Rick Pinkley that (he)

Proofread the following sentences for errors in pronoun selection. If a sentence is correct, write *C* to the right of the sentence.

a. Would you change jobs now if you were him? _he_

b. It was her who designed the program cover. _she_

c. Was it them who were responsible for recruiting volunteers? _they_

d. The officer promoted to captain was she. _C_

e. Them and us are on the team that is ahead by 52 points. _They_ _we_

Objective case pronouns include *me, us, you, him, her, it,* and *them*.

8-3 The **objective case** pronouns include *me, us, you, him, her, it,* and *them*. Use the objective case when the pronoun is the object of a verb. A pronoun is an object if it follows the verb and answers one of these questions: *what? whom? to whom? for whom?*

> Please put *them* in the file. (Put what?)
> Max asked *us* for a contribution. (Asked whom?)
> Sarah gave *him* and *me* a pen. (Gave to whom?)
> Casey bought *them* tickets. (Bought for whom?)

See the Appendix for a more complete list of prepositions.

Use the objective case when the pronoun is the object of a preposition. A **preposition** is a word that joins a noun or pronoun to some other word in the sentence. Many prepositions exist, including the familiar prepositions *among, at, by, for, from, in, on,* and *to*. A pronoun is the object of a preposition if the pronoun follows the preposition. Also, recognize that the words *between, but, like,* and *except* can be used as prepositions. (In the following example sentences P = preposition and O = object.)

>   P O
> Please run your idea by me again.

>   P O
> A package was delivered to us today.

>   P   O   O   P O
> Just between you and me, I think it is a great gift for her.

>   P O
> A friend like him is hard to find.

Use the objective case when the pronoun is the object of an infinitive. An **infinitive** is a phrase containing the word *to* plus the present form of a verb, such as *to run* or *to sing*. When a pronoun immediately precedes or follows an infinitive phrase, use the objective form of the pronoun.

8-2
a. ~~him~~ _he_
b. ~~her~~ _she_
c. ~~them~~ _they_
d. C
e. ~~Them~~ _They_ and ~~us~~ _we_

Carlos expected his coworkers to help them.
(*Them* is the object of the infinitive *to help*.)

Helga wanted to see him before he left for college.
(*Him* is the object of the infinitive *to see*.)

CHECKPOINT 8-3

Proofread the following sentences for errors in pronoun selection. If a sentence is correct, write *C* to the right of the sentence.

a. Are we expected to supervise they as well? *them*

b. Like she and Renn, I am very good at waterskiing. *her* C

c. Vivian showed us her newly decorated office. C

d. We expected Rama to help Susannah and he with registration. *him*

e. The manager asked him to make the announcement for Cindy and I. *me*

© 2000 Ted Goff

"I'm the bad grammar fairy. I've just
broken all your infinitives and
misplaced half your prepositions."

8-4 Use the **possessive case** to show ownership. Possessive pronouns do not contain apostrophes. They include *her/hers, his, its, my/mine, our/ours, their/theirs,* and *your/yours.*

> That is my piano.   The piano is mine.
> It was their fault.   The fault was not theirs.
> Each idea has its own merit.

Possessive case pronouns include *her, hers, his, its, my, mine, our, ours, their, theirs, your,* and *yours.*

Always use the possessive case for a pronoun that immediately precedes a gerund. A **gerund** is a verb form ending in *ing* that is used as a noun. Words such as *running, speaking,* or *eating* can be action verbs; or they can be used as nouns (gerunds).

His **running** for president was a surprise.
Our parents approved of our **volunteering** at the food bank.
Their **asking** to participate in the race helped raise more money.

CHECKPOINT 8-4

Proofread the following sentences for errors in pronoun selection. If a sentence is correct, write *C* to the right of the sentence.

a. You returning by plane really surprised us.

b. The best reorganization plan submitted was theirs. C

c. Is this biology notebook yours or mine? C

d. Because the policy is reasonable, the staff voted for it's adoption right away.

e. With him leaving the company on such short notice, we are behind schedule.

8-3
them
a. ~~they~~
her
b. ~~she~~

c. C
him
d. ~~he~~
me
e. ~~I~~

8-5 A noun or noun phrase that renames another noun or pronoun that immediately precedes it is called an **appositive.** To determine the correct pronoun in this situation, ignore the appositive. Then the pronoun can be identified clearly as either the subject of a verb or an object of a verb or preposition. To determine the correct pronoun in the following sentences, ignore the appositive *auditors.*

> We auditors want to join a professional association.
> (The pronoun *we* is the subject of the verb *want.*)
>
> Magdalena asked us auditors if we were interested in membership.
> (The pronoun *us* is the object of the verb *asked.*)
>
> Will Magdalena pay association dues for us auditors?
> (The pronoun *us* is the object of the preposition *for.*)

8-4

a. You

b. C

c. C

d. it's
his
e. ~~him~~

8-6 **Reflexive pronouns** are pronouns that end in *–self.* These pronouns are used for renaming or for emphasis, and they must be used in combination with the pronoun to which they refer *in the same sentence.* It is incorrect to use reflexive pronouns alone.

renaming	I will send Chelsea a bouquet of roses.
	I will send myself a bouquet of roses.
emphasis	I will read the brief when we receive it.
	I myself will read the brief when we receive it.
incorrect	Send your reponses to myself.
correct	Send your responses to me.

8-7 While you may think it difficult, mastering the pronouns *who* and *whom* and *whoever* and *whomever* is really quite simple. Whenever these pronouns are used, they will be used in a clause. A **clause** always contains

Chapter 8: Grammar Errors: Pronoun Agreement and Selection

a subject and a verb, although the clause may be independent (expressing a complete thought) or dependent (not expressing a complete thought). The key to choosing the correct pronoun is to determine the pronoun's use within the clause, ignoring the rest of the words in the sentence.

If the pronoun is used as the subject of a verb, choose the nominative case pronoun *who* or *whoever*.

> An executive wants an assistant **who** *is dependable*.
> (The pronoun *who* is the subject of the linking verb *is* in the clause *who is dependable*.)
>
> **Who** shall I say *is calling*?
> (The pronoun *who* is the subject of the verb *is calling* in the clause *who is calling*.)
>
> **Whoever** *ate the fruit* should replace it.
> (The pronoun *whoever* is the subject of the verb *ate* in the clause *whoever ate the fruit*. The clause *whoever ate the fruit* is the subject of the verb *should replace*.)

If the pronoun is used as an object of a verb or a preposition, choose the objective case pronoun *whom* or *whomever*. You may need to change the clause to normal order to see the subject-verb-object pattern.

> The person **whom** *you recommended* starts work tomorrow.
> (The pronoun *whom* is the object of the verb *recommended* in the clause *you recommended whom*.)
>
> To **whom** did you wish to speak?
> (The pronoun *whom* is the object of the preposition *to* in the clause *you did wish to speak to whom*.)
>
> We will promote **whomever** *you suggest*.
> (The pronoun *whomever* is the object of the verb *suggest* in the clause *you suggest whomever*. The clause *whomever you suggest* is the object of the verb *promote*.)

WORKPLACE CONNECTIONS

Effective employees edit and revise their writing for correct information, appropriate emphasis, form, grammar, spelling, and punctuation.

> **"** Everything has been said, but not everything has been said superbly, and even if it had been, everything must be said freshly over and over again. **"**
>
> —Paul Horgan

CHECKPOINT 8-5–8-7

Proofread the following sentences for errors in pronoun selection. If a sentence is correct, write *C* to the right of the sentence.

a. Give the extra copy of the book to whomever can use it.

b. This order for copier supplies was taken by who?

c. Our students are considerate of we teachers.

d. We must respect the wishes of whomever is in charge.

e. Who is going to prepare the agenda for the meeting?

f. Please return the survey in the postage-paid envelope addressed to myself.

GENDER-NEUTRAL LANGUAGE

To avoid wordiness, you may use plural constructions rather than resorting to the "his or her" option.

Writers today are careful not to stereotype people with regard to gender. You must be careful to proofread for language that could be considered offensive to some people because of gender reference regarding occupations or other descriptions. Choosing pronoun gender is obvious when you are writing about a specific person. However, using the pronouns *she* or *he* alone to refer to a hypothetical person may be incorrect and reflect stereotyping. Apply the following rules on using gender-neutral language when gender is unknown.

8-8 Use pronouns from both genders when you cannot determine which pronoun is accurate.

> Who is your lawyer, and what is his or her address?
>
> Once you choose a dentist, he or she can call our office to verify insurance benefits.

If possible, use a plural antecedent and the pronoun *their* to avoid using gender-specific pronouns. Remember, the antecedent and the pronoun must agree in number.

> | | A good teacher praises her students. |
> |---|---|
> | *better* | Good teachers praise their students. |
> | *incorrect* | A good teacher praises their students. |

Address the reader in the second person to avoid using gender-specific pronouns.

> [You] Praise your students.

Reword the sentence to avoid the use of gender-specific pronouns by eliminating the pronoun.

> | | Each contestant signed her entry form. |
> |---|---|
> | *better* | Each contestant signed an entry form. |

Use neutral terms when referring to both men and women. The following are examples of the many titles and descriptions to consider when choosing words:

> | salesperson(s), sales representative(s) | *not* salesman/men |
> |---|---|
> | mail carrier(s) | *not* mailman/men |
> | member(s) of Congress, representative(s) | *not* congressman/men |
> | people, humanity, humankind | *not* mankind |
> | worker(s), crew | *not* workman/men |
> | police officer(s) | *not* policeman/men |

8-5-8-7

a. whomever

b. who ^m

c. ~~we~~ us teachers

d. whomever

e. C

f. ~~myself~~ me

Proofread the following sentences for pronoun selection that could be improved. Rewrite if necessary. If a sentence is correct, write *C* to the right of the sentence.

a. She left our company to become a fireman.

b. Each salesman distributed copies of his sales report.

c. We need to ask a doctor for his advice on our ergonomic situation.

d. The survey regarding on-site daycare was given to each parent to get her opinion.

e. Because I do not understand these new tax laws, I am going to ask an accountant for his opinion.

SPELLING APPLICATIONS

8-9 Compare the words in Column A with the corresponding words in Column B. Use the appropriate proofreading symbols to correct the misspelled words. If both columns are correct, write **C** to the left of the number.

	Column A	Column B
1.	committee	comittee
2.	copyright	copywrite
3.	enthuziasm	enthusiasm
4.	miscellaneous	misallaneous
5.	permanant	permanent
6.	psychology	psycology
7.	recognize	reconize
8.	regaurd	regard
9.	relavant	relevant
10.	responsible	responsable

8-8
a. a fireman. *(fighter)*
b. Each salesman . . . his sales report. *(person, or her)*
   All Each salesman . . . *people, their* his sales report. *s, or her*
c. doctor for his advice *(or her)*
   or doctor for his advice
d. each parent to get her opinion. *(his or)*
   or each parent to get her opinion. *(their, s, s)*
e. accountant for his opinion. *(or her)*
   or accountant for his opinion. *(an)*

CHAPTER SUMMARY

Proofread carefully to be sure your documents follow these pronoun selection rules:

♦ Pronouns must agree in number and gender and have a clear reference to their antecedents.

♦ Nominative case pronouns function as subjects of verbs and as subject complements.

♦ Objective case pronouns function as objects of verbs, as objects of prepositions, and as subjects or objects of infinitives.

♦ Possessive case pronouns are used in possessive constructions, including when they immediately precede a gerund.

♦ When appropriate, choose pronouns that reflect neutral gender.

Study these tips, and apply them as you proofread:

♦ Each time you choose a pronoun, consider antecedent agreement, pronoun case, and gender-neutral language.

♦ When choosing a pronoun to place with an appositive, ignore the appositive and consider case only.

♦ Learn which pronouns are nominative case, which are objective case, which are possessive case, and which are reflexive.

♦ Learn which indefinite pronouns are always singular, which are always plural, and which can be either singular or plural depending on their use.

♦ Apply rules of sentence structure so that you can accurately apply rules of pronoun case.

words@work Open *words@work*. Click on the Grammar and Usage tab. In the Lessons menu choose Pronouns. Review the 20-page lesson on pronouns. Then complete the exercises.

Individually or with a classmate, proofread the following paragraphs and use the appropriate proofreading symbols to mark errors you find in grammar, spelling, and gender-neutral language. To aid you in proofreading, the number of errors to be found is indicated in parentheses for Exercises P-1 and P-2; however, you must find the errors on your own in P-3.

P-1 In the next decade many workmen will enter the workforce, some of who will need additional training. Because their skills may not be relavant to the jobs that are being created, employers will find theirselves responsable for training and educating the unskilled. Employers are looking for new ways to meet the employment challenge. One of those ways is to hire people through an employment service on a temporary basis. Employers look for temporary employees who have the skills or aptitude to learn his or her job before being offered a permanant position. This method draws some critisicm from labor advocates, but it has it's advantages for temporary workers. He gets a no-obligation way to see if he wants to work for a particular company.

(11 errors)

P-2 Workers who once took fringe benefits for granted will not have that luxury in this decade. They will have to make critical choices about his or her benefits. Benefits are reguarded as an integral part of an employee's compensation, but it comes with a price. For example, our benefit plan enables we to exchange some healthcare benefits for childcare benefits. Also, contributions to the benefit plan may be applied either to a savings plan or to miscallaneous medical or dependent expenses. Employees themselves can make his or her own decisions about benefits.

(6 errors)

8-9
1. comittee
2. copywrite
3. enthuziasm
4. misallaneous
5. permanant
6. psycology
7. reconize
8. regaurd
9. relavant
10. responsable

P-1
1. workmen
2. some of who
3. relavant
4. theirselves
5. responsable
6. his or her job
7. permanant
8. critisicm
9. it has it's
10. He gets
11. he wants

P-2

1. ~~his or her~~ their benefits.
2. reg~~u~~arded
3. but ~~it comes~~ they
4. ~~we~~ us
5. misc~~a~~llaneous
6. ~~his or her~~ their own

   decisions

P-3

1. who~~m~~ spoke
2. about ~~its~~ their
3. an employee may
   . . . ~~their~~ his or her personal

   schedules.

   or ~~an~~ employees may

   . . . their
4. An assistant who

   has a long com-
   mute to ~~her~~ his or her job

   or ~~An~~ assistants who
   ~~have~~ has a long commute to ~~her~~ their jobs
5. a nurse who is at
   ~~her~~ his or her best

   or a nurses who ~~is~~ are at
   ~~her~~ their best
6. recognise → recognizes
7. perman~~a~~nt → permanent

P-3 Patrick O'Malley, an economist who~~m~~ spoke to our economics class, said that businesses have become more concerned about ~~its~~ their employees' personal time. Today, for example, an employee may often select the hours that fit ~~their~~ his or her personal schedules. An assistant who has a long commute to her job might prefer a 10 a.m. starting time while a nurse who is at her best early in the day would prefer taking the 7 a.m. shift. Many an employer recognise that a 40-hour workweek does not have to be accomplished between the hours of 8 a.m. and 5 p.m. They believe the research that shows that a satisfied employee is a more productive one and is more likely to remain a permanant one.

PROGRESSIVE PROOFREADING

You have applied for a position as an assistant at Virginia State College. Dr. Brianne Layman, your prospective employer, is seeking a person who has exceptional language arts skills. To determine your skills for the job, you are given drafts of typical correspondence to proofread. Dr. Layman uses block letter style with open punctuation.

Virginia State College

989 Johnstown Road
Chesapeake, VA 23320-4961

January 10, 20--

Mr. Greg Washington
4572 East Ninth Street
Chesapeake, Va. 23320-4572

Dear Mr. Washington

Your request for readmission to Virginia State College as a psycology major has been reviewed by members of the Admissions Committee and I at our January 8 meeting.

After the 3d semester a a student must have earned 36 hours, and he must have a grade point average (GPA) of 1.80 to remain in school.

You was enrolled for three semesters 2 years ago. During that time you earned 27 hours with a gpa of 1.67. Consequently, readmission is not possible at this time.

We recommend that you attend summer school as a nonmatriculated student. If you do so, you must take 2 3-hour courses that are relevant to your major area of study. If you receive a grade of C or better in each of these courses, the committee and I will be happy to reconsider you petition for readmission as an psycology major.

Sincerely yours,

Douglas W. Wrenn
Associate Dean

rv

757.555.0164 fax: 757.555.0154 www.virginiastatecollege.edu

Virginia State College

MEMO

TO: All Faculty

FROM: Brianne Layman, Dean

DATE: January 10, 20--

SUBJECT: Computer Requirements for Incoming Students

Associate Dean Douglas Wrenn and I have undertaken a study of computer use on campus. Our findings, which you can read in full at www.virginiastatecollege.edu/deansoffice/, leads us to recommend that all incoming, full-time studnets be required to own a computer. We recognize the potential burden this may place on some students. However, we feel responsible for acknowledging the permanent position technology play in our lives and in the lives of our students.

Several other schools in the state have already instituted this requirement for incoming students. Our neighbors, Lafayette College and St. Martin's, began requiring students to have computers 2 years ago. Administrators at both schools, who I have consulted, said the plan met with very little critisism. Faculty, in particular, appreciates the fact that students no longer have to rely on campus computer labs and its hours.

A task force is being formed to address the minimum requirements of the computer systems and to study options for offering computer systems to students at a discount. Both Lafayette and St. Martin's has agreements with local vendors that allow a 10-20% student discount. The only requirement is that they have the ability to communicate with the college network.

Your feedback is welcome. You may direct it to Douglas Wrenn or myself. In addition, we would like one faculty member from each discipline to serve on the task force. You taking the time to offer your input will be time well spent on an issue that will help place our students in the forefront of their educational fields.

rv

Virginia State College

MEMO

TO: Department Chairmen [person]

FROM: Brianne Layman, Dean

DATE: January 10, 20--

SUBJECT: Parking Regulations

In an effort to improve staff parking conditions, the Campus Traffic Comittee have developed the following parking regulations. Please see that all members of your department receives this information regurading the new regulations.

1. All of the current campus parking permits expire on August 14. As of August 15 staff members are required to have a valid parking permit for the new school year.

2. Staff parking is allowed only in designated areas. Staff is not allowed to park in areas designated for student parking.

3/2. Permanant permits must be displayed in the rear window of all vehicles.

4/3. Any staff member in possession of more than 5 unpaid parking tickets will forfeit their right to park on campus.
        his or her

My thanks go especially to Officer Gonzalez, who has been keenly aware of the numerous parking problems and whom played a significant role on the Campus Traffic Committee. In fact, it was him who suggested that the committee be formed. Officer Gonzalez will continue to monitor parking conditions on campus.

rv

COMPUTERIZED PROOFREADING

Job 4   Edit an e-mail message.

1. Brianne Layman would like to develop an internship program with local businesses. Below are her notes about the possibilities of the program. She has sent e-mail to a faculty member, Dr. Rosemary Schindler, director of academic development, about her ideas.

2. Load file C08JOB4 from the template CD-ROM.

3. Proofread and spell check the e-mail. Correct all errors.

4. Save the e-mail as C08JOB4R.

5. Print the e-mail.

Internships--a variety of local business so students have choices

Areas:

    information management systems

    software development

    graphic design

    CAD/CAM

Potential contacts:

    Stuart Steinman at Learning Design Co.

    Manny Santos, OTC Systems

    Constance Clark-Powers at City Concepts

Issues:

    – What time requirments do businesses have? Is 6 months long enough? Does internship need to be a year?

    – How many hours per week is feasible for students?

    – Internships for seniors only? juniors too? underclassmen?

ERRORS IN WORDS OFTEN CONFUSED

"The difference between the almost right word & the right word is really a large matter—it's the difference between the lightning bug and the lightning." These words, written by Mark Twain in a letter dated October 15, 1888, to George Bainton, explain why you are about to read this chapter. The "almost right word" simply is not good enough.

IMPORTANCE OF DISTINGUISHING BETWEEN SIMILAR WORDS

One of the major difficulties of the English language is that so many words sound similar. They may be spelled differently and have different meanings, but they are often confused and misused because of how they sound. To be a good proofreader, you must be able to distinguish between words that are often confused. This chapter presents 27 groups of words that are commonly used—and commonly misused—in business. Study each group of words, their parts of speech, and their definitions. Read each of the sentences; then write the correct word or form of the word in the space provided in the Checkpoints that follow.

Also presented at the end of the chapter is a section of words that deserve special attention. Challenge yourself to learn the words presented here.

LEARNING OBJECTIVES

- Recognize the correct usage of words that sound alike but have different meanings and spellings.
- Learn a list of challenging words commonly used in business communication.
- Use appropriate proofreading symbols to indicate changes in text.
- Spell correctly a list of commonly misspelled words.

9-1 **a**—*indefinite article (adj.)* used to introduce words or abbreviations that begin with a consonant *sound*; do not use *a* in place of the word *of*

an—*indefinite article (adj.)* used to introduce words or abbreviations that begin with a vowel *sound*

of—*prep.* originating at or from; with reference to

CHECKPOINT 9-1

a. Please bring _____ picnic basket and _____ umbrella.

b. She requested that we send _____ R.S.V.P. to the social committee.

c. What kind _____ party should we expect?

d. This gathering concludes _____ 18-month assignment.

9-1
a. a, an   c. of
b. an   d. an

9-2 **accept**—*v.* to receive; to take

except—*prep.* with the exclusion of

CHECKPOINT 9-2

a. You should _____ the responsibility for completing the payroll.

b. All of the officers _____ the secretary attended the meeting.

c. We will fight the courts about the ruling rather than _____ it.

d. No one _____ Luann can unlock the bank vault.

9-2
a. accept   c. accept
b. except   d. except

9-3 **advice**—*n.* opinion or recommendation

advise—*v.* to give opinion; to counsel

CHECKPOINT 9-3

a. My _____ to you is to find another solution before noon.

b. Nels is willing to pay for _____ about coin collecting.

c. Do you think she will _____ me to attend more classes?

d. We have more _____ than we need to make this decision.

9-3
a. advice   c. advise
b. advice   d. advice

9-4 **adverse**—*adj.* unfavorable; hostile; harmful; contrary to one's welfare or interests

averse—*adj.* feeling of opposition or distaste for something

CHECKPOINT 9-4

a. Your poor review will have an _____ effect on your raise.

b. The plant supervisors are _____ to production delays.

c. Nelda is _____ to working overtime.

d. I also have _____ feelings toward working overtime.

9-4
a. adverse   c. averse
b. averse   d. adverse

9-5 **affect**—*v.* to influence, change, assume

effect—*n.* an outcome or a result; *v.* to bring about or cause to happen

CHECKPOINT 9-5

a. What _____ will the changes in the law have on us?

b. Your driving records will _____ your insurance rates.

c. The plans to _____ a change in policy have been approved.

d. How will her resignation _____ our reorganization plans?

Chapter 9: Errors in Words Often Confused

9-6

already—*adv.* previously

all ready—*adj.* + *noun* all prepared

altogether—*adv.* entirely; completely

all together—*adj.* + *noun* all in one group

always—*adv.* at all times

all ways—*adj.* + *noun* by all methods

CHECKPOINT 9-6

a. We are _____ pleased with the new employees you hired.

b. Sharon _____ trained three new operators yesterday.

c. The team members will work _____ to plan the campaign.

d. Nine new operators are _____ to be trained in our customer service

program so that in _____ they will be able to assist customers.

e. Rory is _____ on time for his appointments.

9-7

anxious—*adj.* wanting or desirous, with a connotation of fear

eager—*adj.* wanting or desirous

CHECKPOINT 9-7

a. The paralegals are _____ to hear the outcome of the trial.

b. We are _____ to get started on the landscaping project.

c. Most of the staff are _____ to begin using their vacation days.

d. Because the results of our certification exams will not arrive until September,

the summer will be an _____ time of waiting for us.

9-8

assure—*v.* to give confidence or remove doubt

ensure—*v.* to make sure or certain

insure—*v.* to secure with insurance against a loss

CHECKPOINT 9-8

a. Which departments still need to _____ their laptop computers?

b. I _____ you that our department has met all insurance requirements.

c. A policy committee will _____ that all requirements are met.

d. Thank you for _____ me of your intention to meet the quota.

Chapter 9: Errors in Words Often Confused

9-8
a. insure   c. ensure
b. assure   d. assuring

9-9 **bad**—*adj.* poor; disagreeable; unpleasant (use following verbs of senses and linking verbs)

badly—*adv.* poorly or in a bad manner

CHECKPOINT 9-9

a. The new employee we assigned to the phones performed _____.

b. Celecia felt _____ about not being able to attend the charity event.

c. The situation looked _____ for us when the phones were ringing and we were rushing to meet the deadline.

d. This critical situation may turn out fine, or it may turn out _____.

9-9
a. badly   c. bad
b. bad   d. badly

9-10 **between**—*prep.* through a position, separating (use when discussing two things or groups)

among—*prep.* in the midst of or surrounded by (use when discussing three or more things or groups)

CHECKPOINT 9-10

a. Only an apology stood _____ Roberto and Flo.

b. Take these reference manuals and distribute them _____ the staff.

c. Professor Thoen asked the class to discuss the chapter _____ themselves before they presented individual ideas.

d. Rather than divide their loyalties _____ family members and their lawyers, the four sisters vowed to keep the secret _____ themselves.

9-10
a. between   d. between,
b. among   among
c. among

9-11 **bring**—*v.* to carry *to* a place

take—*v.* to carry *from* a place

CHECKPOINT 9-11

a. Salim requested that I _____ a tape recorder to the meeting.

b. He and I will _____ refreshments for everyone.

c. The portfolios were available for anyone to _____ home and review.

d. The more ideas I _____ to the discussion, the more ideas Mrs. Guerdo will be able to _____ to the board meeting.

9-12 **can/could**—*v.* ability or power to perform

may/might—*v.* permission or possibility to perform

9-11
a. bring   c. take
b. bring   d. bring, take

CHECKPOINT 9-12

a. With two weeks' notice, the cafeteria _____ cater special events.

b. The vice presidents _____ not want to host the dinner in the cafeteria.

c. You _____ ask Wali for advice if you _____ find him.

d. Mr. Jacowitz said that you _____ plan the banquet for next month.

9-13 **cite**—*v.* to quote or mention

sight—*n.* a view; vision

site—*n.* a location

9-12
a. can or could
b. may or might
c. may, can
d. may

CHECKPOINT 9-13

a. Can you _____ the source of that quotation?

b. As soon as we find a good _____, we will build our headquarters.

c. The Grand Canyon is an inspiring _____.

d. The _____ of the ruins is popular for tourists.

9-14 **complement**—*n.* something that fills up, completes, or makes perfect; *v.* to complete or make perfect

compliment—*n.* recognition; praise; *v.* to praise

9-13
a. cite   c. sight
b. site   d. site

CHECKPOINT 9-14

a. Did you _____ the speaker on his presentation?

b. The drapes and the carpet _____ the color of the walls.

c. I consider that remark to be a _____, and I thank you.

d. When the ship left the shore, it had a full _____ of personnel.

9-14
a. compliment
b. complement
c. compliment
d. complement

9-15 **council**—*n.* an assembly; a governing body

counsel—*v.* to give advice; to advise; *n.* a lawyer; advice

CHECKPOINT 9-15

a. Employees received _____ about compensation benefits.

b. The mayor is the presiding officer of the city _____.

c. Do you know the person who was appointed _____ for the defense?

d. Marie gained leadership experience by serving on the student _____.

9-15
a. counsel c. counsel
b. council d. council

9-16 **every day**—*adj.* + *noun* each day

everyday—*adj.* ordinary; customary

CHECKPOINT 9-16

a. The members of the track team have been jogging _____ this week.

b. Proofreading is an _____ task for the copy editor.

c. Why not use the _____ dishes for the picnic?

d. When you retire from your job, _____ will be a holiday!

9-16
a. every day c. everyday
b. everyday   d. every day

9-17 **fewer**—*adj.* a comparative number (use with countable items)

less—*adj.* a comparative number (use with quantities that cannot be counted)

CHECKPOINT 9-17

a. The stockroom keeps _____ 30-pound paper than 20-pound paper.

b. Reprographics used 100 _____ reams of 30-pound paper last month.

c. They get _____ than six requests per cycle for legal-sized paper.

d. Our paper demand has been _____ than normal.

9-17
a. less   c. fewer
b. fewer d. less

9-18 **good**—*adj.* positive or desirable

well—*adv.* performing in a positive or desirable manner

well—*adj.* good health

CHECKPOINT 9-18

a. Mr. Maurey reported _____ returns from the international sale that

went _____ for our company.

b. He felt _____ about the products our company marketed overseas.

c. However, the long trip abroad left Mr. Maurey not feeling _____.

d. It is a _____ feeling to see our efforts being rewarded so _____.

9-18
a. good, well c. well
b. good   d. good, well

9-19 **imply**—*v.* to offer or suggest

infer—*v.* to deduce or assume

CHECKPOINT 9-19

a. Xavier meant to _____ that he was interested in Sophie's position.

b. We _____ from what Xavier said that he plans to leave the company.

c. Throughout our conversation, I _____ that Kip was angry.

d. Kip insisted he was not angry, but his words _____ otherwise.

9-20 **lay**—*v.* to put or place something (*always* use with an object)

lie—*v.* to recline or rest (do not use with an object); tell a falsehood (this meaning is seldom confused with the other meanings of *lie/lay*)

9-19
a. imply   c. inferred
b. inferred   d. implied

CHECKPOINT 9-20

a. When you are finished, please _____ the stack of files on my desk.

b. Kelly excused herself to _____ down for a nap before dinner.

c. Whenever I _____ my keys down, I lose them.

d. If you are not feeling well, you may _____ down in the nurse's office.

9-21 **loose**—*adj.* not fastened or tight; having freedom of movement

lose—*v.* to fail to win, gain, or keep; to mislay

9-20
a. lay   c. lay
b. lie   d. lie

CHECKPOINT 9-21

a. Too many traffic violations caused Cesar to _____ his license.

b. When the belt is too _____, it will not pull the motor.

c. We lost the key; thus, we will _____ access to the safe-deposit box.

d. The binding on this book is _____; it will _____ more pages.

9-22 **passed**—*v.* past tense of *pass*, meaning to go by or circumvent; to receive favorable results on an examination

past—*n.* the time before the present; *adv.* go beyond

9-21
a. lose   c. lose
b. loose   d. loose, lose

CHECKPOINT 9-22

a. Ying was happy to have finally _____ the statistics test.

b. The bus went _____ my house without stopping.

c. Do you realize that Mandy was _____ up for promotion?

d. A knowledge of the _____ is required to understand the present.

9-22
a. passed   c. passed
b. past   d. past

9-23 **precede**—*v.* to come before in time or rank

proceed—*v.* to go forward; to continue

CHECKPOINT 9-23

a. Move Section C so that it will _____ Section A in the appendix.

b. The knowledge you learned in this lesson _____ the tasks you will learn in the next lesson.

c. The council will _____ to the next item on the agenda.

d. When the doors open, you may _____ to the ticket window.

9-23
a. precede   c. proceed
b. precedes   d. proceed

9-24 **principal**—*n.* a leader; a sum of money; *adj.* highest in importance

principle—*n.* a general or accepted truth; a rule

CHECKPOINT 9-24

a. How much interest will the company have to pay on the _____?

b. Rewarding employees is a _____ concern of our managers.

c. I save diligently because I understand the _____ of compound interest.

d. Are you familiar with the economic _____ of supply and demand?

9-24
a. principal   c. principle
b. principal   d. principle

9-25 **stationary**—*adj.* immobile; fixed in one position

stationery—*n.* materials (paper, pens, ink) for writing

CHECKPOINT 9-25

a. That card shop also sells _____.

b. Rhea enjoys using the _____ bicycle at the health club.

c. I would not recommend colored _____ for a résumé.

d. The interior walls of the cafeteria are not _____.

9-26 **that**—*pron.* refers to people (emphasizing classes or types of people), places, objects, or animals (use to introduce essential clauses)

which—*pron.* refers to places, objects, or animals (use to introduce nonessential clauses)

who—*pron.* refers to people (emphasizing individuality)

9-25
a. stationery c. stationery
b. stationary d. stationary

CHECKPOINT 9-26

a. Phoebe Bayok is the only person _____ can talk Ron into coming.

b. These goats, _____ Sammy took to the county fair, are the ones _____ give us the best milk for cheese.

c. The medical study is to be conducted only on women _____ are over 75.

d. This is the type of job _____ allows me the flexibility I want.

e. My new home, _____ I purchased last month, is east of town.

9-27 **to**—*prep.* in the direction of; *v.* part of an infinitive construction (*to* plus a present tense verb, such as *to run*)

too—*adv.* also; more than enough

two—*adj.* a number, more than one but fewer than three

9-26
a. who   c. who
b. which,   d. that
   that   e. which

CHECKPOINT 9-27

a. Ari and Mikel want to join the committee _____.

b. In my opinion, having _____ bosses instead of one makes the decision-making process _____ difficult.

c. We need to buy a new paper shredder because ours breaks down _____ often.

d. She, _____, will attend the _____-day conference if she can arrange transportation _____ and from the airport.

e. He will have _____ make special arrangements for the auditors.

WORDS DESERVING SPECIAL CONSIDERATION

9-28 The following words may be particularly challenging for business communicators. Although these words may not be confused with other words or spellings, proofreaders must consider how the words are used so they can make correct word choices and grammar decisions.

9-27
a. too   d. too, two,
b. two, too   to
c. too   e. to

All right. This is always spelled as two words. Think of it as you would think of *all wrong*. You would never write *alwrong*.

▮   The terms of this contract seem all right to me.

Etc. *Etc.* is an abbreviation that stands for *et cetera*, which means "and other things." The use of *etc.* implies that many further examples could be given. Do not use the word *and* before *etc.* Instead of using *etc.* in formal writing, use the words *and the like* or *and so on*.

▮   On the farm we have cows, pigs, turkeys, geese, chickens, etc.

but   The report discusses the student survey regarding campus parking, class registration, library use, and so on.

Like. *Like* can be used as a verb or a preposition. Used as a verb, *like* is not troublesome. (I like you. You like me.) Used as a preposition, *like* should be used to introduce words or phrases, *not* clauses. To introduce clauses, use the words *as* or *as if*.

▮   I like cake. You like pie. We like ice cream. (used as a verb)

     I just peeked outside; it looks like snow. (used as a preposition)

but   It looks as if it will snow.

Regardless. This word is sometimes incorrectly pronounced and written *irregardless*. *Irregardless* is a substandard form of the word and should not be used.

▮   We will not change our position, regardless of the outcome.

Retroactive to. Always use the preposition *to* following the word *retroactive*, *not* the preposition *from*.

▮   Your salary adjustment will be retroactive to July 1.

Unique. The word *unique* means that something is one of a kind; therefore, do not use this word to mean "unusual or out of the ordinary." When using *unique* in a comparison, be sure to use special modifiers such as *more nearly* or *virtually* because the word itself cannot otherwise be compared.

▮   You are a unique individual in this sea of people.

but   This vase is a virtually unique glass creation.

9–29 Compare the words in Column A with the corresponding words in Column B. Use the appropriate proofreading symbols to correct the misspelled words. If both columns are correct, write **C** to the left of the number.

	Column A	Column B
1.	expereince	experience
2.	February	Febuary
3.	imediately	immediately
4.	ocasionally	occasionally
5.	omitted	ommitted
6.	prerequisite	prerequisite
7.	receiving	recieving
8.	reference	reference
9.	temperament	temperment
10.	valueable	valuable

CHAPTER SUMMARY

♦ When in doubt about the meaning, spelling, or usage of a word or word group, consult a dictionary or reference manual. Using words correctly shows that you have proofread your communication carefully and enables the reader to understand the intended message.

♦ Be aware of the standard pronunciation of words because mispronunciation frequently leads to misspelling and misuse of words.

words@work Open *words@work*. Click on the Resources tab; then click Grammar and Usage. Choose Frequently Misused and Confused Words to review the confusing words discussed in the chapter and to see additional words that are frequently misused.

9-29

1. expe~~rie~~nce
2. Feb~~r~~uary
3. i~~m~~mediately
4. oc~~c~~asionally
5. om~~m~~itted
6. C
7. re~~ie~~ving
8. C
9. temper~~a~~ment
10. valu~~e~~able

Proofread the following ads using the appropriate proofreading symbols to mark errors you find in word usage or spelling. To aid you in proofreading, the number of errors to be found is indicated in parentheses for the first three ads.

P-1 THE PRICE IS RIGHT!

Well-built two-story house on 3-acre sight, complimented by professional landscaping. House overlooks a lush green valley— a beautiful sight to see everyday. This valueable property is already for occupancy. Price: $212,000. Directions: Precede 1 mile passed the water tower on Highway 28; first house on the right. For additional information, call Kendra at Four-Star Realty, 555-0146.
(8 errors)

P-1

1. ③-acre *sp*
2. ~~sight~~ *site*
3. compl~~i~~mented *e*
4. see every~~day~~ *#*
5. valu~~e~~able
6. ~~already~~ *all ready*
7. ~~Precede~~ 1 mile *Proceed*
8. ~~passed~~ *past*

P-2 OUR LOSS—YOUR GAIN

Must sell personal items, including valueable date-of-issue stamped envelopes; boxes of bond stationary; exercise equipment; books on principals of type and temperment, psychology, investment advise, ways to loose weight, art (some valuable first editions); and more items to numerous to list. Saturday from 8 a.m. to 11:30 a.m. at 3153 Highland Avenue.
(7 errors)

P-2

1. valu~~e~~able
2. bond stationa~~r~~y *e*
3. ~~principals~~ of type *principles*
4. temper~~a~~ment
5. investment advi~~s~~e *c*
6. ways to lo~~o~~se
7. t~~o~~ numerous *o*

P-3 ADMINISTRATIVE ASSISTANT NEEDED

Administrative Assistant, City Council. Principle duties include writing and/or transcribing correspondence, council minutes, and memorandums. Travel is necessary ocassionally. Prerequisits for the job include three years of experience, good keyboarding skills, and excellent grammar and proofreading skills. Applicants should be able to except every day administrative responsibilities with minimum supervision. Send résumé, including referances, to Personnel Department, City Hall, 401 Sixth Street, Sioux City, IA 51101.
(6 errors)

NOTICE TO CITIZENS

The City Council will be receiving comments about the redistricting proposal at its Febuary 3 meeting. The counsel members voted on the proposal at the last meeting; however, the city attorney adviced members that the vote was not binding for two reasons:

1. The item was ommitted from the announced agenda.

2. A quorum was not present at the meeting.

Citizens wishing to express their views on this proposal should meet in Room 207 of City Hall 30 minutes proceeding the Febuary 3 meeting.

P–3
1. ~~Principle~~ Principal
2. ocassionally   (c / s)
3. Prerequisits (e)
4. ~~except~~ accent
5. every day
6. referances (e)

P–5  Learn to use difficult word pairs. Visit the web site http://englishplus.com/ where you will find Grammar Slammer. Choose "Common Mistakes and Choices." Create a worksheet by choosing ten different word pairs not already listed in this chapter and writing sentences for each word. Leave a blank space to fill in the correct word. Exchange worksheets with a classmate, and use Grammar Slammer to help you choose the correct words.

P–4
1. Febuary 3   (r)
2. The ~~counsel~~ council
3. adviced (s)
4. ommitted (r)
5. ~~proceeding~~ Preceding
6. Febuary 3   (r)

PROGRESSIVE PROOFREADING

One of your duties as an administrative supervisor in the Ridge Hills Real Estate office is to proofread the correspondence. You proofread not only for the usual keyboarding, spelling, and number expression errors but also for errors in grammar and word usage. Ridge Hill uses modified block letter format and mixed punctuation.

Job 1 Proofread the e-mail carefully.

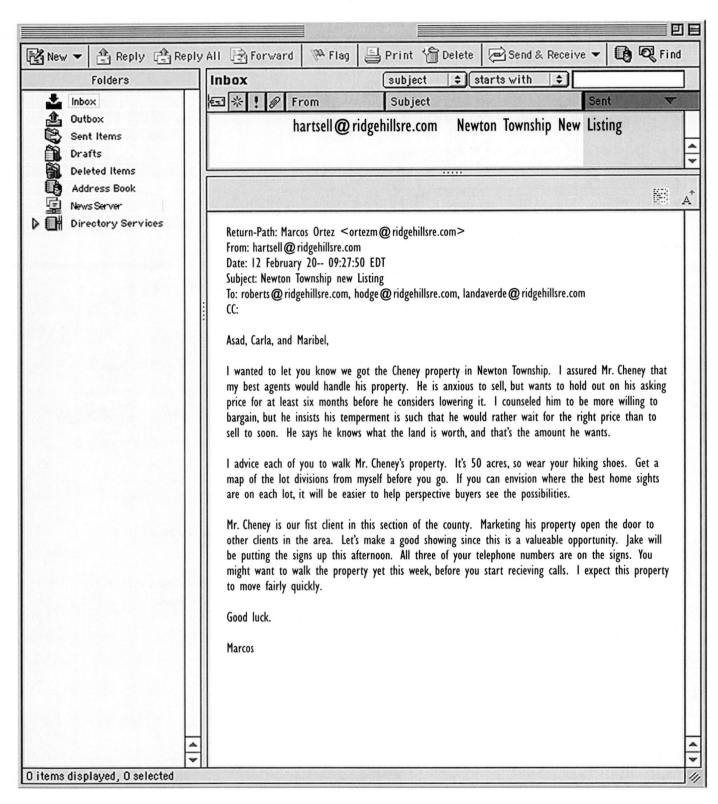

New ▼ | Reply | Reply All | Forward | Flag | Print | Delete | Send & Receive ▼ | Find

Folders
- Inbox
- Outbox
- Sent Items
- Drafts
- Deleted Items
- Address Book
- News Server
- Directory Services

Inbox subject ⬍ starts with ⬍

From | Subject | Sent

hartsell@ridgehillsre.com   Newton Township New Listing

Return-Path: Marcos Ortez <ortezm@ridgehillsre.com>
From: hartsell@ridgehillsre.com
Date: 12 February 20-- 09:27:50 EDT
Subject: Newton Township new Listing
To: roberts@ridgehillsre.com, hodge@ridgehillsre.com, landaverde@ridgehillsre.com
CC:

Asad, Carla, and Maribel,

I wanted to let you know we got the Cheney property in Newton Township. I assured Mr. Cheney that my best agents would handle his property. He is anxious to sell, but wants to hold out on his asking price for at least six months before he considers lowering it. I counseled him to be more willing to bargain, but he insists his temperment is such that he would rather wait for the right price than to sell to soon. He says he knows what the land is worth, and that's the amount he wants.

I advice each of you to walk Mr. Cheney's property. It's 50 acres, so wear your hiking shoes. Get a map of the lot divisions from myself before you go. If you can envision where the best home sights are on each lot, it will be easier to help perspective buyers see the possibilities.

Mr. Cheney is our fist client in this section of the county. Marketing his property open the door to other clients in the area. Let's make a good showing since this is a valueable opportunity. Jake will be putting the signs up this afternoon. All three of your telephone numbers are on the signs. You might want to walk the property yet this week, before you start recieving calls. I expect this property to move fairly quickly.

Good luck.

Marcos

0 items displayed, 0 selected

RIDGE HILLS REAL ESTATE

3168 NORTHWOOD DRIVE
RUSTON, LA 71270-6653
318-555-0190
www.ridgehillsre.com

Febuary 19, 20--

Miss Bethany Whitley
Plant Manager
Toggs Manufacturing Co.
P.O. Box 7022
Indianapolis, IN 46208-9865

Dear Miss Whitley:

The one hundred-acre site on Five Mile Rd. you considered for your new plant is still available. The owners have all ready rejected some offers, but new circumstances have made the owners anxious to sell. I believe they are prepared to except the offer that you and me discussed.

If you still wish to obtain this property, I suggest that you submit a offer immediatly. Interest rates are not likely to decrease any more this year. In fact, it is likely to increase.

Remember, the owners are insisting on a cash transaction. As a prerequisit, I would suggest that you obtain advise from legal council regaurding about the best way to finance the principle loan and to handle the transfer. Please call me to discuss your plans about this matter.

Sincerely yours,

Marcos Ortez
General Manager

yn

Job 3
Compare the keyed memo on the next page with the handwritten draft below. Use the appropriate proofreading symbols to mark all errors on the keyed version.

Please key this memo.
Make corrections if needed.
Thanks.
Marcos

To: All Personnel

Please join me in congratulating Maribel Landaverde, who has received the Louisiana Realtors' Association salesperson-of-the-Year award. Maribel's performance this passed year has certainly been deserving of recognition. I am proud that the Association choose her for the award.

Maribel has been with Ridge Hills Real Estate for 9 years. During that time, she has increased her sales by at least 14% each year. The year Maribel started, she broke the company's sales records for a first-year agent. Taking a wider perspective, Maribel's performance has a positive affect on the whole company. Her drive and enthuziasm can inspire all of us. In addition, her award brings attention to the company from all over the state.

Thank you, Maribel, for your outstanding work. We are proud to be your colleagues.

3168 NORTHWOOD DRIVE
RUSTON, LA 71270-6653
318-555-0190
www.ridgehillsre.com

INTEROFFICE MEMORANDUM

TO: All Personnel
FROM: Marcos Ortez
DATE: July 14, 20--
SUBJECT: Congratulations

Please join me in congratulating Maribel Landaverde, who has recieved the Louisiana Realtors' Association salesperson-of-the-Year award. Maribel's performance this passed year has certainly been deserving of recognition. I am proud that the Association choose her for the award.

Maribel has been with Ridge Hills Real Estate for nine years. During that time, she has increased her sales by at least 14 percent each year. The year Maribel started, she broke the company's sales records for a first-year agent. Taking a wider prospective, Maribel's performance has a positive affect on the whole company. Her drive and enthuziasm inspire all of us. In addition, her award brings attention to the company from all over the state.

Thank you, Maribel, for your outstanding work. We are proud to be your colleagues.

yn

COMPUTERIZED PROOFREADING

Job 4 Proofread a memo with a table.

1. Load the file C09JOB4 from the template CD-ROM. The document consists of a memo that includes a table. The table was compiled from data in the financial statements shown below.
2. Proofread the message for errors in abbreviations, spelling, grammar, number expression, format, and confusing words. Check the accuracy of the figures and text in the table by comparing them to the printed statements. Check all totals as well.
3. Send the memo to **Jill Carmichael, Advertising Manager,** from **Marcos Ortez, General Manager.** The subject is **Review of Advertising Costs from 2002 to 2004;** the date is **February 27, 20--.** Format as a standard memorandum, and include the table as an attachment. Format the table attractively on a separate page with a 1 1/2″ top margin.
4. Save the revised document as C09JOB4R.
5. Produce the document by following the standard procedures.

2004	
OPERATING EXPENSES:	
ADVERTISING	
TELEVISION	$19,588.52
CIRCULARS	5,047.90
HOMEBUYER'S GUIDE	3,885.12
NEWSPAPERS	14,589.70
RADIO	1,409.61
MISCELLANEOUS	961.80
	$45,482.65
2003	
OPERATING EXPENSES:	
ADVERTISING	
TELEVISION	$15,947.50
NEWSPAPERS	12,785.63
CIRCULARS	4,672.30
HOMEBUYER'S GUIDE	2,933.88
RADIO	1,180.12
MISCELLANEOUS	769.44
	$38,288.87
2002	
OPERATING EXPENSES:	
ADVERTISING	
CIRCULARS	$ 3,597.28
HOMEBUYER'S GUIDE	2,292.18
NEWSPAPERS	11,096.79
TELEVISION	14,795.72
RADIO	870.08
MISCELLANEOUS	641.20
	$33,293.25

PUNCTUATION ERRORS, PART I

Missing commas after introductory elements and in compound sentences are the most frequent types of errors in student writing (Lunsford and Connors 2000). No wonder, then, that comma usage frustrates even experienced business writers.

A seasoned editor once quipped, "The only thing worse than a writer who doesn't use commas is one who uses too many." So where is the middle ground? The middle ground is laid out in this chapter.

IMPORTANCE OF CORRECT PUNCTUATION

Punctuation makes the meaning of messages clear and precise. When punctuation is omitted or used incorrectly, messages may become confusing, distorted, or inaccurate. Consider the change in meaning in the following sentences:

The protester, claimed the newscaster, was trampled by an angry mob.

The protester claimed the newscaster was trampled by an angry mob.

As you can see, a proofreader must know how to use punctuation to enable readers to interpret a written message correctly.

In this chapter you will review the correct use of terminal punctuation and the most common internal punctuation mark, the comma. Other marks of punctuation are reviewed in Chapter 11.

TERMINAL PUNCTUATION

Terminal punctuation is used to indicate a distinct pause in the voice and, therefore, helps to clarify the meaning of a message. Terminal punctuation marks include the period, the question mark, and the exclamation point. One of these marks is used to terminate, or end, every independent clause. An independent clause contains a subject and a predicate, and an independent clause makes complete sense.

LEARNING OBJECTIVES

- Identify errors in terminal punctuation.
- Identify errors in using commas to separate words.
- Identify errors in using commas to separate sentence parts.
- Identify errors in using commas with essential and nonessential sentence elements.
- Use appropriate proofreading symbols to indicate changes in text.
- Spell correctly a list of commonly misspelled words.

Terminal punctuation marks are the period, the question mark, and the exclamation point.

Terminal punctuation provides the strongest breaks possible, while internal punctuation provides varying levels of softer breaks.

Use the following proofreading symbols to indicate changes in punctuation:

Symbol	Meaning	Example
⊙	Insert a period.	Please answer the telephone⊙
?/	Insert a question mark.	Who did you say is calling?/
!/	Insert an exclamation point.	I just won the lottery!/
✗	Delete a terminal punctuation mark.	She will not go, will she✗?/

In a keyed or word-processed document, terminal punctuation is usually followed by two spaces. However, one space is becoming more widely accepted, especially when a document is desktop-published.

Whether you use one space or two spaces after terminal punctuation, be consistent within a document.

10-1 Use a **period** at the end of a statement, a command, an indirect question, and a polite request. A command usually contains the "understood *you*" as the subject. An indirect question is a statement that reports someone else's question. A polite request is in the form of a question, but instead of looking for an *answer*, it looks for an *action*.

Statement:	The sun is shining today.
Command:	Be sure to make the reservation this morning. (understood *you* is the subject)
Indirect question:	Malay asked if we had already eaten dinner.
Polite request:	Would you please find the Backoula file for me. (looks for an action instead of an answer)

10-2 Use a **question mark** after a direct question or a statement that is intended to sound like a question. Also, use a question mark for a short direct question appended to a statement or for short questions that independently follow a sentence or question.

Direct question:	How much money have you saved this month?
Statement phrased as a question:	You really think your plan will work? And they said they agreed with your plan?
Appended direct question:	I think this furniture arrangement will work just fine, don't you?
Independent direct questions:	What is your objective? To avoid failure? To protect your ego?

10-3 Use an **exclamation point** to express strong emotion, surprise, or urgency or to give emphasis after an interjection. Use this mark sparingly in business writing.

> Ramon won the scholarship!
>
> Congratulations! You have completed your course work.

INTERNAL PUNCTUATION—THE COMMA

Internal punctuation is used when a brief rather than a distinct pause is needed. Internal punctuation marks include the comma, the colon, the semicolon, the dash, parentheses, quotation marks, the underscore, and the apostrophe. Each internal punctuation mark has a specific function. The proofreader should know the function of each and keep in mind that punctuation is used to make the meaning of the message clear.

Use the following proofreading symbols to mark corrections in the use of the comma:

⌃ Insert a comma.	Our company has openings for computer operators but we do not expect to begin hiring until next month.	
⁄ Delete a comma.	The manager will interview all qualified candidates and choose from among them.	

#@%&!@#

Clear, but for want of a comma (or two):

He was a master mind you at fooling his friends.

Connie was that girl wearing your jacket?

USING THE COMMA TO SEPARATE WORDS

To provide the greatest clarity in written messages, use commas to separate words as you would use pauses or inflections in the voice if speaking the same message. Study the following rules that separate words or word groups with commas.

10-4 Use commas to set off a name or title addressed directly to the reader or listener.

> Jack, please assist me with conference registration.
>
> Allow me, sir, to take your coat.

10-5 Use commas to set off contrasted elements.

> The president, not the board, made the decision.
>
> Glennis, rather than Lana, will make the presentation.

When a contrasted element is considered essential to the meaning of the sentence, the contrasted element is not set off by commas.

> It was a busy but enjoyable trip.
>
> Working on this year's Red Cross campaign was a tiring although worthy venture.

10-1—10-3

a. door?

b. C

c. C

d. Business communication.

e. schedule!"

f. do you

10-6 Insert commas to provide clarity and to prevent sentences from being misread.

> *Confusing:*   Inside the house was a mess.
> *Better:*   Inside, the house was a mess.
>
> *Confusing:*   To Jo Kurt seemed the right person for the job.
> *Better:*   To Jo, Kurt seemed the right person for the job.
>
> *Confusing:*   In short people seem to have the right idea.
> *Better:*   In short, people seem to have the right idea.

The main purpose of a comma is to provide clarity. Think about your reader as you finalize a document. Ask yourself what your reader needs to be able to understand the message.

10-7 Insert commas to separate identical or similar words, except when the addition of a comma would increase the awkwardness of the sentence.

> It had been a long, long while since we talked.
>
> For the user, user-friendly instructions are always appreciated.
>
> He felt that that statement was not in good taste.

Proofread the following sentences for errors in the use of the comma. If a sentence is correct, write *C* to the right of the sentence.

a. Above all this program must be revamped if it is to succeed.

b. We think but we really don't know that he may resign next month.

c. To a perfectionist like Carol Anne would not be acceptable for the assignment.

d. What it was, was an oversight on Brad's part.

e. The trip to Madrid not the trip to Moscow is my choice, Akemi.

f. I am happy, Shimon that you achieved your goal.

10-8 Insert a comma to indicate a word or words omitted in a sentence. Use this construction carefully and only when the meaning is absolutely clear.

> Two years ago we sent employees to 92 seminars and training meetings; last year, 72 employees to seminars alone.
> (omitted words: *we sent*)

> The truth is, we did not expect the idea to work.
> (omitted word: *that*)

10-9 Use a comma to separate two consecutive adjectives that modify the same noun. A comma is needed between the two adjectives if they can be joined by *and*. However, do not use a comma and the word *and* in the same construction unless it is a series (three or more).

> This has been a long, hard trip.
> (The sentence could read *This has been a long and hard trip.*)

but This has been a stressful, long, and hard trip.

> She bought a good used car.
> (*Good* modifies the idea expressed by the combination *used car.*
> It is not a good and used car.)

10-10 Insert a comma to separate unrelated adjacent numbers when both are written in figure form or both are written in word form.

> In 1999, 174 people attended the city's budget conference.

> Please note that on page 15, 32 different kinds of birds are named.

> Although the table was set for only four, five guests were seated.

10-4—10-7

a. Above all⌃this

b. We think⌃but we
   really don't know⌃
   that

c. like Carol Anne⌃

d. C

e. Madrid⌃not the trip
   to Moscow⌃is my

f. Shimon⌃that

Clarity is always the test. If your readers may misread the text, a comma may help.

10-11 Use commas to separate parts of addresses and geographical elements when *two* or more appear together within text. Also, use a comma to separate the city and state within an inside address on a letter. Note that in writing addresses, the state and the ZIP Code are separated by a space but no comma; this rule applies to both an inside address using the two-character abbreviation and an address given within text when the state name is spelled out. When these elements fall within the sentence, not at the end, be sure to insert a comma both before and after the last item.

Do *not* place a comma between a state name or abbreviation and a ZIP Code. This rule applies to inside addresses, addresses in text, and addresses on envelopes.

Inside address on a letter:	Travis St. James 10 Hollow Springs Road Boise, ID 83744
Address within text:	Write to me at busytsj@focus.net or at 10 Hollow Springs Road, Boise, Idaho 83744.
Geographical items within text:	I enjoyed visiting San Antonio, Texas, last year. This year I will travel to Bogata, Columbia, in South America, for an excursion.

CHECKPOINT 10-8–10-11

Proofread the following sentences for errors in the use of the comma. If a sentence is correct, write *C* to the right of the sentence.

a. Many people choose real estate as a challenging, second career.

b. Wanting to work together as a husband and wife team, Alan and Alicia chose to become real estate agents; Trent and Carma real estate brokers.

c. At Home Parade 2001 1,300 real estate agents in the cities of Dallas and Fort Worth, Texas received new leads for potential buyers from outside the state.

d. The law requires people to hold a genuine up-to-date license to sell real estate.

e. In Cleveland, Ohio 687 homes were sold last month; in Cleveland, Tennessee only 3.

f. During 2001 227 homes were listed in that area, including the one at 320 Desert Way, Euless, Texas, 76039.

10-12 Use commas to separate parts of dates when *three* or more elements appear together, but do not insert a comma between the month and the day. Count the month, day, and year as separate elements; count the name of a holiday or another designation for a special date as one element. When these elements fall within the sentence, not at the end, be sure to insert a comma both before and after the last item.

We were married on April Fool's Day, April 1.

We met on Tuesday, September 10, 1990, at 4 p.m.

but We met in September 1990 during a sales convention in Atlanta.

10-13 Use a comma to separate degrees or abbreviations that follow a person's name. Do not use commas for abbreviations that follow a person's or an organization's name (such as *Jr.*, *Sr.*, or *Inc.*) unless you know it is the person's or organization's preference. Note the use of commas before and after the element when it falls within the sentence.

Cheree Price, D.V. M., opened a new clinic last year.

Love Inc. is a charitable organization operating in nine cities across Canada.

We invited both Bryan Sr. and Bryan Jr. to join us.

The contract was landed by Smith, Barlow & Routhe, Ltd. Smith, Barlow & Routhe, Ltd., will probably hire a hundred people to help them meet their new deadlines.
(Smith, Barlow & Routhe, Ltd., uses a comma in its legal name.)

10-14 Use a comma to introduce a short quotation. A short quotation is generally one sentence.

Stewart replied, "The computers we bought a year ago already are obsolete."

10-15 Use a comma to separate three or more elements in a series if the items do not contain internal commas. If the elements of the series contain internal commas, use a semicolon to separate them. (Semicolons will be discussed in Chapter 11.) Elements of a series can be words, phrases, or clauses. Always use a comma before a conjunction, such as *and* or *or*, preceding the last item in the series.

Word series:	We reward qualities such as integrity, sincerity, adaptability, and initiative in our employees.
Phrase series:	She said Paula could pick up the tickets, deliver the tuxedoes, or check on the flowers.
Clause series:	You should call the meeting to order, Marcelo should distribute the agenda and portfolios, and Maurice should record the minutes.

Locate a source document to determine whether a person or company prefers a comma before a designation such as *Jr.* or *Inc.*

10-8—10-11

a. challenging, second

b. Trent and Carma real estate brokers.

c. 2001 1,300 . . . Fort Worth, Texas received

d. genuine up-to-date

e. Cleveland, Ohio 687 homes . . . Cleveland, Tennessee only 3.

f. During 2001 227 homes . . . Texas, 76039.

Newspaper journalists adhere to AP, or Associated Press, style, which does not use a comma before the last item in a series. In business correspondence, however, writers and editors should use the final comma in a series.

Proofread the following sentences for errors in the use of the comma. If a sentence is correct, write *C* to the right of the sentence.

a. Morgan Forsey Sr., says "Specialty temporary services in accounting, in computing and in medical technology will continue to grow in the next decade."

b. This trend is increasing because hiring costs are lower, fringe benefits do not have to be provided and workloads can be handled more easily in peak periods.

c. A nationwide survey released on Tuesday, May 12 indicated that temporary workers may expect to receive health insurance, retirement plans tuition assistance and child care benefits.

d. National placement agency Holland & Heart Inc., stated that temporary workers will face more extensive pre-employment testing for personality, general aptitudes, and computer skills.

e. Masey Heart, Ph.D. of Holland & Heart often states, "The temporary workforce of today is the permanent workforce of tomorrow."

f. Holland & Heart placed approximately 600 temporary workers from Tuesday May 1, through Thursday May 31.

USING THE COMMA TO SEPARATE SENTENCE PARTS

Remember, independent clauses contain a subject and a predicate and they make sense. Dependent clauses contain a subject and a predicate, but they need to be connected to independent clauses to make sense and, therefore, to achieve grammatical completeness. A phrase contains either a subject or a verb, but not both.

Business messages include sentences written in various forms, which makes the writing more interesting to readers. Writers use **simple sentences** (one independent clause), **compound sentences** (two independent clauses), **complex sentences** (one dependent clause and one independent clause), and **compound-complex sentences** (two dependent clauses and one independent clause) to convey their message and engage their readers.

Other combinations of sentence parts also contribute to writing in forms other than a simple subject and predicate. For instance, a sentence could be made up of an introductory verbal phrase plus a subject and a predicate. Commas are used to separate sentence parts so that the message can be clearly communicated. Learn to identify sentence parts and to insert commas where necessary to achieve clarity of written communication.

10–16 Use a comma to separate the main clauses of a compound sentence connected by the coordinating conjunctions *and, or, but,* or *nor.* (The words *so, for,* and *yet* are infrequently used coordinating conjunctions as well.) The comma comes before the conjunction. In the following examples the subject and verb of each independent clause are identified and the conjunctions are highlighted in bold.

10-12—10-15
a. Sr. says, "Specialty . . . in computing and
b. provided and
c. Tuesday, May 12 indicated . . . retirement plans tuition assistance and child care benefits.
d. Inc. stated
e. Ph.D. of Holland & Heart,
f. Tuesday May 1, through Thursday May 31.

> S   V   S V
> Ralph Waldo Emerson was a famous poet, **and** I am a huge fan of his work.
>
> S   V   S   V
> Betty Jimenez will attend the meeting, **or** she will send a substitute.
>
> S   V   S   V
> Many resources were available, **but** we decided to use a computer search.
>
> S V   V S
> I am not a member of that group, **nor** will I become a member.

If both clauses are short (four words or fewer), a comma is not necessary.

> S   V   S   V
> I copied the reports **and** he distributed them.

Do not mistake a compound sentence for a simple sentence with compound verbs. Such a sentence requires no comma before the conjunction.

> S   V   V
> The software tracks our expenses **and** provides an accurate record.
>
> S   V   V
> Sweeny arranged for an after-hours conference room **and** ordered dinner for the crew who was working late.

WORKPLACE CONNECTIONS

Good writers use a variety of sentence styles to make their writing engaging. Editors and proofreaders must ensure the accuracy of those sentences.

CHECKPOINT 10-16

Proofread the following paragraph for errors in the use of the comma.

You can now purchase ultrasonic humidifiers or you can still buy the warm-mist models. A humidifier can soothe dry throats, and help keep plants from withering. Low humidity allows static electricity to build up, and that accounts for minor electrical shocks received when you touch a metal object. An acceptable humidity range is between 40 and 60 percent but higher ranges may cause paper to absorb moisture. Set correctly, either one you choose will be able to provide the right amount of moisture, and provide a comfortable environment.

10-17 Use a comma after most introductory elements, such as transitional words, prepositional phrases, and verbal (participial) phrases. However, do not use a comma after a short (four words or fewer) prepositional phrase. In the following examples the word(s), phrases, or clauses being discussed are highlighted in bold.

Introductory transitional word:	**However,** we can call you on June 4 to remind you of the appointment.
Introductory prepositional phrase:	**Before the first staff meeting of each month,** we always send a reminder memo.
Short introductory prepositional phrase:	**After our announcement** the partners held their own meeting.
Introductory verbal phrase:	**Commuting by vanpool,** Fiona and Rich made good time on the interstate.

CHECKPOINT 10-17

Proofread the following paragraph for errors in the use of the comma.

In the West, many farms are irrigated by water brought from the mountains to the fields. Reservoirs hold the water that melts from the winter's snowfall on the mountains. After the canals are opened up each spring farmers begin to use the water to prepare their fields and to water their crops. Without the water provided by irrigation crops cannot thrive in the arid climates in the West. Thankfully snow always falls in the winter and melts in the spring.

10-18 Use a comma after an introductory dependent clause, which begins the sentence, or an internal dependent clause, which falls within the sentence. While all clauses contain subjects and verbs, some clauses— including dependent clauses—contain *implied* subjects and/or verbs. In the following examples the dependent clauses are highlighted in bold; the implied subjects and verbs in the third example sentence are set in brackets:

10-16

humidifiers or

throats, and

percent but

moisture, and

provide

Introductory dependent clause:	**When you arrive in Denver,** please call my assistant to pick you up.
Internal dependent clause:	After Quinton called, **as you said he would,** we figured out the message.
Internal dependent clause with implied subject and verb:	My favorite meal is seafood gumbo, **when [*it is*] hot,** and mint tea, **when [*it is*] cold.**

Generally, do not use a comma with a terminal dependent clause, which is a dependent clause that falls at the end of the sentence. However, if the terminal dependent clause sounds like an afterthought, use a comma to separate it from the independent clause.

> Please call my assistant to pick you up **when you arrive in Denver.**
>
> I believe Trevor's plan will work **because Trevor is committed to its success.**
>
> We will send our shipment by ground freight, **if that is acceptable to you.**

10-17

In the West, many

spring farmers

irrigation crops

Thankfully snow

CHECKPOINT 10-18

Proofread the following paragraph for errors in the use of the comma.

Have you considered using a spreadsheet program to keep track of your accounts payable and receivable? However busy you can find time to investigate software options. Automatic calculation functions and the ability to write formulas which most operators appreciate, are just a couple of features to consider. Although the learning curve may take a little time at first you can save time in the long run by using a spreadsheet software package. I would be happy to help you shop for a software package to fit your business needs if you would like my assistance.

10-19 Do not use a comma after phrases or clauses that function as the subject of the sentence. If the subject is difficult to determine, locate the verb first. Then you can more easily locate the clause functioning as the subject. The phrases or clauses that function as subjects in the following examples are highlighted in bold.

>   S   V
> **Finding the lost contact lens** is their goal.
> (gerund phrase used as subject)
>
>   S   V
> **To accept sole credit for the idea** would be unfair.
> (infinitive phrase used as subject)
>
>   S   V
> **What he learned in school** has helped him throughout his life.
> (noun clause used as subject)
>
>   S   V
> **Whomever Madeline chooses as a running mate** will have a lot of work to do.
> (dependent clause used as subject)

WORKPLACE CONNECTIONS

Many employees are expected to be able to express complex thoughts clearly. Such expression may call for the use of complicated sentences, the meaning of which depends on accurate comma use.

Proofread the following paragraph for errors in the use of the comma.

Writing a résumé, does not have to be an overwhelming task. All it takes, is for a job seeker to highlight his or her best qualities. Skills developed through work experience and/or education, need to be highlighted for a potential employer to review. Remember, a neat, attractive format, helps to create interest in a résumé. Also, remember that even a small error on an otherwise spotless résumé, will almost always result in the résumé ending up in the "circular file," i.e., the trash can.

10-18

However busy you

formulas which

first you

needs if you

ESSENTIAL AND NONESSENTIAL ELEMENTS

An **essential element,** or *restrictive* element, is a word, phrase, or clause that is necessary to the meaning of the sentence. A **nonessential element,** or *nonrestrictive* element, is a word, phrase, or clause that provides additional information but is not necessary to the meaning of the sentence. Nonessential elements include nonrestrictive elements, transitional expressions, and appositives; they are separated from the rest of the sentence by commas.

To determine whether an expression is essential or nonessential, try omitting it from the sentence. If you can leave the expression out without changing the basic meaning of the sentence, the expression is a nonessential expression and should be set off with commas.

10-20 Use commas to set off nonessential elements. Nonessential elements provide additional descriptive information about the nouns or pronouns they modify. The nonessential elements in the following examples are highlighted in bold.

> We knew that, **late or not,** we were expected to attend the briefing.
>
> The new automated information delivery system, **which was installed last Thursday,** can function as a telephone receptionist and voice mail system.
>
> Dr. Benita Moore, **who is president of the Georgia Business Education Association,** has provided excellent leadership to business teachers.

Do not use commas to set off elements that are essential to the meaning of the sentence. Without the essential element the sentence may be grammatically correct, but it lacks the definition the essential element gives. The essential elements in the following examples are highlighted in bold.

10-19

Writing a résumé,

does

All it takes, is for

education, need

format, helps

résumé, will

The student **who studies hard and completes all assignments** should make a good grade.
(The restrictive words identify the student to whom the sentence refers.)

The book **that is lying on the table** must be returned to the library. (The restrictive words identify the book to which the sentence refers.)

CHECKPOINT 10-20

Proofread the following paragraph for errors in the use of the comma.

A skill you should acquire to build your career portfolio which is what you will need for job interviews, is that of writing promotional literature. Not every company, doing business in the global market today, has a marketing department. Some companies rely on administrative staff to prepare newsletters, brochures, news releases, and home pages. Although you may not have been formally trained, to prepare these types of promotional literature, a person, who routinely reads brochures and other promotional literature, actually has more experience than he or she thinks.

10-21 Use commas to set off nonessential parenthetical expressions (such as *on the other hand, first, in fact, to tell the truth, however, that is, then, therefore,* and *for example*) when they begin, interrupt, or change the flow of the sentence. The nonessential elements in the following examples are highlighted in bold.

You are able, **theoretically,** to make the experiment work.

The person who received the recognition, **if you recall,** was the supervisor.

However, you may choose to spend the extra time watching a television special.

The Red Riders, **on the other hand,** won the division title.

CHECKPOINT 10-21

Proofread the following paragraph for errors in the use of the comma.

Many experts recommend drinking eight glasses of water a day. However when people exercise or are outdoors in the heat, they need even more water. Consider the eight glasses, therefore as a starting point for daily water consumption. To figure the total ounces of water you need each day, divide your weight by two. For example a person who weighs 150 pounds should drink 75 ounces of water a day. The important point, ultimately is to drink water for your health's sake.

10-20

portfolio which

company, doing

. . . today, has

trained, to prepare

person, who . . .

literature, actually

"'I don't need computer skills,' I said.
'I can do all my work with a pad and
pencil,' I told them."

10-22   Use commas to set off **appositives.** An appositive is a word or phrase that renames or can be substituted for the noun or pronoun that immediately precedes it. The appositives in the following examples are highlighted in bold.

> Rafael Velazco, **vice president, Sun Rise Software,** has been invited to give a presentation at the fall education conference.

> Panama City Beach, **one of my favorite vacation spots,** is very crowded during Memorial Day weekend.

> Theresa Wodzinski, **a benefits consultant with Higgins Co.,** reported that only a small percentage of companies allow unused vacation time to accrue.

> Next Tuesday, **November 6,** we will allow everyone extra time at lunch to vote.

Do not use commas to set off a one-word appositive when it contains information that is essential to the meaning of the sentence or has a close relationship to the preceding word.

> Her daughter **Olivia** was promoted to second lieutenant. (She has more than one daughter, but Olivia is the one who was promoted.)

> The doctor **himself** did the testing.

10-21

However when

glasses, therefore

as

For example a

point, ultimately

is to

Proofread the following paragraph for errors in the use of the comma.

All students who want to receive financial aid to attend college must fill out a federal student aid report the FAFSA. Using the FAFSA, students, the ones who will attend college report their income and other personal information. The federal government determines how much financial contribution students can make to their education expenses and how much money they the students, can receive in federal student loans. Work study funds, funds that students can earn to apply toward education expenses are also calculated based on the FAFSA. If parents have the information, they can fill out the FAFSA for their children; however, the students, themselves, must sign the FAFSA before submitting it.

SPELLING APPLICATIONS

10-23 Compare the words in Column A with the corresponding words in Column B. Use the appropriate proofreading symbols to correct the misspelled words. If both columns are correct, write **C** to the left of the number.

	Column A	Column B
1.	amateur	ameteur
2.	arrangment	arrangement
3.	changeable	changable
4.	fulfill	fullfill
5.	itinerary	itinerery
6.	liesure	leisure
7.	liasion	liaison
8.	occurrence	occurence
9.	priviledge	privilege
10.	transferred	transfered

10-22

1. report the FAFSA
2. attend college report
3. they the students,
4. education expenses are
5. students, themselves, must

CHAPTER SUMMARY

Proofread carefully to be sure your documents follow these punctuation rules:

♦ Use periods, question marks, and exclamation points for terminal punctuation.

♦ Use commas to indicate pauses and to achieve clarity in written messages.

♦ Generally, use commas in these situations: direct address; contrasted elements; adjacent identical words; omitted words; consecutive adjectives; unrelated adjacent numbers; dates, addresses, and geographical elements; and degrees and abbreviations after a person's or an organization's name. Also, use commas to introduce short quotations and to separate items in a series.

♦ Generally, use commas to separate sentence parts in these situations: compound clauses, introductory elements, and introductory or internal dependent clauses. Use commas with terminal dependent clauses when they sound like afterthoughts.

♦ Use commas to set off nonessential elements; do not use commas to set off essential elements.

♦ Use commas to set off appositives; do not use commas with one-word, closely related appositives.

Study these tips, and apply them as you proofread:

♦ Punctuation marks are used in order to make the meaning of a sentence clear. Proofread to eliminate confusion caused by errors in punctuation.

♦ Keep a reference guide close by in case you need to refer to it.

words@work Open *words@work*. Click on the Grammar and Usage tab. Click on Lessons; then click on Punctuation. Read page 1 of the lesson; then proceed to page 2. Use the links provided to review terminal punctuation and comma use.

Proofread the following paragraphs. Use the appropriate proofreading symbols to mark errors you find in terminal punctuation, comma usage, or spelling. To aid you in proofreading, the number of errors to be found is indicated in parentheses for Exercises P-1 and P-2.

P-1 Do you routinely use an automatic teller machine (ATM) to withdraw money from your checking account. To transfer funds between accounts. To pay regular monthly bills? Most of us are no longer amaters at this form of electronic funds transfer, and find it a convenient flexible method of banking. Did you know that these services may be available, even if you are thousands of miles from your bank's ATM. Many of the thousands of ATMs in our country are linked into statewide, regional or national networks.
(8 errors)

P-2 The small plastic card you use at your ATM is actually a debit card. It allows you, the bank customer to withdraw from your account electronically without writing a check. Would you like to be able to use your debit card right at the cash register. You can. Simply put your debit card through a processing scanner, enter your personal code and depress a button on the scanner. The amount of your purchase is immediately deducted from your checking account, and transfered to the store's account.
(5 errors)

P-3 The development of point-of-sale debiting has caught on quickly in the United States, and has the enthusiasm of many people. Retailers get their money almost immediately, and chances of a theft are diminished because money is deposited in the store's bank account rather than into its cash register. Moreover customers enjoy the priviledges of paying faster, carrying less cash and not having to wait for check approval. For retailers then the use of debit cards means efficiency; for customers convenience.

10-23
1. ameteur — a
2. arrangment — e
3. changable — e
4. fullfill
5. itinerary — a
6. liesure
7. liasion
8. occurence — r
9. priviledge
10. transfered — r

P-1
1. checking account. ?/
2. between accounts. ?/
3. amaters — u
4. transfer/ and find
5. convenient flexible
6. available, even if
7. your bank's ATM. ?/
8. regional or
   national

P-2

1. you, the bank customer to
2. cash register. /?/
3. code and
4. account, and
5. transfered

P-3

1. States, and
2. Moreover customers
3. priviledges
4. less cash and
5. For retailers then the
6. for customers convenience.

P-4

1. current relevant
2. All-in-One card /?/
3. California, 90024-8765.
4. February 15, 2003
5. credit card has

PROGRESSIVE PROOFREADING

You are the manager of Mercado Travel Agency. You confer with customers and make travel reservations, but you are also responsible for seeing that all communication is correct. Today you have five documents to proofread. Follow the instructions provided with each document. Your office uses block letter format and open punctuation.

Mercado Travel Agency

November 5, 20--

Mrs. Nyela Weiss
1166 Norwood Street
Cleveland, OH 44197-8032

Dear Mrs. Weiss

Thank you for your letter requesting brochures, price lists and information sheets about cruises leaving from Miami, FL. Your inquiry comes at a time, when a number of interesting exotic cruises are available at fabulously low prices.

You should receive up-to-date information within the next few days from three cruise lines about their winter cruises. When you are making a choice, consider each line's total cost the cost of air travel to the point of departure, and the itinerary. As you will see prices for a seven-day cruise range from $1195 to $3,150 per person.

The enclosed brochure provides helpful information about choosing a cruise. After you make your decision about the cruise, fill out and return the data sheet. You can then leave everything in our hands and rest assured that satisfactory arrangements will be made.

We look forward to serving as you laision to the cruise line of your choice.

Sincerely

Miss Cassandra E. Spellman
Marketing Manager

dp

4500 West Kennedy Boulevard • Tampa, FL 33609-3421 • www.mercadotravel.com
Phone: 800.555.0113 • Fax: 813.555.0133

Add Art

PARADISE ISLAND
"Your Bahamas Getaway Vacation"

Ask about our:
• Golf and tennis clinics.
• Island dance lessons.
• Honeymoon packages.

From $299
3 days/2 nights including air
(3 nights from $329 including air)

1-800-555-0113

Mercado Travel Agency
4500 West Kennedy Boulevard
Tampa, FL 33609-3421

Please rush FREE brochures and information to:
NAME _____

STREET _____

CITY_____ STATE ___ ZIP_____

PARADISE ISLAND
"Your Bahamas Getaway Vacation"

Ask about our:
 • Golf and tennis clinics.
 • Honymoon packages

1-800-555-0113

Mercado Travel Agency

4500 West Kennedy Boulevard
Tampa, FL 33609-3421

From $299
* 3 days/3 nights including air
(3 nights from $339 including air)

Please rush FREE brochures and information to:

NAME _____

STREET _____

CITY_____ STATE __ ZIP_____

Job 3 Check the following copy for errors. Be sure that all words are spelled correctly.

CHOOSING THE RIGHT CRUISE FOR YOU

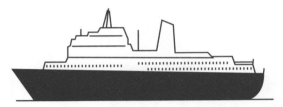

As the winter cruise season approaches, discounts on ship fares are plentiful. Smart consumers are taking advantage of the special bargains. Now is the time to consider taking a liesurely cruise. It may fullfill a lifetime dream for you? If you have never pictured yourself as a passenger on a cruise ship, consider the following facts:

Passenger Profile

Once cruises were a pastime for the rich and the retired. Today cruises are taken by individuals from all walks of life and all income levels. Forty-eight percent of cruise passengers now earn less than $40,000 a year. Nearly half are under forty-five years of age, and ten percent areunder twenty-five.

More than a million and a half people will take cruises on about one hundred cruise ships this year and cruise lines are competitively vying for this business. Two qualities of the cruise experience is being stressed: value and convenience. Now is a great time to participate in what some refer to as the "cruise revolution."

Cost and Convenence

Consider the price of the average cruise. The price that you pay includes accomodations, baggage handling, meals, entertainment (including first-run movies and live performances), room service, daily activities ranging from computer lessons to aerobics classes, travel to any number of ports and reduced round-trip airfare to and from the port city.

Convenients is another factor, that you must consider as you contemplate taking a cruise. In what other way can you travel from one country to another without having to unpack and repack your bags? Where else can you spend days or weeks without having to open your wallet or purse constantly. And you don't have to worry, about arranging travel schedules, making plane reservations, or waiting long hours in airports.

Activities on Board

So that a cruise meets your expectations, you should take time to find out what various cruise lines offers and to who they cater. For example, some cruise lines cater to families with children and make special provisions for them. Other lines cater only to adults. Some provide for academic pursuits, while others provide primarily entertainment and recreation.

Give some thought to the types of activities that you enjoy. Do you want entertainment. Do you want physical fitness programs? Do you want to learn something? At least one cruise ship regularly doubles as a floating university. There is no pressure to participate in any of the activities provided by the cruise line. If you wish, you can relax on deck with a book or watch television in your own cabin. You can choose your own recreation.

Some passengers desire the traditional dining room experience where guests dress in formal attire. Others prefer a more relaxed dining atmosphere where casual dress is alright. Both tastes can be accomodated on today's cruises.

Cruise Itinarary

Another important criterion that will effect your selection of a cruise is the planned itinarary of the ship. Consider the number of stops the ship will make and the ports you can visit. Is there particular cities you have always wanted to tour. Your travel agent can provide you with a detailed list of port choices and itinerary options to help you decide on the best cruise.

How to Get Started

After you have made some of the major decisions reguarding your preferences in a cruise, see your travel agent. The agent can help determine which cruise suits your specific needs, and provide answers to any other questions that you might have. In other words, your travel agent is the liason between you and the cruise line. Contact your travel agent today and take the worry out of traveling.

Job 4   Proofread the following e-mail message to a client.

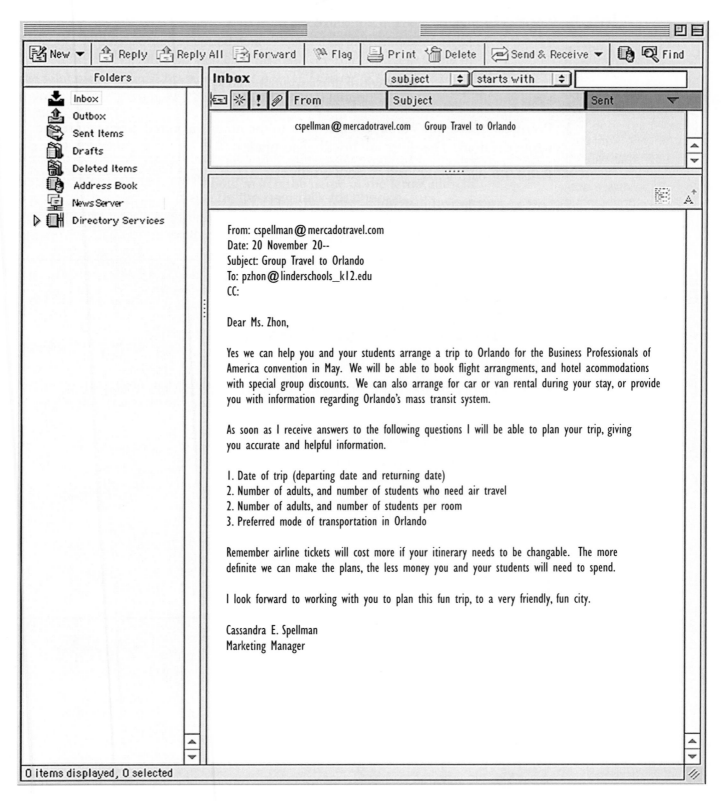

From: cspellman@mercadotravel.com
Date: 20 November 20--
Subject: Group Travel to Orlando
To: pzhon@linderschools_k12.edu
CC:

Dear Ms. Zhon,

Yes we can help you and your students arrange a trip to Orlando for the Business Professionals of America convention in May. We will be able to book flight arrangments, and hotel acommodations with special group discounts. We can also arrange for car or van rental during your stay, or provide you with information regarding Orlando's mass transit system.

As soon as I receive answers to the following questions I will be able to plan your trip, giving you accurate and helpful information.

1. Date of trip (departing date and returning date)
2. Number of adults, and number of students who need air travel
2. Number of adults, and number of students per room
3. Preferred mode of transportation in Orlando

Remember airline tickets will cost more if your itinerary needs to be changable. The more definite we can make the plans, the less money you and your students will need to spend.

I look forward to working with you to plan this fun trip, to a very friendly, fun city.

Cassandra E. Spellman
Marketing Manager

COMPUTERIZED PROOFREADING

Job 5 Proofread a memo.

1. Cassandra Spellman, the marketing manager, has written a memo to the firm's travel agents about the upcoming season.

2. Load the file C10JOB5 from the template CD-ROM.

3. Proofread Cassandra's draft, comparing it to the notes she jotted down before she wrote the draft. The notes are brief but accurate.

4. Finish formatting the memo using standard memo format.

5. Save the file as C10JOB5R.

6. Produce the document by following the standard procedures.

Mercado Travel Agency

weather map--tell them to be sure and check Mich., OH, Ind., Ill., and Wisc.

Bahamas, 10% discount, no-frills cruises
don't confuse these with other cruises

agent incentive--10 days to Tahiti
from 12/1 to 2/27

PUNCTUATION ERRORS, PART 2

A sentence without punctuation is like a road without signs or traffic signals. As a driver, how would you know where to go or how to behave without signs and road signals? Punctuation marks provide the same type of guidance for readers, telling them when to stop, when to start again, or when to just pause. Using punctuation marks according to certain rules and conventions gives your readers a helpful path to follow. Without accurate punctuation marks, readers are likely to end up confused and in the ditch.

PUNCTUATION TO CLARIFY

As previously discussed, punctuation marks have specific, prescribed functions. Punctuation helps the reader interpret the meaning of the communication. The proofreader must know the function of each mark of punctuation to be able to evaluate its use in clarifying the message.

Chapter 11 reviews the use of semicolons, colons, apostrophes, quotation marks, underscores and italics, dashes, parentheses, and brackets. Use the following proofreading symbols to mark errors in the use of these punctuation marks:

⨝	Insert a semicolon.	Join us for dinner tonight we're having steak.
⩚	Insert a colon.	You will need to bring three things notepaper, pen, and pencil.
ⱽ	Insert an apostrophe or a single quotation mark.	Tennessees economic climate is continually improving.
⟨⟨ ⟩⟩	Insert quotation marks.	When interest rates are down, invest in stocks advised the broker.
ital	Set underscore or italics.	The word _articulate_ should be included in the list.

Symbol	Instruction	Example
⌄	Insert a dash.	The thief took everything my car, my wallet, and my luggage.
( )	Insert parentheses.	The committee's findings are published in their April meeting minutes(pages 6-7)
[ ]	Insert brackets.	"*The Post* reported that Senator Bob MacInerny lost her[*sic*]seat on the budget committee."

SEMICOLON

A semicolon provides a stronger pause than a comma.

A semicolon is used when a sentence needs a stronger break than would be provided by a comma. The semicolon is not as strong as a period and does not signal the end of a thought as a period does. The semicolon is a strong separator and is used only between equal parts. A semicolon is followed by one space.

11–1 Use a semicolon to separate independent clauses of a compound sentence when the clauses are not joined by a conjunction, including the coordinating conjunctions *and, but, or,* and *nor.* Use this construction when the clauses are closely related and a break softer than a period is desired.

> I must leave now to vote; the polls close in an hour.

> Please send the report by overnight delivery; we need an answer tomorrow.

The clauses on either side of a semicolon must express complete thoughts.

11–2 Use a semicolon to separate two independent clauses joined by the coordinating conjunctions *and, but, or,* and *nor* when at least one of the clauses contains an internal comma. The semicolon provides a stronger break between the two clauses and provides clarity to the message.

> When you receive the document, sign it; but do not mail it until Friday, March 10.

> I requested files for Carlson, Kramer, and Davison; and Matthew requested files for Carlsen, Kraemer, and Davidson.

A comma is often sufficient to provide clarity between two independent clauses even though one contains an internal comma. However, a semicolon is also correct and may be used if a stronger break is desired.

> My brother lives in Sao Paulo, Brazil, but he will return to the United States next year.

> Marcus and Josefina served on the holiday committee last year; however, they do not want to serve again.

> **Give to the world the best you have and the best will come back to you.**
>
> —Madelaine Bridges

11-3 Use the semicolon to separate independent clauses of a compound sentence joined by an adverbial conjunction or a transitional expression such as *accordingly, consequently, furthermore, hence, however, in fact, likewise, on the other hand, otherwise, then, therefore,* and *thus.* Follow an adverbial conjunction or a transitional expression with a comma unless it is only one syllable.

> It was past midnight; consequently, they had to adjourn before the issue was settled.
>
> He ran the race in record time; then he decided to celebrate.

11-4 Use the semicolon to separate items in a series when at least one of the items contains a comma.

> Copies of the report were sent to Janet Carpenter, president; Edwin Wukman, vice president; and Trilby Mays, secretary.

A semicolon separates items in a series when one of those items contains an internal comma.

CHECKPOINT 11-1–11-4

Proofread the following sentences for errors in the use of commas and semicolons. If a sentence is correct, write *C* to the right of the sentence.

a. Budgeting is crucial to financial planning, however most people do not enjoy the record keeping.

b. I will carry only the essentials, the nonessentials require too much space.

c. I like to visit California, Nevada and New Mexico but, Kansas and Oklahoma will be my destinations this year.

d. I detest dieting; it takes too much willpower.

e. Imperial Airlines serves Miami, Florida, Atlanta, Georgia, Birmingham, Alabama, and Raleigh, North Carolina.

COLON

A colon represents a break that is stronger than the semicolon but less strong than the period. Usually, a writer uses the colon after a statement to introduce and emphasize what follows. Two spaces follow a colon used to introduce an enumeration, a listing, a question, or a quotation.

11-1—11-4

a. planning,
   however,

b. essentials; the

c. Nevada, and New
   Mexico, but,
   Kansas

d. C

e. Miami, Florida;
   Atlanta, Georgia;
   Birmingham,
   Alabama; and
   Raleigh, North
   Carolina.

A colon provides a stronger break or pause than a semicolon.

When introducing a list or series, structure the introductory sentence to avoid using a colon after a preposition or a verb.

If list items are complete sentences, punctuate them as sentences. If list items are not sentences, start each one with a capital letter but do not close with a period.

11-5   Use a colon to introduce a question or a quotation of two sentences or longer.

> The speaker raised an interesting question: Which comes first, enthusiasm or success?

> The consultant made these recommendations: "First, reorganize the workstations to be more convenient and to incorporate ergonomic principles. Second, restructure the lighting to provide adequate light for the new workstation arrangements."

11-6   Use a colon after an introduction to a clause when the second clause explains or defines the first clause. The first word of a main clause following a colon may be capitalized for emphasis.

> Mr. Wong's philosophy was simple: Give the best service, strive for superior performance, and respect the individual.

11-7   Use a colon to introduce a horizontal list or a series preceded by introductory words such as *namely* and *for example*.

> I would like you to contact the following airlines: United, American, Delta, Southwest, and Northwest.

> The production schedule includes many variables: namely, employee vacations, availability of parts, equipment maintenance, and power outages.

Note: Do not use a colon to introduce a list that immediately follows a preposition or a verb. Instead, either omit the colon or insert words such as *the following* or *as follows*.

Incorrect:	The supervisor has the responsibility to: assist the staff, establish procedures, and resolve conflicts.
Correct:	The supervisor has the responsibility to assist the staff, establish procedures, and resolve conflicts.
Correct:	The supervisor has the responsibility to do the following: assist the staff, establish procedures, and resolve conflicts.

Use a colon to introduce a vertical list. Use periods after items in a vertical list if the items are stated as independent clauses.

> The steps to operate the MK410 are as follows:
>
> 1. Flip the red switch to the ON position.
> 2. Wait for the blinking green light to remain solid.
> 3. Rotate the power knob to the No. 7 position.
> 4. Wait 10 minutes before using the machine.

These criteria are considered important:

- A quality education
- Meaningful work experience
- Leadership experience
- A strong work ethic

11-8 Use a colon to separate hours and minutes expressed in figures. Do not include a colon and two zeros to indicate on-the-hour time.

> Dinner will be served at 5:30, the show will start at 7, and dessert will be served at 8:30.

In many industries employees create product documentation and training materials. Documents of this type frequently include numbered and bulleted lists. The format must be accurate and consistent throughout many volumes of the documents.

11-9 Use colons in formatting business documents. In correspondence use colons to follow the salutation when mixed punctuation is used and to punctuate reference initials if the author's initials are included. In memos use colons to follow the introductory words *To*, *From*, *Date*, and *Subject*.

> *Reference initials:* JP:df *or* jp:df *(writer:preparer)*
>
> *Salutation:* Dear Miss Feinstein:
>
> *Introductory words:* To: Barry Weeman

Reference initials also may be keyed using just the preparer's initials; for example, *df.*

CHECKPOINT 11-5–11-9

Proofread the following sentences for errors in the use of commas, semicolons, and colons. If a sentence is correct, write *C* to the right of the sentence.

a. It's as true with documents as it is with people: First impressions count.

b. Three criteria are used when booking a hotel; location, value, and reputation.

c. The policy manual states, "Under certain circumstances spouses may be asked to voluntarily terminate their employment. Spouses will not be permitted to continue their employment when one of them occupies a confidential position."

d. At 12:00 noon the article was sent to the following newspapers. *The Jerusalem Post, The Miami Herald, The New York Times,* and *The Washington Post.*

e. This is what she asked me, "How do you know the president's plans?"

11-5—11-9

a. C

b. hotel location

c. states

d. 12:00 noon . . .

   newspapers

e. me

APOSTROPHE

An apostrophe is used to form possessives and some plurals. It is also used to indicate the omission of letters and figures. The apostrophe is followed by a single space unless the next character is part of the same word.

11–10 Use an apostrophe and *s* to form the possessive case of a noun—singular or plural—that does not end in an *s* sound. Add only the apostrophe to form the possessive case of a noun that already ends in an *s* sound and *does not* add an extra syllable when possessive. Add an apostrophe and *s* to form the possessive case of a singular noun that ends in an *s* sound and *does* add an extra syllable when possessive.

Janie's friend	(friend of Janie)
the dog's bark	(bark of the dog)
a year's work	(the work of a year)
ten years' work	(the work of ten years)
Nadia's hat	(the hat of Nadia)
James' hat	(the hat of James)
Gus's hat	(the hat of Gus)
my boss's desk	(one desk of one boss)
my two bosses' desks	(two desks of two bosses)

In most circumstances avoid awkward possessions by not using the possessive form and by not creating possessions for inanimate objects.

	The car that belongs to my uncle's attorney.
not	my uncle's attorney's car
	The legs of that chair are badly scratched.
not	the chair's legs

11–11 Use an apostrophe and *s* to form the possessive case of an indefinite pronoun.

anyone's guess   everybody's friend   somebody's glove

Note: A personal pronoun does not require an apostrophe.

her/hers	my/mine	your/yours
his	our/ours	
its	their/theirs	

This notebook is mine; yours is on the desk.

The building has exceeded its capacity.

WORKPLACE CONNECTIONS

Accurate use of apostrophes when forming possessives shows care and attentiveness. These qualities will come through in your written correspondence and inspire confidence in your readers.

Confusion between *its* and *it's* is common. If the words *it is* make sense in your sentence, you need to use the contraction *it's,* with the apostrophe in place. However, use contractions sparingly in business writing.

11-12   Use an apostrophe and *s* to form the possessive case of an irregular noun, which is a noun that does not form its plural by adding *s* or *es*.

children's field trip	(field trip of the children)
men's hats	(hats of the men)
women's coats	(coats of the women)

11-13   To form the possessive of a compound noun, make the final element possessive.

my daughter-in-law's book	(the book of my daughter-in-law)
somebody else's problem	(the problem of somebody else)
the notary public's seal	(the seal of a notary public)

If the compound is a plural possessive (it is both plural and possessive), first make the compound noun plural; then make it possessive. To make a compound word plural, make the principal element of the compound plural. The principal element may be any word in the compound. If necessary, consult a dictionary to determine the plural of a compound word.

my daughters-in-law's books	(the books of my daughters-in-law)
the notary publics' seals	(the seals of more than one notary public)

In compound nouns that are plural and possessive, make the principal element plural; then make the final element possessive.

11-14   To show joint ownership, make the final name possessive. To show separate ownership, make each name possessive.

Marvin and Joyce's home	(one home owned by both)
Brent's and Ben's rackets	(two rackets—one belongs to Brent, one belongs to Ben)
husband's and wife's signatures	(two signatures—one belongs to the husband, one belongs to the wife)

11-15   Use an apostrophe to form the plural of the capital letters A, I, M, and U and the plural of all lowercase letters. Also, use an apostrophe to form the plural of abbreviations made up of lowercase letters. Use an apostrophe in combinations even though you may not use an apostrophe with one of the elements in an isolated case. On the other hand, do not use an apostrophe if no confusion results from its omission.

Apostrophes are used to form plurals in only a few situations.

A's and S's	p's and q's	dot your i's and cross your t's

My stencil collection is missing two Js, five Ks, and one O.

11-16 Use an apostrophe to indicate the omission of letters or figures. This includes words formed as contractions.

Have you ever written a report about the 1960s? about the 1600s? Note that you do *not* need an apostrophe when you identify decades or centuries with numerals.

OK'd	(okayed)
o'clock	(of the clock)
class of '06	(class of 2006)
it's	(it is)
won't	(will not)

CHECKPOINT 11-10–11-16

Proofread the following sentences for errors in the use of the apostrophe. If a sentence is correct, write *C* to the right of the sentence.

a. Managers need to spend more time with clients as the nation's economy becomes more service oriented.

b. Someones briefcase was left in my office's doorway.

c. Let's celebrate Teri's and Joe's wedding anniversary with a party.

d. My three brothers-in-law attended the wedding, and parking tickets were placed on all three of my brother-in-laws' cars.

e. Her paper did not receive one of the As in the childrens' literature class because the professor stated she failed to dot her i's and cross her ts in the composition.

QUOTATION MARKS

It is unethical to use someone else's exact words without indicating that you are doing so. Using quotation marks is the right thing to do, whether quoting someone else's spoken or written words.

Quotation marks are used to enclose words quoted (spoken or written), some titles, and words used in an unusual manner. Use either a comma or a colon to set off words that are quoted.

11-17 Use quotation marks to enclose a direct quotation.

Mrs. Guerrero said, "I will introduce the new CEO at our next board meeting."

"All correspondence should be answered," said the manager, "within two days."

Note: Place a question mark or an exclamation point outside the quotation marks if the entire statement is a question or an exclamation. Place a question mark or an exclamation point inside the quotation marks if only the quoted material is a question or an exclamation. Always place commas and periods inside quotation marks.

Ross asked, "Is it time to leave?"

Which supervisor said, "No one can clock out until 4 p.m."?

Erika exclaimed, "I won the debate!"

I thoroughly enjoyed hearing him sing "America the Beautiful"!

11–18   Use single quotation marks to enclose a quotation within a quotation.

In his speech to the graduating class, Dean Stanhope remarked, "I believe that, as John Kennedy said, 'It is time for a new generation of leadership . . . for there is a new world to be won.' "

11–19   Use quotation marks to enclose titles of book chapters; articles in journals, magazines, or newspapers; and other parts of complete works. (Use italics or underscore titles of books, magazines, newspapers, or other complete works.)

One of the most popular columns in *The News and Observer* is "Under the Dome."

The article "Microimage Methods" in the April issue of *Administrative Management* provides an analysis of film and electronic technologies.

11–20   Use quotation marks to enclose words and expressions that are used in a special manner, such as the words *Fragile* and *Handle with Care* when they are introduced by words such as *marked* or *stamped*. Expressions that follow words such as *marked* or *stamped* are keyed with initial capital letters.

Please mark the envelopes containing photographs "Do Not Bend" and the large boxes containing pottery "Fragile."

Also use quotation marks for special words that may be unfamiliar to the reader. This technique should be used sparingly, or it will lose its effectiveness. In these constructions only proper nouns are keyed with initial capital letters.

Wohl stated that many companies have "Adidas networks," in which you run the diskette down the hall to your coworker.

In prior days "computer phobia" caused many managers to communicate poorly with their work groups.

11-10—11-16

a. C
b. Someone's . . . my the office's doorway to my office
c. Let's celebrate Teri's and Joe's
d. my brother-in-laws cars.
e. As in the childrens . . . dot her i's and cross her t's

Word processing programs may allow you to choose between two styles of quotation marks—straight quotes ("A") and smart (curly) quotes ("A"). This option is usually available in a Tools menu. Smart quotes give a document a more polished, professional look.

When you use a word or phrase in a special way and enclose it in quotation marks, treat that word or phrase the same way throughout a document.

UNDERSCORE AND ITALICS

The underscore is used to give special emphasis to certain words or expressions. In typewritten copy, italics are indicated by underscoring. A printer sets all underscored words in italic type. With word processing software, creating underscores or italics requires the same effort, so it is often a matter of author preference. Even though underscore and italics mean the same thing, be sure to use your choice of style consistently.

Many writers prefer to use italics for word emphasis. They reserve underscoring for emphasis of formatting, such as side headings in a report.

11-21   Use the underscore or italics to set off titles of published works, including books, journals, magazines, newspapers, and audio and video recordings. Also, use the underscore or italics for plays, movies, and musical compositions.

> Our library subscribes to *The Wall Street Journal* and numerous periodicals, including *Modern Office Technology* and *Personal Computing*.
>
> We wanted to rent the DVD <u>The Sound of Music</u>, but no copies were available.

11-22   Use the underscore or italics to set off words being emphasized, defined, referred to, or used as examples. Foreign words should be underscored or italicized if they are likely to be unfamiliar to the reader, with or without a parenthetical explanation of the word. Because some foreign words are commonly used in business writing, be sure to check a dictionary or reference manual to determine whether underscoring or italics should be applied to the word.

> You were instructed to turn <u>left</u> at milepost 12.
>
> *Glower* means "to look with sullen annoyance or anger."
>
> For example, <u>imminent</u> should be included in the appendix with other confusing words.
>
> She added an <u>s</u> to my name.
>
> They traveled *a pied* (on foot) to the Eiffel Tower.
>
> *but*   Rudy was now considered a bona fide member of the team.

> " What I like in a good author is not what he says, but what he whispers. "
>
> —Logan Pearsall Smith

Proofread the following sentences for errors in the use of quotation marks, the underscore, and italics. If a sentence is correct, write C to the right of the sentence.

a. Gwen asked, "Would you please define <u>ergonomics</u> for our management class".

b. Facsimile systems were discussed in the article Facsimile Storage and Delivery, which appeared in the May issue of *Office Systems*.

c. Jens asked, "Did you rent the movie Star Wars last night"?

d. The flight attendant asked: "Would you like a copy of 'Newsweek' or the 'San Francisco Chronicle'?"

e. We all wish we could "undo" our spoken words just as easily as we can our written words.

DASH

The dash, an informal mark of punctuation, always emphasizes the word or words it sets off. Use a dash to indicate a sudden change in thought and to emphasize what follows. Use this mark sparingly so that it does not lose its impact. Create a dash by depressing the hyphen key twice. No space precedes or follows a dash.

11-23   Use a dash to indicate a sudden change in thought or direction of speech.

> The best way—perhaps the only way—to meet the demand is to work overtime the next two weeks.

> The political impact of Rishi's action—and that's what counts—cannot be measured.

11-24   Use a dash in place of commas to set off a nonessential element when your purpose is to give emphasis to the text.

> That person is a thief—and I can prove it!

> Successful organizations have a common source of power—people.

Certain fonts in some word processors will change two hyphens keyed together as an em dash, or a dash the length of capital M. No matter how a dash is used in a sentence, it never has a space before or after it. In other words, dashes are set "closed up" to the words around them.

Refer to Chapter 4 for treatment of a dash at the end of a line of type.

11-25 Use a dash in place of a semicolon for a stronger but less formal break between two independent clauses in a sentence.

> Frequently when people get upset, they don't expect you to provide answers—they just need to unleash their feelings.

11-26 Use a dash in place of a colon to introduce an explanatory word or words, phrases, or clauses when a stronger but less formal break is desired.

> Patience—it is an important personal quality.
>
> Today we experienced a variety of weather—hail, rain, sunshine.
>
> Jeff had to sell everything—his car, his house, and his furniture.

11-27 Use a dash when a list comes *before* the explanation or definition.

> A dictionary, a thesaurus, and a reference manual—these are tools a writer needs to have within easy reach.

11-28 Use a dash to attribute a quote when the author's name (or the word *anonymous* if the author is unknown) appears on a separate line.

> Learning is not attained by chance; it must be sought for with ardor and attended to with diligence.
>
> —Abigail Adams

11-17—11-22

a. class(*'s*)

b. "Facsimile Storage and Delivery," (or ital)

c. <u>Star Wars</u> last night(*?*) (or ital)

d. "<u>Newsweek</u>" or the "<u>San Francisco Chronicle</u>" (or ital)

e. "<u>undo</u>" (or ital or C)

CHECKPOINT 11-23–11-28

Proofread the following sentences for errors in the use of the dash. If a sentence is correct, write *C* to the right of the sentence.

a. Mail merge, templates, and macros. These are the features of word processing that I want to master.

b. Fourteen games of chess were played in the tournament—and fourteen games of chess were won by the same master.

c. I wish we could vacation in Hawaii—no, in France, to celebrate your graduation.

d. In the United States at least one thing stands in the way of a company's becoming a monopoly in the marketplace—antitrust laws.

e. We purchased software packages, a word processing program, a spreadsheet program, and a database program—that will accomplish the basic needs of our office.

PARENTHESES

Parentheses are used to enclose nonessential, supplementary, or illustrative information. Unlike dashes, parentheses de-emphasize information. Use punctuation—internal and terminal—with material in parentheses. In other words, if the material within the parentheses is an independent clause, use a terminal punctuation mark inside the end parenthesis; if the material is a fragment or a phrase, do not use terminal punctuation.

11–29 Use parentheses to separate nonessential information from the rest of the sentence when your purpose is to de-emphasize the material.

> To obtain your complimentary pass, stop at the first ticket booth (the one with the red flag on it).

or To obtain your complimentary pass, stop at the first ticket booth. (It is the one with the red flag on it.)

11–30 Use parentheses to explain an abbreviation or to enclose periods of time.

> An immediate 10 percent salary increase will be given to any person with a CPS (Certified Professional Secretary) rating.

> The latter part of the twentieth century (1990–2000) was a period of immense growth and change.

11–31 Use parentheses to enclose characters in a run-in enumeration. Be sure to use both beginning and ending parentheses in this construction in addition to the punctuation you would normally use with a series.

> To enter the contest, you must (1) fill in the application form, (2) pay an entry fee, and (3) mail your entry.

BRACKETS

Brackets are used specially for parenthetical information within quoted material. Brackets indicate that the inserted material comes from the author or editor, not the original writer or speaker. Do not confuse parentheses with brackets; each has its own distinct purpose.

11-23—11-28

a. macros These
b. C
c. —no, in France
d. C
e. packages, a word

Information enclosed in parentheses should be less important than the information in the related sentence.

Placing information in parentheses can provide clarity to the text. If parentheses are overused, however, they lose their effect and may cause confusion.

When proofreading, make a point to check for punctuation that comes in pairs—quotation marks, parentheses, and brackets. You may do this manually, or your word processor's grammar check function may help.

11-32 Use brackets to enclose parenthetical information within a quotation. The brackets demonstrate that the material was not in the original quotation; rather, the material is intended to give additional information to the reader.

> Martina concluded her remarks by saying, "Once we have reached this month's sales goals [$157,000], we will initiate the new incentives program immediately."

11-33 Use brackets and the word *sic* to indicate an error you are repeating from original text. Obviously, this construction is used only when quoting from a source. Use italics for the word itself, if available, but do not underscore.

> Mayor Felicia Baca squelched rumors of her bid for reelection this week when she said, "I will not run for a second term as mayor, irregardless [*sic*] of swelling public support."

11-34 Use brackets to explain any change you make to quoted material, such as boldface or underscore, when these changes are made to give emphasis to a portion of the quoted text.

> Grant Fosley testified, "The policy specifically states on page 3, paragraph 5, that <u>benefits for weight loss are not covered</u>." [Emphasis added.]

#@%&!@#

Sometimes a correctly spelled word is just the wrong word.

When he became sick, he went into a comma. I don't know where he went, but when he came out of it, he was a changed man.

CHECKPOINT 11-29–11-34

Proofread the following sentences for errors in the use of parentheses and brackets. If a sentence is correct, write *C* to the right of the sentence.

a. Randall Kilgore receives a good income (more than $75,000 a year working as a financial planner for Estrada & Kading).

b. Two years ago she began charging $45 an hour [or $30 a half hour] for private lessons on the cello.

c. The curriculum was presented at the OSRA Office Systems Research Association convention held in March.

d. Fritz Bilderback says of his company, "Managing this company (Argo Kinetics, Inc.) by keeping it growing, profitable, and abreast of technology is a giant balancing act."

e. To prepare your photocopy jobs, 1) remove the staples, 2) make sure the pages are in order, and 3) fill out a copy request form.

© 2001 Ted Goff

"Oh-oh. You misspelled privacy again."

11-29—11-34

a. (more than $75,000 a year) . . Kading).

b. (for $30 a half hour))

c. OSRA (Office Systems Research Association)

d. [Argo Kinetics, Inc.]

e. (1) remove the staples, (2) make sure the pages are in order, and (3)

SPELLING APPLICATIONS

11-35 Compare the words in Column A with the corresponding words in Column B. Use the appropriate proofreading symbols to correct the misspelled words. If both columns are correct, write **C** to the left of the number.

	Column A	Column B
1.	acheivement	achievement
2.	anylasis	analysis
3.	bankruptcy	bankrupcy
4.	debter	debtor
5.	noticeable	noticable
6.	paralell	parallel
7.	permissible	permissable
8.	pursuit	persuit
9.	repetition	repetition
10.	undoutedly	undoubtedly

CHAPTER SUMMARY

Proofread carefully to be sure your documents follow these punctuation rules:

♦ Semicolons separate independent clauses of a compound sentence when the clauses are not joined by a conjunction. Semicolons separate independent clauses joined by the conjunctions *and*, *but*, *or*, or *nor* when at least one of the clauses contains an internal comma. Semicolons separate independent clauses when the clauses are joined by an adverbial conjunction or a transitional expression.

♦ Colons introduce questions, long quotes, explanatory clauses, and lists. Colons also separate hours and minutes and aid in formatting elements of business documents.

♦ Apostrophes form possessives, form some plurals, and indicate omitted characters in words such as contractions.

♦ Quotation marks enclose direct quotations and titles of book chapters, articles, and other parts within published works. Quotation marks also enclose special words and expressions.

♦ Underscores and italics have the same purpose and can generally be used interchangeably. Use them to indicate titles of separately published works or words being emphasized or defined.

♦ Dashes set apart and emphasize words or word groups from the regular text. They may be used between independent clauses to give a stronger break than a semicolon or comma, to introduce explanatory words or word groups, and to attribute a quote.

♦ Parentheses set apart and de-emphasize words or word groups from the regular text.

♦ Brackets are used to enclose parenthetical information within quoted material that has been added to the original quotation.

Study these tips, and apply them as you proofread:

♦ Check to be sure that punctuation marks convey the proper meaning. Query the originator if necessary.

♦ Check to be sure that substitutions have been entered where words have been crossed out.

♦ As part of the second step of the three-step process of proofreading, proofread for punctuation marks that appear in pairs (brackets, dashes, parentheses, and quotation marks) to be sure both marks are included in the text.

words@work Open *words@work*. To reinforce the rules presented in this chapter, click on Grammar and Usage, then on Lessons. The Punctuation section discusses the use of internal punctuation marks and provides practice.

PROOFREADING APPLICATIONS

Individually or with a classmate, proofread the following paragraphs and use the appropriate proofreading symbols to mark errors you find in punctuation and spelling. To aid you in proofreading, the number of errors is indicated in parentheses for Exercises P-1 and P-2.

P–1   Please read the article titled <u>The Anatomy of a Merger</u>. A noticable point in the article is that most mergers fail. Undoutedly there are some false assumptions about mergers. One such assumption is: top performers will remain with an organization. Actually, the explanation for most merger failures is people problems. People are often given the lowest priority during merger activity, therefore, they often dont stay with the new organization. The result may lead to problems with debtors or even bankrupcy. During a merger its permissible to communicate nonclassified information to employees so that uncertainty is reduced.

(8 errors)

P–2   Fifty percent of office time is spent communicating: talking, writing, or listening. It is the latter activity listening that constitutes the majority of communication time. Contrary to popular belief, listening is not a passive activity, it involves more than just hearing. For the listener it also includes: using lag time to repeat the speaker's words and relating the words to personal experience. An active listener provides feedback to the speaker by nodding or saying, Yes or I see. Most people would be surprised at the difference listening can make in job acheivement and in interaction with others.

(6 errors)

11–35
1. achievement
2. anylasis
3. bankrupcy
4. debter
5. noticable
6. paralell
7. permissable
8. persuit
9. C
10. undoutedly

P–1
1. The Anatomy of a Merger
2. noticable
3. Undoutedly
4. is: top
5. activity, therefore,
6. dont (or do not)
7. bankrupcy
8. its (or it is)

P-2

1. activity listening
   that
2. passive activity, it
3. includes, using
4. saying, "Yes"
5. or "I see."
6. achievement

P-3

(or ital)
1. "Presentations
   Plus,"
2. visually, 13
   percent through
   hearing,
3. words alone words
   (or ital)
4. The Secretary
5. International (PSI),
6. ([flip charts])
7. images,

P-4

1. sulking: ——
2. isnt (or is not)
3. negative, in fact
4. speaking then
5. graciously and
   do makes

P-3 In my analysis of the book "Presentations Plus," I learned that people gain 75 percent of what they know visually: 13 percent through hearing: and only 12 percent through other senses. A picture is three times more effective than words alone words and pictures together are six times more effective than words alone. The current issue of The Secretary, published by Professional Secretaries International PSI, provides suggestions for preparing effective visual presentations. Whether using nonprojected visuals [flip charts] or projected visuals (transparencies, slides, and computer-projected images, the key to a successful presentation is preparation.

P-4 Making excuses, arguing, counterattacking, or sulking: these are unproductive ways people react to criticism. It's not easy to take criticism, but we can expect to receive it as long as we interact with people. Realize that criticism isnt always negative, in fact it can be a catalyst for personal growth. Listen carefully when a critic is speaking then paraphrase what you heard. Ask pertinent questions about what you could do differently. Accepting criticism graciously and that's hard to do makes both you and your critic winners.

PROGRESSIVE PROOFREADING

You work for the Department of Tourism for the state of Georgia, which publishes an annual travel guide. As assistant to the Associate Commissioner for Tourism, one of your responsibilities is to make sure there are no errors in the travel guide and related correspondence. Proofread the following documents for errors in spelling, grammatical construction, punctuation, number usage, and format. Your office uses block letter style with open punctuation.

DISCOVER YOUR PLACE IN THE GARDENS

If you havent seen Colonial Gardens yet you are in for a treat. Discover the natural wonder of 10,000 acres of lakes, woodlands, gardens, and wildlife. Enjoy golf on our 18-hole, par-73 championship course. Take advantage of all the extras Colonial has to offer, tennis, swimming, nature trails, riverboat rides, and fishing.

All 210 of our rooms at the Colonial Inn has a waterfront or forest view, private balconies, and comfortable furnishings. If you're planning a meeting put us in your plans. We have more than 11,000 square feet of meeting space. You also can enjoy our charming cottages, or romantic villas.

Colonial. It's for families, couples, and friends. It's for people who appreicate natures beauty.

Call 1-800-555-0107 for reservations or information.

Job 2 Proofread the calendar of events by comparing it to the correct information on the registration cards shown on pages 191 and 192. Correct any mistakes you find. Assume the information on the cards is correct.

State of Georgia
Department of Tourism

7653 Peachtree Road, NE
Atlanta, GA 30308-9873
www.state_of_georgia.com

20-- CALENDAR OF EVENTS
SOUTHEAST GEORGIA

March

10–17	St. Patricks Day Celebration Dublin Bobbie Whitehead	478/555-0197
26–27	Harness Festival Hawkinsville Dana Morriw	478/555-0130

April

14–28	Dogwood Festival Jessup Kita Hagino	912/555-0192

May

10–24	Vidalia Onion Festival Vidalia Lewis Green	912/555-0111

June

15–28	Blueberry Festival Alma Deweese Arnold	912/555-0158

July

4	Fantastic Fireworks Extraavaganza Dublin Andre Southern	478/555-0144

October

6	Great Pumpkin Festival Cochran Joann Keena	478/555-0163
27	Georgia Sweet Potato Festival Ocila Gail Madigan-Boggs	229/555-0185

20-- CALENDAR OF EVENTS
Registration Card

Date(s) _May 10—24, 20--_   City/County _Vidalia_

Event Title _Vidalia Onion Festival_

Location _Vidalia_

Contact Person _Lewis Green_   Phone (_912_) _555-0111_
                                   area code

20-- CALENDAR OF EVENTS
Registration Card

Date(s) _October 6, 20--_   City/County _Cochran_

Event Title _Great Pumpkin Festival_

Location _Cochran_

Contact Person _Joanne Keena_   Phone (_478_) _555-0163_
                                   area code

20-- CALENDAR OF EVENTS
Registration Card

Date(s) _March 10—17, 20--_   City/County _Dublin_

Event Title _St. Patrick's Day Celebration_

Location _Dublin_

Contact Person _Bobbie Whitehead_   Phone (_478_) _555-0197_
                                   area code

20-- CALENDAR OF EVENTS
Registration Card

Date(s) _April 14-28_   City/County _Jesup_

Event Title _Dogwood Festival_

Location _Jesup_

Contact Person _Kita Hagino_   Phone (_912_) _555-0129_
                                   area code

20-- CALENDAR OF EVENTS
Registration Card

Date(s) __October 27, 20--__   City/County __Ocilla__

Event Title __Georgia Sweet Potato Festival__

Location __Ocilla__

Contact Person __Gail Madigan-Boggs__ Phone (__229__) __555-0185__
                                              area code

20-- CALENDAR OF EVENTS
Registration Card

Date(s) __July 4, 20--__   City/County __Dublin__

Event Title __Fantastic 4th Fireworks Extravaganza__

Location __Dublin__

Contact Person __Andre Southern__   Phone (__478__) __555-0144__
                                            area code

20-- CALENDAR OF EVENTS
Registration Card

Date(s) __June 14—28, 20--__   City/County __Alma__

Event Title __Blueberry Festival__

Location __Alma__

Contact Person __Deweese Arnold__   Phone (__912__) __555-0158__
                                            area code

20-- CALENDAR OF EVENTS
Registration Card

Date(s) __March 26—27, 20--__   City/County __Hawkinsville__

Event Title __Harness Festival__

Location __Hawkinsville__

Contact Person __Dana Morrow__   Phone (__478__) __555-0130__
                                         area code

Job 3   Proofread the following letter.

State of Georgia
Department of Tourism

7653 Peachtree Road, NE
Atlanta, GA 30308-9873
www.state_of_georgia.com

August 4, 20--

Ms. Gladys McCoy, Director
Macon Tourism and Trade
410 Riverside Drive
Macon, GA 31204-3798

Dear Ms. McCoy:

We;re getting ready to publish next years addition of *Georgia—A Peach of a State.* You undoubtably will want to provide updated copy for our article on central Georgia.

Please provide current information [avoid repitition of last year's material] on planned activities, festivals, and so on, on the enclosed form by September 30th so that we can incorporate your ideas into next years' publication and calender of events.

Will Macon participate as usual in "Georgia Days, which will be held at Cumberland Square in Atlanta from June 17–21 of next year. Please use the enclosed for to submit your registration and exhibit needs so that we can reserve appropriate space for you.

I understand you had record attendance at the Cherry Jubilee Street Party last month. Congradulations on the excellent job you do in organizing and motivating your volunteers.

Sincerely

Carter B. Tamara
Associate Commissioner for Tourism
State of Geo.

sj

COMPUTERIZED PROOFREADING

Job 4 Proofread and revise a travel article.

1. Load the file C11JOB4 from the template CD-ROM.

2. Proofread the article to be included in the travel guide, and make any corrections.

3. Format the article as an unbound report.

4. Save the article as C11JOB4R.

5. Produce the article by following the standard procedures.

CAPITALIZATION ERRORS

HAVE YOU EVER RECEIVED A MESSAGE IN ALL CAPITAL LETTERS, LIKE THIS? HOW DID IT MAKE YOU FEEL? Perhaps it startled you. Perhaps it was difficult to read. It no doubt grabbed your attention, though. And attention is what capital letters are all about.

Important words—words that deserve attention—begin with a capital letter. Proper nouns begin with capital letters. People's names begin with capital letters as well as names of towns, schools, and streets. However, overemphasizing something can be as ineffective as not emphasizing it at all.

FUNCTIONS OF CAPITALIZATION

Capitalization calls attention to words, distinguishes them, and gives them importance. However, do not overuse capitalization or its emphasis will be lost. The general rule for applying capitalization is to capitalize only when you have a specific rule or reason to do so.

Use the following symbols to indicate changes in capitalization:

≡   Use a capital letter.   Rocky mountains
≡

╱   Use a lowercase letter.   Sincerely Yours

SENTENCES, WORDS, AND HEADINGS

The following are the most common situations that require the use of capital letters.

12–1   Capitalize the first word of a sentence, a question, or a direct quotation. Do not capitalize the first word of the second part of an interrupted quotation.

> Eat a balanced diet every day.
>
> How did you know where to go?
>
> The memo read, "Vacation requests are due by Friday."
>
> "I was not aware," he said, "of any new agenda items."

Capitalize a phrase or a single word that expresses a complete thought.

> Not ever? Why?

12-2 Capitalize the first word after a colon if that word begins a complete sentence.

> I had a surprise: My friends gave me a birthday party.

> She had one purpose in mind: to get the job.

CHECKPOINT 12-1, 12-2

Proofread the following sentences for capitalization errors. If a sentence is correct, write _C_ to the right of the sentence.

a. Eleanor pursues an interesting hobby: Stamp collecting.

b. Have you completed the student interest survey?

c. Always walk against traffic. do you know why?

d. "My boss," grinned Emile, "Is gone for two weeks."

e. The most important rule in business writing is this: be concise.

12-1, 12-2

a. $\cancel{S}$tamp

b. C

c. do
   ≡

d. $\cancel{I}$s

e. be
   ≡

#@%&!@#

From the headlines:
- Electrical Engineers Needed for Generation of Electrical Power
- Students Cite Classes as Reason for Poor Grades

12-3 Capitalize names of people, and follow the style preference of people, if known.

> Margaret Mead   Robert S. McNamara
>
> Seymour R. Cray   Walter J. de la Mare
>
> Martin Luther King, Jr.   J. R. Cabrillo

Capitalize well-known descriptive names or nicknames that are used to designate particular people.

> the First Lady   Slammin' Sammy Sosa

12-4 Capitalize a personal or professional title that comes _before_ a person's name.

> Please ask Miss Kwan to come in.

> The meeting was called to order by Chairperson Rita Andruzzi.

Capitalize a title in an address or a signature line.

> Mrs. Leslie Winn, Vice President

> Willis Chambers, Manager

Do not capitalize a title when it *follows* the person's name in a sentence or is used in place of the name or when it is used in a general sense. Do not capitalize job titles when they stand alone.

> Libby Swanson, editor, received the Outstanding Journalist Award.
>
> The facilitator, Rocco Ely, called the meeting to order.
>
> The president of the credit union is leaving town tomorrow.

Regardless of where it appears in the sentence, capitalize an official title that refers to a specific person and is a title of high distinction.

> the President of the United States   the Pope
>
> the Governor of Arizona   the Premier

An exception to the rule: In formal minutes, rules, or bylaws, professional titles are always capitalized.

Some titles, such as those for heads of state, are always capitalized.

CHECKPOINT 12-3, 12-4

Proofread the following sentences for capitalization errors. If a sentence is correct, write *C* to the right of the sentence.

a. Will the secretary of state accompany former President Carter to the conference?

b. Will Governor Tate be the after-dinner speaker at the banquet?

c. Margaret Thatcher served as Great Britain's prime minister from 1979 until 1990.

d. Rod has been elected President of Office Systems Research Association.

e. Ms. Marrero is a Translator for a textbook company.

12-5 Capitalize proper nouns. A proper noun refers to a *specific* person, place, or thing.

> Colorado River   *but* the river
>
> University of Tennessee   *but* the university
>
> Billings Chamber of Commerce   *but* the chamber of commerce

Capitalize the personal pronoun *I*.

> Jameel and I met the client at the airport.

12-6 Capitalize proper adjectives, which are derived from proper nouns.

> Georgia → Georgian   Greece → Greek

Note: Some derivatives change to lowercase through frequent use.

> french fries   plaster of paris
>
> diesel engine   bone china

Many word processing programs can detect the pattern [space] i [space] and automatically capitalize the i if it has been keyed in lowercase.

12-3, 12-4

a. secretary of state

b. C

c. prime minister

d. President

e. Translator

12–7 Capitalize only those parts of a hyphenated word that are proper nouns or proper adjectives. Do not capitalize prefixes or suffixes connected to proper nouns.

ex-Governor Arhar	Mayor-elect Cox
French-American cuisine	mid-Atlantic
North-South game	Spanish-speaking students

CHECKPOINT 12-5–12-7

Proofread the following sentences for capitalization errors. If a sentence is correct, write *C* to the right of the sentence.

a. What we call garbage cans, the british call "dustbins."

b. The Marshall Plan was put into effect in the Post-World War II era.

c. The Snake river runs through Grand Teton National park.

d. Most American businesses observe seven or eight holidays a year.

e. The town's Carnegie Library now serves as a Community Center.

Articles include *a, an, the;* conjunctions include *and, but, nor,* and *or;* prepositions include *of, for,* and *in.* See the Appendix for a list of common prepositions.

12–8 Capitalize the first and last words and all important words in titles and headings. Do not capitalize articles, conjunctions, and prepositions that contain fewer than four characters unless they are the first or last words.

Book:	*Small-Business Web Sites*
Magazine:	*The Saturday Evening Post*
Newspaper:	*St. Petersburg Times*
Article:	"Difficult Colleagues: How to Get Along"
Artistic works:	*Phantom of the Opera*

CHECKPOINT 12-8

Proofread the following sentences for capitalization errors. If a sentence is correct, write *C* to the right of the sentence.

a. I just read an interesting article entitled "Career Jobs for the over and Under."

b. Betsy's latest book is *Information Processing for the New Century.*

c. Did you see this month's issue of *The Journal of The Arts*?

d. The movie *Driving Miss Daisy* received many Oscar Nominations.

e. I read about the Dogwood Festival in *The Knoxville news-Sentinel.*

NAMES OF THINGS AND PLACES

Just as we capitalize names of people, names of things and places also deserve capitalization. These rules apply to names of things and places when they are specific names, not general names. Again, articles, conjunctions, and prepositions that contain fewer than four characters within the name of a thing or place are not capitalized.

12-9 Capitalize names of organizations. Also, capitalize organizational words that refer to specific departments or groups within the originator's own organization. Do not use capitals when referring to a department or group in another organization.

> The Nature Conservancy's headquarters are in Arlington, Virginia.
>
> Please forward this memo to Marcia in our Marketing Department.
>
> Zahin got a job in the advertising department of Delta Company.

12-10 Capitalize specific brand names but not the product types.

> Dove soap   Jantzen swimsuits
>
> Kleenex tissue   Macintosh computer

12-5-12-7

a. british
   ≡
b. P̸ost-World War II

c. river . . . park
   ≡   ≡
d. C

e. C̸ommunity C̸enter

12-8

a. over
   ≡
b. C

c. T̸he Arts

d. N̸ominations

e. *news-Sentinel.*
      ≡

CHECKPOINT 12-9, 12-10

Proofread the following sentences for capitalization errors. If a sentence is correct, write *C* to the right of the sentence.

a. Do you use an AccuCall Cellular Phone?

b. Call human resources about the cafeteria plan benefits.

c. Eileen traded her Buick Regal Car for a Dodge Caravan.

d. We ordered four large Pizzas from Pizza Hut.

e. This article says that Sheaffer Fountain Pens are making a comeback.

12-11 Capitalize points of the compass when they refer to definite regions of the country or are part of a proper noun. Check a dictionary for exact location names. Do not capitalize these words when they indicate a direction.

> The Peihams moved to the West Coast.
>
> The library's main branch is on North Fifth Street.
>
> Ray lives east of the campus.

Capitalize words such as *southern* or *northeast* when they refer to the customs, cultural or political activities, or residents of the region.

> Sherm believes the Western vote is generally more liberal.

but The hurricane did damage in several southern states.

CHECKPOINT 12-11

Proofread the following sentences for capitalization errors. If a sentence is correct, write *C* to the right of the sentence.

a. Trina Robinson plans to develop an industrial park West of the city.

b. Moving from northern Wisconsin to Northern Ireland was more than culture shock.

c. Connor is exhibiting true Southern hospitality.

d. To see the university's tulip beds, drive East for eight miles.

e. Babbler Inc. has been purchased by western Pacific Company.

12-9, 12-10

a. Ȼellular/Ƥhone

b. human resources

c. Ȼar

d. Ƥizzas from

   Pizza Hut

e. Ƒountain/Ƥens

Some grammar checkers recognize certain proper nouns. The checker will query you if, for example, you key *monday* instead of *Monday*.

12-12 Do not capitalize names of seasons of the year unless they are part of a proper noun or are personified, as in poetry.

> This spring, at the end of the first quarter, we will set our goals.

> The Summer Symphony Series ends on Labor Day weekend.

> Old Man Winter will call Spring to awake before he himself goes to sleep.

12-13 Capitalize names of days of the week, months of the year, and holidays.

> School is closed on Monday because of Presidents' Day.

> In September some of my neighbors observe Yom Kippur.

CHECKPOINT 12-12, 12-13

Proofread the following sentences for capitalization errors. If a sentence is correct, write *C* to the right of the sentence.

a. Farmers' crops are in desperate need of spring rains this year.

b. To see New England in the Fall is one of my dreams.

c. For many Americans, independence day means parades and picnics.

d. New Year's Day falls on a Monday this year.

e. Would you like to travel to Switzerland next Winter for some skiing?

Chapter 12: Capitalization Errors

12-14   Capitalize the name of an academic degree immediately following a personal name. The degree name is usually abbreviated but may be written in full.

> Keith Kamara, M.D.
>
> Muriel Bloom, Doctor of Philosophy

Do not capitalize an academic degree when it is used in general terms or with the word *degree*.

> Margarita just received her master's in education.
>
> Does a bachelor of arts degree guarantee a good job?

You may want to review the rule on abbreviating academic degrees presented in Chapter 3, page 23.

12-15   Capitalize names of specific course titles, which often appear with a course number. Do not capitalize general areas of study unless the name includes a proper noun or a proper adjective.

> Keyboarding I   military history
>
> Computer Science 201   American history
>
> Trey attends Advanced Geometry 346 each day, where he studies advanced geometry.

12-11

a. X̷West

b. C

c. C

d. E̷ast

e. western
   ≡

CHECKPOINT 12-14, 12-15

Proofread the following sentences for capitalization errors. If a sentence is correct, write *C* to the right of the sentence.

a. Phil has earned his B.S. Degree in chemistry.

b. This quarter I am taking a Programming class and English 201.

c. The university awarded more than two thousand Bachelor's Degrees at its commencement exercises.

d. At my company top-level managers are expected to have a master's degree.

e. Inglis F. Duckett, Doctor of Education, has authored nine books.

ADDITIONAL CAPITALIZATION RULES

The following guidelines are presented to help you apply capitalization rules to nouns followed by numbers, to lists, and to outline entries.

12-16   Capitalize most nouns followed by numbers or letters except common nouns such as *line*, *note*, *page*, *paragraph*, *size*, *step*, and *verse*. The numbers may be preceded by the abbreviation *No.*

12-12, 12-13

a. C

b. F̷all

c. _independence_day
   ≡   ≡

d. C

e. X̷Winter

12-14, 12-15

a. Ɗegree

b. Ƥrogramming

c. Ɓachelor's

Ɗegrees

d. C

e. C

Chapter 5	page 6	Room A
Route 95	paragraph 2	Model No. x-102
Flight 1034	verse 63	Check No. 1428

12-17 Capitalize the first word of each item in a vertically displayed list.

Order the following supplies:

Paper
Envelopes
Staples

12-18 In an outline, first-level entries are in all capital letters. Second-level entries have initial capital letters on main words. Third-level and subsequent entries have only the first word capitalized.

I. FIRST-LEVEL ENTRY

    A. Second-Level Entry

    B. Second-Level Entry

        1. Third-level entry

        2. Third-level entry

II. FIRST-LEVEL ENTRY

CHECKPOINT 12-16—12-18

Proofread the following sentences for capitalization errors. If a sentence is correct, write *C* to the right of the sentence.

a. I. ADMISSION REQUIREMENTS

    A. Completion of 45 Semester Hours

    B. Overall Average of 2.5 on a 4.0 Scale

   II. Petition for Admissions

b. Did Gabriel order Model No. 2166 or 2266?

c. Refer to table 3.1, page 10, for more information.

d. While driving east on highway 258, Edna saw the exit for route 66.

e. Prior to departure, make sure you have all of these articles:

   • Plane ticket

   • Boarding Pass

   • itinerary

SPELLING APPLICATIONS

12-19 Compare the words in Column A with the corresponding words in Column B. Use the appropriate proofreading symbols to correct the misspelled words. If both columns are correct, write *C* to the left of the number.

	Column A	Column B
1.	aknowledgment	acknowledgment
2.	apologize	apolagize
3.	embarrass	embarass
4.	empasize	emphasize
5.	equiped	equipped
6.	fascinate	fassinate
7.	gratitude	gratitude
8.	insistent	insistant
9.	miniture	miniature
10.	perseverance	perserverance

12-16—12-18

a. Petition for
   Admissions

b. C

c. table

d. highway
   . . . route 66

e. Boarding Pass
   itinerary

CHAPTER SUMMARY

♦ Unless you can apply a definite rule that calls for capitalization, do not capitalize.

♦ Do not confuse proper nouns with common nouns. A proper noun refers to a *specific* person, place, or thing. A common noun provides a reference to a *general* person, place, or thing.

♦ In titles and headings capitalize the first and last words and all important words.

♦ Test a compass-point word by asking yourself, "Does this tell me *in what direction* something went?" If it does, the word should *not* be capitalized.

♦ If your workplace has a style guide for the use of capital letters, follow it.

words@work Test your knowledge of capitalization rules by completing the capitalization exercises in *words@work*. To get there, click on Grammar and Usage, then Exercises, then Capitalization. Or if you prefer to review the rules, read them in the Lessons section of Grammar and Usage.

Proofread the following documents, and use the appropriate proofreading symbols to mark errors you find. To aid you in proofreading, the number of errors to be found is indicated in parentheses for the first two exercises. You must find the errors on your own in the third one.

12-19
1. aknowledgment
    C
2. apologize
     ^ o
3. embarass
         r
4. empasize
       h ^
5. equiped
      ^ p
6. fassinate
        ^ c ^
7. C
8. insisjant
         e
9. miniture
      a ^
10. perserverance

P-1

Dear Mrs. McMurray:

You are invited to an autograph-signing party for Sheldon Brenneman. Mr. Brenneman, author of <u>Laughter Is The Best Medicine</u>, will be at Village bookstore on Thursday, May 3, from 2 to 5 p.m. The store is located in South Hills mall, which is one mile North of the downtown area.

Because of the popularity of the book, it has been printed for Non-English-speaking people and in miniture copies for carrying ease.

We at Twin Elms publishing company are happy to make it possible for you and your friends to meet Mr. Brenneman.

Sincerely yours,

(7 errors)

P-2

Business Travel is a mixed blessing. On one hand it allows people to see places they might not otherwise see. Those places include vast Corporate Parks with the usual ponds and geese that have become native to American business life. Or *lucky* travelers might get to see a bustling downtown area—From high atop the office building where they are cooped up, working with people they hardly know.

At the same time, business travel takes people away from their homes, families, and other pleasures and obligations. One Executive's solution is to charge a premium when his clients require him to travel. "Traveling is an inconvenience," he says, "And I charge for that inconvenience."

For those who enjoy travel, it is an advantage to be able to blend work and travel. For those who resent travel, the only answer is to learn to enjoy a good book, no matter where you are—Boston Logan, LA international, Newark International, Hartsfield Atlanta.

(6 errors)

P-1

1. Laughter Is ~~T~~he Best Medicine
2. Village ~~b~~ookstore
3. South Hills ~~m~~all
4. ~~N~~orth
5. ~~N~~on-English- speaking
6. mini~~a~~ture
7. publishing company

P-2

1. ~~T~~ravel
2. ~~C~~orporate ~~P~~arks
3. ~~F~~rom
4. ~~E~~xecutive's
5. "~~A~~nd I charge
6. ~~international~~

P-3

1. Washington ~~county~~
2. emba~~r~~assed
3. Volunteers ~~O~~f
4. ~~M~~athematics
5. ~~I~~nformational ~~M~~eeting
6. ~~room~~ 121
7. p~~re~~severance

P-3

Attention Retired Teachers:

Can you imagine being an adult and not being able to read? Twenty percent of the adults in Washington county fall into that category. You don't know about them because they are embarassed. They get by, but they need your help.

To erase illiteracy, the Literacy Volunteers Of Washington County need people with skills in reading, writing, and Mathematics to work as tutors. Refresher courses emphasizing these skills will be provided for tutors.

An Informational Meeting will be held on May 18 at Eastern Middle School, located on Route 13, beginning at 8 p.m. in room 121. Nina Shannon, Ph.D., will lead the discussion.

We express our gratitude to all who offer their time and skills to this program. Through preseverance we can conquer illiteracy.

P-4

 The Paradigm Online Writing Assistant is an online writer's guide and handbook distributed over the World Wide Web. Access the site at http://www.powa.org/. On the home page, click "Editing Your Writing." From the menu on the left, choose "Capitalization." Review the rules presented. Copy the activity from the site into a blank document in your word processing program. Complete the activity; then exchange papers with a classmate. Check each other's work, marking any changes with appropriate proofreading symbols.

PROGRESSIVE PROOFREADING

You are employed as an assistant to Sameera Dharia, the director of Diamond Hills Senior Community Center. The center keeps in touch with its members by means of e-mail, letters, and bulletin board notices. Ms. Dharia uses block letter style with open punctuation. Proofread the letters and notifications carefully for keyboarding, spelling, number expression, punctuation, grammar, abbreviation, word usage, and capitalization errors.

Job 1 Proofread the following e-mail message.

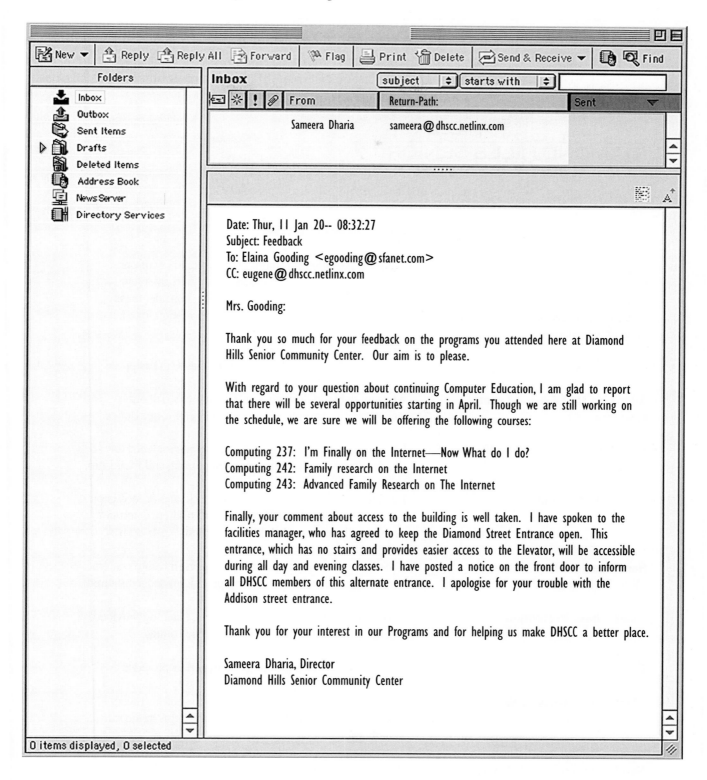

Date: Thur, 11 Jan 20-- 08:32:27
Subject: Feedback
To: Elaina Gooding <egooding@sfanet.com>
CC: eugene@dhscc.netlinx.com

Mrs. Gooding:

Thank you so much for your feedback on the programs you attended here at Diamond Hills Senior Community Center. Our aim is to please.

With regard to your question about continuing Computer Education, I am glad to report that there will be several opportunities starting in April. Though we are still working on the schedule, we are sure we will be offering the following courses:

Computing 237: I'm Finally on the Internet—Now What do I do?
Computing 242: Family research on the Internet
Computing 243: Advanced Family Research on The Internet

Finally, your comment about access to the building is well taken. I have spoken to the facilities manager, who has agreed to keep the Diamond Street Entrance open. This entrance, which has no stairs and provides easier access to the Elevator, will be accessible during all day and evening classes. I have posted a notice on the front door to inform all DHSCC members of this alternate entrance. I apologise for your trouble with the Addison street entrance.

Thank you for your interest in our Programs and for helping us make DHSCC a better place.

Sameera Dharia, Director
Diamond Hills Senior Community Center

DIAMOND HILLS SENIOR COMMUNITY CENTER

397 ADDISON STREET
SAN FRANCISCO, CA 94131-3507
415-555-0126
WWW.DHSCC.COM

January 13, 20--

VOLUNTEER OPPORTUNITIES

Volunteerism is an important part of our community, especially for seniors. Therefore, many of our Diamond Hills Seniors are very active in volunteer activities. Their involvement ranges from a few hours a month to a few hours a day. If you haven't yet found your volunteering niche, consider these opportunities. See Micki in the main office for telephone nos. and other contact information for each of these Organizations:

Organization	Types Of Volunteer Duties Or Tasks
American Red Cross—Local Chapters	Assist with blood drives in the Bloodmobile; fill out paperwork; answer phones; oversee general office duties.
Community Partners For Youth	Meet with a local youth whose interests are matched to your's to provide companionship, mentoring, and friendship.
Children's hospital	Read to or play games with children; hold and/or feed babies; run errands for parents of hospitalized children; entertain siblings of hospitalized children.
San Francisco Bay National Wildlife Refuge	Greet vistors; conduct tours of the Andersen nature center; perform general office work [computer knowledge required].
Elder Abuse Prevention	Answer Crisis lines; provide councilling (training provided); assemble mailings; perform general office duties.
Literacy Alliance—South Bay	Tutor illiterate adults (training and materials provided).
Meals On Wheels of San Francisco	Deliver midday and/or evening meals to shut-ins (every effort is made to match volunteers with clients in the same neighborhood)
San Francisco Bay Girl Scouts counsel	Support a Brownie or Girl Scout troop by conducting a special class, chaperoning outings, or assisting with arts and crafts projects.

Job 3 Proofread the following letter.

DIAMOND HILLS SENIOR COMMUNITY CENTER

397 ADDISON STREET
SAN FRANCISCO, CA 94131-3507
415-555-0126
WWW.DHSCC.COM

January 20, 20--

Ms. Julia Gorham
San Francisco Bay Girl Scouts
538 North 152d Avenue
San Francisco, CA 94188-6242

Dear Ms. Gorham:

As you and I thought would happen, we had many Diamond Hills seniors respond to our call for volunteers, which we posted a week ago. About a dozen senior women wish to volunteer with the San Francisco Bay girl scouts. I would like to invited you to come to Diamond Hills to speak to this group of volunteers.

In particular, these women have questions about how to chaperoning outings. They need to feel comfortable with the rules and guidelines of the Girl Scouts Organization. The arts and crafts will be a pleasure for these women, as most of them spend a great deal of time working on crafts. In fact, several of the women recently constructed a minature dollhouse and are now working on its furnishing. They thought the girls might be interested in a project such as this.

Many of the women who are interested in volunteering were once Girl Scouts themselves, and they expressed graditude for the role the Girl Scouts played in their lives. I am happy that Diamond Hills can coordinate a volunteer effort between our seniors and the San Francisco Bay Girl Scouts.

Would you be able to speak to our volunteers next Tuesday or thursday? If not, we will do our best to accomodate your schedule. I look forward to hearing from you.

Sincerely Yours,
Sameera Dharia

Job 4 Proofread both the handwritten and printed versions of part of the Senior Community Center's class schedule. Check the accuracy of the schedule by comparing it to the handwritten draft. Assume the information in the draft is accurate, though it may not be formatted correctly.

Winter Schedule

DHSCC Course Offerings

January 3–March 30

(All classes last for two hours unless otherwise noted. All classes are held at DHSCC unless otherwise noted. Meeting rooms may change. call to confirm.)

Course	Time	Fee (if any)	Room
Arts 277: Flower Arranging	Wednesday 10:30	$12.00	134
Arts 427: Hand Papermaking	Wednesday 3–6:00	$15	130
Arts 428: Advanced Papermaking	Wednesday 6:00–9:00	$22	130
Computing 101: Why Do I Need A Computer?	Tuesday 8:00 Wednesday 12:00 Friday 2:00	--	222
Computing 102: Buying a Computer	Tuesday 10:30 Wednesday 2	--	222
Computing 103: Setting up and Hooking up	by appointment	--	--
Computing 210: Why Do I Need the Internet?	Tuesday 12 Thursday 4	--	216
Cooking 111: Cooking for One	Monday 10:30 Thursday 6	$35	DHSCC kitchen
Cooking 118: Recipes to Freeze and Eat Later	Monday 10:30	$35	DHSCC kitchen
Cooking 208: Canning and Preserving–Modern and Simple	Tuesday 2:00	$40	DHSCC kitchen

Chapter 12: Capitalization Errors

Winter Schedule

DHSCC Course Offerings

January 3–March 30

(All classes last for two hours unless otherwise noted. All classes are held at DHSCC unless otherwise noted. Meeting rooms may change. call to confirm.)

Course	Time	Fee (if any)	Room
Arts 277: Flower Arranging	Wednesday 10:30	$12.00	134
Arts 427: Hand Papermaking	Wednesday 3–6	$15	130
Arts 428: Advanced Papermaking	Wednesday 6–9	$22	122
Computing 101: Why Do I Need A Computer?	Tuesday 8:00 Wednesday 12:00 Friday 2:00	--	222
Computing 102: Buying a Computer	Tuesday 10:30 Wednesday 2	--	222
Computing 103: Setting up and Hooking up	by appointment	--	--
Computing 210: Why Do I Need the Internet	Tuesday12 Thursday 4	--	216
Cooking 111: Cooking For One	Monday 10:30 Thursday 6	$35	DHSCC kitchen
Cooking 118: Recipes to Freeze and Eat Later	Monday 10:03	$35	DHCSC kitchen
Cooking 208: Canning and Preserving—Modern and Simple	Tuesday 3	$40	DHSCC kitchen

COMPUTERIZED PROOFREADING

Job 5 Proofread a course announcement.

1. Load the file C12JOB5 from the template CD-ROM.

2. Proofread the announcement. Check it against the notes that Sameera Dharia jotted down when she spoke to the course instructor.

3. Format the announcement with 1.5″ margins. Center the two-line heading at the top of the page.

4. Save the revised announcement as C12JOB5R.

5. Produce the document by following the standard procedures.

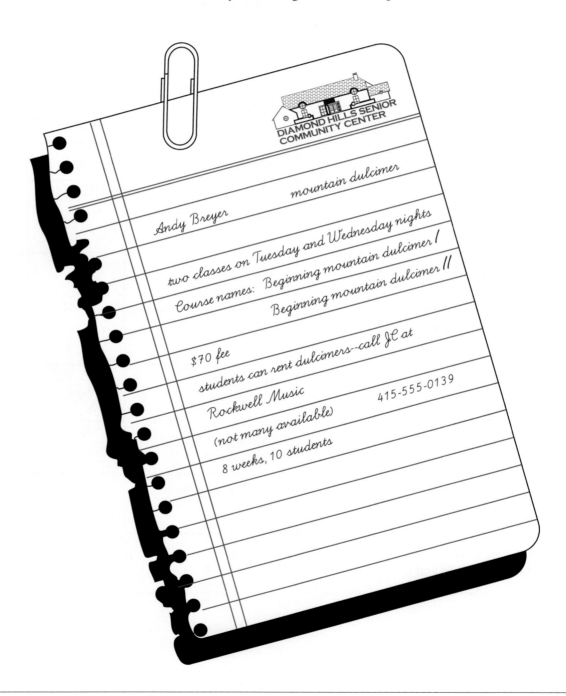

Chapter 12: Capitalization Errors

CHAPTER 13

EDITING FOR CONTENT

I n an e-mail message, a writer forgets to include the room number for a meeting. The error of omission may cause confusion, or it may inconvenience the recipients. What is the impact when errors are published in thousands of copies of books? Yes, even professionals in the textbook industry make errors. Some are simple typographical errors. Others are more serious content errors. In a 1999 textbook review, one state review committee discovered that Christopher Columbus sailed for the New World in 1942. In another book the Statue of Liberty was said to be made of bronze, rather than copper. And one world history text omitted an entire Chinese dynasty. (*Carolina Journal*, June–July 1999, Vol. 8, No. 6)

Of course, anyone can make an error—and everyone does at one time or another. The point of proofreading, though, is to eliminate errors—or at least to minimize them. Whereas mechanical or format errors may cloud a message, content errors may completely obscure it. Do not let that happen to messages that you proofread.

EDITING FOR CONTENT

The real measure of a proofreader's skill lies in his or her ability to proofread written communication for meaning and accuracy and to edit and revise ineffective communication. While previous chapters have dealt primarily with mechanical and grammatical errors, the remaining chapters in this text deal with editing to make messages clear for the reader. This chapter in particular addresses the need to proofread for content errors—errors that affect the correctness of the message.

Content errors include incorrect facts, inconsistencies, and missing information. The skillful proofreader must be able to identify these problems, make necessary changes, and bring questionable items to the originator's attention. You have already learned the appropriate symbols for making corrections to copy and for presenting a query to the originator of the document. Use these symbols when editing for content.

LEARNING OBJECTIVES

- Identify errors caused by incorrect facts, inconsistencies, and missing information.

- Use appropriate proofreading symbols to indicate changes in text.

- Spell correctly a list of commonly misspelled words.

INCORRECT FACTS

When copy contains incorrect facts, confusion and frustration may result. Recognizing such errors is not always easy unless a rough draft or source document can be used for comparison. Some items should always be checked for accuracy. If the copy makes reference to Wednesday, June 16, and June 16 is actually on Thursday, there is an obvious error. However, the proofreader must research to find out the actual intended date. He or she must not just assume it is one or the other.

By paying close attention, you can sometimes recognize errors in figures by using reason and common sense. For example, social security numbers always contain nine digits and ZIP Codes always contain either five digits or five digits plus four. Invoice numbers, telephone numbers, dates, and other items of special importance should always be checked.

In the same manner, do not assume the spelling of people's names. Seek a source document to spell names correctly. Be especially careful to check unfamiliar, foreign, or similarly spelled names for accuracy. Notice the varied spellings of these names:

WORKPLACE CONNECTIONS

Names are very important in business relationships. Whether you are a salesperson or chair of the board, learning—and using—the names of the people around you makes a positive impression.

Andres, Andreas	Sara, Sarah
Hansen, Hanson	John, Jon
Hernandes, Hernandez	

Johnsen, Johnson, Johnston, Johnstone, Jonson

Schneider, Schneiter, Snider, Snyder

Schmid, Schmidt, Schmit, Schmitt

13–1 Eliminate incorrect facts by correcting inaccuracies in dates, figures, addresses, names, and numbers or by querying the originator. Note the incorrect facts in the following examples:

> The Dow Jones Industrial Average rose from 10,910 to 10,942, a gain of 22 points.

> The play is scheduled for February 15–30.

CHECKPOINT 13-1

Proofread the following sentences for incorrect facts.

a. Former President Bill Clinton attended a party for Republican campaign workers.

b. The deadline for registering to vote in the next election is Tuesday, April 31.

c. Send the proposal to ACS, 1144 Meade Street, Vienna, WV 2610.

d. At $2.39 apiece, six packages of pens will cost $15.34.

e. You may request a free copy by calling (800) 555-015.

INCONSISTENCIES

Whenever reference is made to specific information more than once in a document, be sure the information appears consistently. For example, if a word has two acceptable spellings, use the same spelling throughout. If numbers are transferred from one document to another, be sure the numbers have been keyed correctly. If a term has been defined in a document, be sure the abbreviation, *not* the term being defined, is used throughout the remainder of the document. If block format is chosen for a letter, make certain the format conforms to block style throughout the letter.

13–1
Democratic
a. ~~Republican~~

b. April ③① ?

c. WV ②⑥①⓪ ?

d. $1⁴3.34

e. 555 ⓪①⑤ ?

13–2 Eliminate inconsistencies in copy by checking words, figures, and format for any discrepancies. Note the inconsistencies in the following examples:

> Mr. Dakas was elected mayor in 1986; Dacas has been an exemplary public official.

> This CD player can be purchased for only $189. Where else can you find a unit like this for $199?

Consistency in format and usage is a sign of professionalism. It also shows the reader that the writer cares about a particular piece of business communication—and its recipient.

CHECKPOINT 13-2

Proofread the following sentences for inconsistencies.

a. Ruby Petersen has started her own company. Next Monday Peterson's Copying Service will open for business, with operating hours of 6 p.m. to midnight seven days a week and delivery hours of 9 a.m. to 7 p.m. Monday through Friday.

b. Dillon's Department Store is advertising a sale on its men's and women's suits. Men's suits priced at $340 are reduced 35 percent, a savings of $112.20. Ladies' suits ranging from $150 to $250 are reduced 20 percent, a savings of $30 to $50. The sale is open to charge customers on Tuesday, July 3; it is open to the public on Thursday, July 6.

c. The North Central Education Association (NCEA) sponsors an insurance program through Statewide Insurance Group for NCAE members. Statewide covers not only the North Central Education Association but also Tarrant County Educators and Educators United of Bristol County.

d. Only 23 of the 35 members attended the regional meeting. President Hasseim was hopeful that all 37 members would be able to attend the local meeting next month.

MISSING INFORMATION

Errors of omission may be the most difficult to detect.

13-2

a. Petersen or Peterson /?
   6 p.m. to midnight
b. women's or ladies /?
   ~~$112.20~~ 119
   Tuesday, July 3
   . . . Thursday, July 6. /?
c. . . . NC(AE) members. Statewide ^Insurance Group covers not only the ~~North Central~~ NCEA Education Association
d. 35 or 37 members /?

Because the meaning of a message may be affected when words, phrases, or even complete lines or sentences are omitted unintentionally, you must compare the final copy with the rough-draft copy to be sure nothing has been deleted. Sometimes information may be missing from the original draft. This may happen if a writer assumes the reader will understand a message. If you, as the proofreader, do not understand the message in a document you are proofreading, the receiver of the message may not understand it either. A proofreader should edit the message, filling in missing information that makes the meaning clear. If the proofreader is not authorized to edit and make changes, he or she must query the originator about any errors that prevent the meaning of the message from being clear.

13-3 Eliminate confusion in copy by checking for missing information. In the example sentence below, if the word *this* was not explained within the context of the document, only the writer—and not the reader—would understand the message.

> To get to the airport, turn right on **this** road.

CHECKPOINT 13-3

Proofread the following sentences for missing information.

a. On the first day of the conference, we scheduled a no-host social in the Gold Room of the Plaza Hotel at six and a dinner in the main dining room of the Hilton, the conference hotel. Please plan to meet me there.

b. To get to our office, travel six blocks east and turn at the Willow Street intersection. After traveling about three blocks, you will see a sign; turn right at the sign and travel one more block. Our building is the third one.

c. All bids for the contract must be in no later than Wednesday, November, at 5 p.m. Bids can be faxed only to the special line we set up at the joint project headquarters, not to either company's regular fax numbers. Only faxes received by midnight will be considered.

d. To delete the highlighted text from the computer screen, press the key. If you change your mind and want to retrieve the text you just deleted, use the undo.

e. You will need an 8 x 10 mat for that job. Call Bob at the construction warehouse and ask him to send you a mat.

13–4 Compare the words in Column A with the corresponding words in Column B. Use the appropriate proofreading symbols to correct the misspelled words. If both columns are correct, write **C** to the left of the number.

	Column A	**Column B**
1.	advantageous	advantangous
2.	analyst	analist
3.	cordinate	coordinate
4.	effeciency	efficiency
5.	fluctuating	fluctuating
6.	implemented	emplemented
7.	independant	independent
8.	insurence	insurance
9.	productivaty	productivity
10.	programer	programmer

13–3

a. dinner (when?) /?
   meet (where?) /?

b. travel six blocks
   east (from
   where?) /?
   turn at the Willow
   Street intersection
   (which way?) /?
   you will see a sign
   (that says what?)
   /?
   the third one (third
   one where?) /?

c. November (date?)
   /?
   faxed only to the
   special line (what
   number?) /?
   received by 5 p.m.
   or by midnight /?

d. press the key
   (which one) /?
   use the undo
   (key? icon?) /?

e. 8 × 10 (inches?
   feet?) /?
   Bob (more than
   one Bob?) /?

CHAPTER SUMMARY

♦ Read the copy with a questioning mind by asking yourself these questions: Is the message perfectly clear? Are there any inconsistencies in the presentation of facts? Are there omissions?

♦ Control the environment in which you proofread. Noise and movement, as well as insufficient light, are distractions.

♦ Use the three-step process of proofreading. Verify the spelling of names, addresses, numbers, and facts as a separate step.

♦ When revising copy, cross out all unnecessary original copy.

PROOFREADING APPLICATIONS

 Individually or with a classmate, proofread the following exercises and use the appropriate proofreading symbols to mark errors you find in content and spelling. To aid you in proofreading, the number of errors to be found is indicated in parentheses for Exercises P-1 and P-2.

P-1

DRIFTWOOD RESTAURANT OPENS NEW FACILITY

The Driftwood Restaurant, a popular eating place since opening in 1973, began serving breakfast at 6 a.m. Sunday, July 1, 2001, at its new location, 4100 Trade Street. The restaurant now has more parking and greater seating capacity than the 25-year-old Banks Street location, according to Sonny Hostetler, the owner.

The restaurant is open daily from 6 a.m. to 11 a.m. You can order the famous Early Bird Special from 3:30 p.m. to 5:30 p.m. every day. This Thursday Sonny Hostetler invites you to take advantage of Driftwood's Fourth of July special. Place your order for Driftwood's take-out picnic special for a family of four, with a choice of either fried chicken or, and pay only $24.99 instead of the regular price of $34.99. That's a 20 percent savings on a wonderful picnic that you won't need to cook. Stop by the Drift Restaurant soon.

(6 errors)

P-2

Miss Vidya Powell
429 Butler Street
Jacksonville, NC 2610-0429

Dear Miss Vidya:

We appreciate your interest in becoming an independent Dana dealer.

Because of the depressed market in South Carolina for Dana products, no new Dana dealerships are being impliminted at this time.

Mr. Powell, we will your name on file so we can notify you if a dealership does become available in your area.

Sincerely yours,

(6 errors)

P-3

TO: Electronic Publishing

FROM: Judith Dempsey

DATE: July 17, 20--

SUBJECT: System 40-X Overview Meeting

A meeting has been scheduled for Thursday, July 26, from 10:15 to 12 a.m. to review the System 40X capabilities for the Electronic Publishing Department. Please plan to attend.

Suzie Chirombole will instruct us on the applications that will benefit us, and she will field your questions. Our Dallas branch saw a 7 percent increase in productivaty the first month after its system was installed. I'm sure we will benefit tremendously from the insight Susie has gained from her previous experience as programer and system analist.

Lunch will be provided immediately after the training session for all who attend. We can continue the question-and-answer session with Suzie during that time.

P-2

1. 2610-0429 ?
2. Miss Vidya: Powell
3. South Carolina North
4. implemented (e)
5. Mr. Powell Miss
6. will your name keep

PROGRESSIVE PROOFREADING

You are the assistant to Hugh Ireland, manager of TOPS (Temporary Office Personnel Services) in Seattle, Washington. This office is one of three branches of a new business venture and is owned by Mazie Dunstan, who resides in Tacoma, Washington. Your office provides two services to local business firms: It provides temporary office help, and it contracts to provide certain office jobs to be done in-house. At the present time you are to proofread all work that has been done at the Seattle office. The agency uses block letter format with open punctuation.

P-3

1. 10:15 to 12 a.m. noon
2. System 40-X . . . System 40X ?
3. Suzie . . . Susie ?
4. productivaty (i)
5. programer (m)
6. analist

Job 1 Verify the accuracy of the invoice by comparing it to the items ordered on the purchase order on the next page. Unit prices and extensions are entered automatically by the computer. However, TOPS telephoned and requested that the order for **Zip disks** be changed to **3 1/2-inch diskettes** at **$68/box.** Also, the price of print cartridges has been raised to **$26.50;** this price has not been entered into the computer. Other information you will need to check is as follows:

Order No.: **LA19284**
Shipped by: **UPS**
Terms: **2/10, n/30**

B&B Supply Company
P.O. Box 5314
Phoenix, AZ 20721-8011

INVOICE

TOPS
909 South 35th Street, NW
Seattle, Washington 98121-1974
Phone (564)555-0191   Fax (564)555-0141

Date: August 15, 20--

Order No.: LA19284

Shipped By: UPS

Terms: 2/10, n/20

Quantity	Description	Unit Price	Total
1	Print cartridge	24.95	24.95
5 boxes	Zip diskettes	41.95	209.75
6 boxes	T-III vanila file folders	8.79	52.74
12 reams	G-P dual-purpose paper, 20 lb	5.25	63.00
12 reams	G-P copier paper, 20 lb	6.65	79.80
12 rolls	Magnetic tape, 1/2 inch	1.89	22.68
5 doz	Express pens, violet ink	9.12	45.60
			503.97

TOPSTOPS

(Temporary Office Personnel Services)
909 South 35th Street, NW
Seattle, Washington 98121-1974
Phone (564)555-0191   Fax (564)555-0141

PURCHASE ORDER

B&B Supply Company
P.O. Box 5314
Phoenix, AZ 20721-8011

No: LA19284

Order No.: August 9, 20--

Terms: 2/10, n/30

Shipped By: UPS

Quantity	Description	Unit Price	Total
1	Print cartridge	24.95	24.95
5 boxes	Zip diskettes	41.95	209.75
6 boxes	T-III manila file folders	8.79	52.74
12 reams	G-P dual-purpose paper, 20 lb	5.25	63.00
12 reams	G-P copier paper, 20 lb	6.65	79.80
12 rolls	Magnetic tape, 1/2 inch	1.89	22.68
1	Tape dispenser	5.45	5.45
5 doz	Express pens, violet ink	9.12	45.60
			503.97

By _____   Purchasing Agent

Job 2 Please check the accuracy of Rebecca D. Chou's Travel Expense Report by verifying its figures against the receipts and the handwritten list of expenses. Also, verify the totals.

<table>
<tr><td colspan="11" align="center">TRAVEL EXPENSE REPORT</td></tr>
<tr><td colspan="11">Travel Authorization No.

239407</td></tr>
<tr><td colspan="6">Employee Name

Rebecca D. Chow</td><td colspan="5">I.D. Number

T6103</td></tr>
<tr><td colspan="6">Destination

Portland, Oregon</td><td colspan="5">Date(s)

8/25/-- to 8/27/--</td></tr>
<tr><td colspan="11">Purpose of Trip

AMS meeting; meeting with managers of TOPS</td></tr>
</table>

Date	From To	Transportation				Meals		Lodging		Total	
		Miles	Amount	Air	Taxi						
8/25	Seattle/ Portland	129	45	15	--	--	22	50	80	00	147	65
8/26	Travel within Portland	165	57	65	--	--	53	20	80	00	190	85
8/27	Portland/ Seattle	129	45	15	--	--	7	25	--		61	70
Totals		147	95				82	95	160	00	390	90

Signature   Date   Total Expenses $390.90
(Attach Receipts)

_____   8/29/--

Seattle – Portland Trip

8/25	Seattle-Portland 129 miles at 35 cents per mile	
	AMS Dinner Meeting at The Jackson Inn	$22.50
	Room – The Jackson Inn	
8/26	Breakfast	$8.50
	Drive within Portland; meeting with local managers of TOPS; visit employers— 165 miles	
	Lunch	$18.75
	Dinner at the Inn	$26.45
	Room at Jackson Inn	
8/27	Breakfast	$7.25
	Lunch	$9.30
	Mileage from Portland-Seattle	

Please prepare an expense report. Fill in anything I have left out. My receipts are attached.
RC

```
THE JACKSON INN
        ROUTE 20, EAST                              (503)555-0122
           PORTLAND, OR 97268

ROOM        LAST NAME        FIRST              MIDDLE INITIAL
329         CHOU,              REBECCA               D.
ADDRESS        1805 ST. CHARLES AVENUE         ROOM RATE
               SEATTLE, WA 98198                  $80.00

ARRIVAL              AUGUST 25, 20--            NO. IN PARTY
DEPARTURE            AUGUST 27, 20--                 1

     DATE                DESCRIPTION              AMOUNT
     8/25               RESTAURANT                 22.50
     8/25               ROOM, TAX INCLUDED         80.00
     8/26               RESTAURANT                  8.50
     8/26               RESTAURANT                 26.45
     8/26               ROOM, TAX INCLUDED         80.00
     8/27               RESTAURANT                  7.25
                                      TOTAL      $224.70
                                       PAID      $224.70
                                    BALANCE       000.00
```

Guest Receipt **Rainbow Café**

Date *8/26* Amount *$18.75*

Guest Receipt *Quintana's*

Date *8/27* Amount *$9.30*

(Temporary Office Personnel Services)
909 South 35th Street, NW
Seattle, Washington 98121-1974
Phone (564)555-0191   Fax (564)555-0141

August 21, 20--

Mrs. Mazie Dunstan
2001 King Alfred Drive
Tacoma, WA 98411-0045

Dear Mazie

At last week's meeting you stated that your goal was, to make sure that our temporary office personnel stand out above all the rest. You said that you wanted the hallmark of TOPS personnel to be their excellent communication skills. Think about the following idea for how we can accomplish this goal.

We should provide training in proofreading and editing for our temps. As you know 93% of the temps we place in offices produce letters, memos, and reports while out on assignment. Marketing our temps as "trained in proofreading would be a terrific angel. I made a few calls, and found that none of the other temp agencies in the Seattle area provides training in proofreading.

For training material, I suggest we use a book from South-Western Educational Publishing entitled "The Basics of Proofreading." The text contains 15 chapters and is written for either classroom instruction or individualized training. I found Chapter 9 dealing with format issues to be especially useful.

We could offer the class as an independant study or we could cordinate classes at one of the branch office in the evenings. If this recommendation is emplemented, the payoff in our temps' productivity and accuracy would well worth the cost of the books and training. After all, 90 percent is a large number of temps who needs these skills.

I am anxious to hear what you think; please contact me when you have time to discuss this idea.

Sincerely

Hugh
Seattle Branch Manager

plp

COMPUTERIZED PROOFREADING

Job 4 Edit a report.

1. A TOPS employee has been assigned to key some reports for a client who prefers that the employee do the work at the TOPS office. One of the reports is about telework. Load the file C13JOB4 from the template CD-ROM.

2. Proofread the report carefully for mechanical and content errors. Check the resources cited against the handwritten note below from the client.

3. Format the document as a two-page unbound report. Format the main and side headings in bold.

4. Save the report as C13JOB4R.

5. Produce the report following the standard procedures.

Please key this report--double-spaced. At the end, list these sources. Thank you.

"Telecommuting (or Telework): Alive and Well or Fading Away?" International Telework Association & Council. 1 Aug. 2001 <http://www.telecommute.org/aboutitac/alive.shtm>.

"Telework America (TWA) 2000: Research Results." International Telework Association & Council. 1 Aug. 2001 <http://www.telecommute.org/twa2000/research_results_summary.shtml>.

EDITING FOR CONCISENESS

Formal writing once meant using big words and fancy phrases. Today, however, formal writing—writing for business—means just the opposite. Readers are interested in your message. Help readers comprehend your message quickly and efficiently by eliminating redundancy, using precise words, and avoiding clichés and obsolete expressions. Take a look at this paragraph. How could you make the meaning clearer?

Congratulations on a job well done. We put our noses to the grindstone to come up with a win-win situation. We ran our new marketing campaign up the flagpole, and the results were super. Our new campaign now reaches a wider public audience than ever before. This campaign will really put us on the map.

EDITING FOR CONCISENESS

The first draft of a written business communication usually needs to be edited for conciseness. Many people think that the more words they use, the more effective their writing will be. Actually, the opposite is true. In business writing, the more concise your message is, the better chance you have of communicating effectively.

Conciseness means using as few words as possible to convey the message completely. Conciseness does not mean being curt or abrupt; but it does mean getting to the point, eliminating unnecessary information, and generally writing short sentences.

One of the proofreader's tasks may be to edit business documents for conciseness. When doing this, the proofreader should try to eliminate any unnecessary words or phrases. In particular the proofreader should edit clichés, obsolete expressions, jargon, redundancies, and passive voice.

LEARNING OBJECTIVES

- Identify errors caused by clichés, imprecise words, obsolete and redundant expressions, and passive voice.
- Use appropriate proofreading symbols to indicate changes in text.
- Spell correctly a list of commonly misspelled words.

When you edit for conciseness, watch for overused expressions so you can eliminate or replace them.

CLICHÉS AND IMPRECISE WORDS

Although you should use simple, familiar words in business writing, be careful that you do not fall into the habit of using overused words and expressions. These clichés have become trite and boring through overuse.

WORKPLACE CONNECTIONS

By avoiding clichés and imprecise words, writers produce work that is original, fresh, and accurate. That kind of writing stands out among the many business messages workers encounter each day.

Imprecise words are ambiguous; for example, your reader may have a different meaning for *soon* than you do. Your business writing will be more interesting if you avoid clichés, and the meaning of your message will be clearer if you avoid imprecise words.

14-1   Edit for clichés that have lost their clear meanings through overuse. Edit for imprecise words, which may not convey your message clearly.

Cliché:	Our company has grown *by leaps and bounds* during the past year.
Concise:	Our company has grown *by 5 percent* during the past year.
Imprecise:	Darlene appears to be a *good* candidate for the position of branch manager.
Precise:	Darlene appears to be a *well-qualified* candidate for the position of branch manager.

Avoid these clichés and imprecise expressions:

rat race	dog-eat-dog
between a rock and a hard place	face the music
good, great	soon
by leaps and bounds	sound out
manner of speaking	the bottom line
super	very
turn over a new leaf	awful
fish out of water	can of worms
water under the bridge	bite the bullet
take the bull by the horns	really
straight from the shoulder	track record
shoot from the hip	

#@%&!@#

Watch for clichés gone wrong.

This new procedure opens up a real kettle of worms.

The chairman was, in a matter of speaking, out of his league.

CHECKPOINT 14-1

Proofread the following sentences for clichés and imprecise words. If a sentence is correct, write *C* to the right of the sentence.

a. He was caught between a rock and a hard place in making a decision about a new career.

b. Carlota decided to bite the bullet and go ahead and work on her MBA degree.

c. I felt like a fish out of water when I was promoted to assistant manager.

d. Quinn really needs your request for training dates soon.

e. We need to tighten our belts because there is no wiggle room in this year's budget.

f. Before you open that can of worms, find out what really happened to the files.

g. My new chair is awesome.

h. He was hired because his track record was very good.

OBSOLETE AND REDUNDANT EXPRESSIONS

Obsolete expressions are terms that are out of date. They should not be used in today's business writing. Many writers mistakenly think that these dull, pompous terms make their written communication more effective. Interestingly, these same writers would never use these obsolete terms when talking with others.

Redundant expressions are those that repeat themselves. Most obsolete and redundant expressions are wordy and can be avoided by using more precise words or phrases.

14-2 Edit for obsolete expressions by choosing modern, more concise expressions.

Obsolete:	We are in receipt of your manuscript.
Concise:	We received your manuscript.
Obsolete:	Enclosed please find the booklet you requested.
Concise:	Enclosed is the booklet you requested.
Obsolete:	Kindly advise us of your decision as soon as possible.
Concise:	Please let us know your decision by [state a date].

The following obsolete words, phrases, and clauses should be edited to reflect more concise, present-day business writing standards.

Obsolete Terms	**Concise Terms**
acknowledge receipt of; are in receipt of	received
as per your request	as you requested
at the present time; at this point in time	now
at your [*or* earliest] convenience	[state a date]
attached herewith	attached
despite the fact that	although, despite
due to [*or* in view of] the fact that	because
enclosed please find	enclosed
hoping to hear from you soon	—
. . . I remain—Sincerely yours	Sincerely yours
in closing	—
in the event that	if
in the near future	[state a date]
in view of the fact that	because
kindly advise	please tell
meet with your approval	approve
permit me to say	—
please be advised that	—
take the liberty	—

14-1
(sample revisions)
a. He found it difficult to make a decision . . .
b. Carlota decided to work on her MBA degree.
c. I felt uncomfortable with my new responsibilities when I was promoted . . .
d. Quinn needs your request for training dates by Friday.
e. We need to spend carefully because this year's budget does not include extra money.
f. First, find out what happened to the files.
g. My new chair fits me well.
h. He was hired because of his proven ability to close a sale.

Thank you for your cooperation in this matter.	Thank you for [insert specifics].
thanking you in advance	thank you
trusting you will find	you will find
under separate cover	separately
until such time as	until
we regret to inform you	unfortunately
we would ask that you	please
would like to recommend	recommend

14–3 Edit for redundant or wordy expressions by eliminating unnecessary words to make the writing more concise.

Redundant: Please explain the past history of this account.

Concise: Please explain the history of this account.

Redundant: We expect the witness to tell the honest truth.

Concise: We expect the witness to tell the truth.

Wordy: I am writing this letter to tell you that I will be able to attend the NBEA conference in May.

Concise: I will attend the NBEA conference in May.

CHECKPOINT 14-2, 14-3

Proofread the following sentences for obsolete terms. If a sentence is correct, write _C_ to the right of the sentence.

a. Enclosed please find a coupon certificate for $10 to apply toward your first monetary purchase at King's Department Store.

b. Kindly inform us of your intentions to list your home with our firm despite the fact that you do not plan to move until September.

c. Let us hear from you at your earliest convenience so that you can begin enjoying your Readers' Guild books.

d. Due to the fact that our conference is in Los Angeles, only 12 of our marketing representatives will be able to attend.

e. We are trusting you will find the enclosed information helpful as you make a decision.

f. The nine copies of the brief are being sent by UPS today under separate cover.

g. Mr. Wilhelm will return Erin's call despite the fact that he has never spoken with her.

h. Permit me to say that I have never enjoyed a dinner meal meeting as much as I enjoyed this one.

© 2001 Ted Goff

"Your report is great. It just
needed a little editing."

PASSIVE VOICE

While certain circumstances in business writing are appropriate for passive voice, generally, business writing should be written in active voice. **Active voice** emphasizes the *subject*, and the subject performs the action described by the verb. **Passive voice** emphasizes the *action* rather than the doer of the action. Active voice gets right to the point and tells *who* did *what*. Passive voice tells *what* action took place but often neglects to say *who* performed the action.

In active voice the subject usually comes before the verb and the word being acted on (the object) follows the verb.

> Cleo jammed the photocopier this morning.

In passive voice the doer of the action is either not mentioned or is de-emphasized by being placed *after* the verb. Notice that a form of the helping verb *to be (was)* is combined with the verb *jammed*.

> The photocopier was jammed this morning.

> The photocopier was jammed this morning by Cleo.

Active voice creates a sharper, clearer picture in the mind of the reader than passive voice does. Generally, avoid passive voice verbs. However, you may use passive voice verbs when you want to avoid criticism or a negative statement or when you do not intend to mention the doer of the action.

14-2, 14-3
(sample revisions)

a. Enclosed is a certificate for $10 toward your first purchase . . .

b. Please let us know if you intend to list your home with our firm although you do not plan . . .

c. Let us hear from you this month so that you . . .

d. Because our conference . . .

e. You will find the . . .

f. . . . of the brief are being sent separately by UPS today.

g. . . . Erin's call although he has never . . .

h. I have never enjoyed a dinner meeting as much . . .

14–4 Edit for passive voice by using active voice verbs.

Passive:	A survey on distance learning was conducted.
Passive:	A survey on distance learning was conducted by Rahim.
Active:	Rahim conducted a survey on distance learning.
Passive:	A complete line of voice messaging equipment is currently being offered.
Passive:	A complete line of voice messaging equipment is offered by CompuCall.
Active:	CompuCall offers a complete line of voice messaging equipment.

The use of passive voice is sometimes necessary, such as when a writer prefers not to name the doer of an action. In general, however, writers should avoid passive voice for business writing.

CHECKPOINT 14-4

Edit the following sentences by changing passive voice to active voice. Provide a doer of the action, if necessary. If a sentence is correct, write *C* to the right of the sentence.

a. More than $1,000 is spent annually by the firm on office products and services for each employee.

b. Technology phobia can be overcome by companies with an organized approach.

c. The continuing legal education conference was attended by more than 200 attorneys and their staff.

d. It was recommended that our department correct its ergonomic shortfalls.

e. Beautiful color copies can be made on our new Prestige 3500 copier.

f. More than a dozen foot-long sandwiches were ordered for the lunch meeting.

g. The conference call will be originated by our receptionist at 3:15 this afternoon.

h. Reports from all three satellite offices were combined by Frederick into one report; the report was then submitted to the Board of Directors.

Chapter 14: Editing for Conciseness

SPELLING APPLICATIONS

14-5 Compare the words in Column A with the corresponding words in Column B. Use the appropriate proofreading symbols to correct the misspelled words. If both columns are correct, write **C** to the left of the number.

	Column A	Column B
1.	announcement	announcement
2.	benefited	benefitted
3.	definitely	definately
4.	dominent	dominant
5.	entrapraneuer	entrepreneur
6.	ingrediant	ingredient
7.	management	managment
8.	manageing	managing
9.	rhythm	rythym
10.	strickly	strictly

14-4
(sample revisions)

a. The firm spends more than $1,000 annually on office products and services for each employee.

b. Companies can overcome technology phobia with an organized approach.

c. More than 200 attorneys and their staff attended the . . .

d. A consultant recommended that our department correct . . .

e. We can make beautiful color copies on our . . .

f. She ordered more than a dozen . . .

g. Our receptionist will originate the conference call . . .

h. Frederick combined reports from all three satellite offices; he then submitted his report to the Board of Directors.

CHAPTER SUMMARY

♦ Avoid using overworked expressions (clichés).

♦ Select updated rather than obsolete expressions.

♦ Generally, use active voice rather than passive voice.

♦ Edit business messages for conciseness while ensuring that messages convey your meaning.

words@work Open *words@work*. Click on the Grammar and Usage tab. Under Lessons, choose Editing, Proofreading, and Spelling. This lesson highlights editing for conciseness, then reviews basic spelling rules. The exercises that follow also reinforce those skills.

14-5

1. C
2. benefitted
3. definetely
4. dominent
5. entrapraneuer
6. ingrediant
7. managment
8. manageing
9. rythym
10. stricly

PROOFREADING APPLICATIONS

Proofread the following paragraphs. Use the appropriate proofreading symbols to mark errors in the use of clichés, obsolete expressions, redundancies, passive voice, and spelling. To aid you in proofreading and editing, sample revisions are provided for these exercises.

P–1 To get out of the rat race, you have decided to go into business for yourself. You know what your product or service will be. At this point in time, you have made two of the most important business decisions you will ever make. Additional decisions will have to be made, however, to make sure your business gets started on the right foot. These decisions deal with how you organize your business, what goals you set, with whom you will work with, and how you attract your first customers or clients.

P–2 After deciding what type of business you want, seek help in starting your business. Basic business and legal questions can be answered by outside professionals, such as a lawyer and an accountant. If you are planning a business that is likely to grow by leaps and bounds, consider consulting with a banker, a compensation specialist, or even a marketing expert. After putting together the right outside team, make sure the right people are hired.

P–3 If you are planning a one-person business, consider a sole proprietorship. This type of organization enables an entrepraneur to avoid the can of worms that comes with incorporating. In the event that your business will require hiring employees and selling products or services that could cause harmful injury, you should consider incorporating. Help for determining the best type of business organization for your business can be obtained from your attorney or your accountant.

P–1
(sample revisions)
1. You have decided to go into business for yourself.
2. You have now made two of . . .
3. You will have to make additional decisions, however, to make sure your business gets a good start.
4. These decisions deal . . . with whom you will work, and how you . . .

P–2
(sample revisions)
1. Outside professionals, such as a lawyer and an accountant, can answer basic business and legal questions.
2. If your business grows rapidly and steadily, consider consulting . . .
3. After putting together the right outside team, hire the right people.

P-4 After organizing your company, you must toot your own horn. A new company has a definite advantage over more established businesses. Because there is no past company history for others to refute, your only problem as a new business owner is to get your share of the marketplace. A variety of low-cost marketing tactics can be taken advantage of by a young company. You should beat the bushes giving talks and seminars that highlight your service or product. As a final thought, just be sure to direct your efforts to the right audience— potential customers or individuals who can refer customers.

P-3

(sample revisions)

1. This type of organization enables an entrepreneur to avoid some of the difficulties and complications that come with incorporating.
2. If your business will require . . . that could cause injury, . . .
3. Your attorney or your accountant can help you determine the best type of organization for your business.

P-4

(sample revisions)

1. After organizing your company, you must promote it.
2. Because there is no company history for . . .
3. A young company can take advantage of low-cost marketing tactics.
4. You can promote your company by giving talks and seminars that highlight your service or product.
5. Finally, be sure . . .

PROGRESSIVE PROOFREADING

You are the assistant to Ada Carlton, the personnel manager in the law firm Richards & Armon. You assist the personnel manager with the hiring and managing of all nonattorney staff. Additionally, she has given you editing privileges for all her writing. Proofread the following documents for all errors, and edit the documents for content and conciseness. Your firm uses the simplified letter format.

Job 1 Proofread the following form letter that will be sent to job applicants.

RICHARDS & ARMON
Attorneys at Law
One Radisson Square, Suite 1500
Houston, Texas 77022-3626   richardsarmonlaw.com
Telephone (713)555-0103   Fax (713)555-0151

[insert date]

[insert applicant's name and address]

Thank you for your interest in a position at Richards & Armon.

[paragraph A]
We have reviewed your résumé and are impressed with your credentials. Despite the fact that you are very well qualified for an administrative assistant position with our firm, at this point in time we are completely staffed. We will keep your application in our current files for the next three months. If a position opens within that time, we will contact you to arrange an interview. If you do not hear from us, you may apply with us again after the three-month period.

[paragraph B]
We have reviewed your résumé and note that while you have [insert number of years] years of [insert specific type of experience or just say "office"] experience, you lack training or education specific to a legal office. We highly recommend the legal office training program at the Houston School of Technology (HST). HST offer day and evening classes in legal terminology, transcription, and legal office technology. The legal office program at HST also cordinates internships for its students so they can begin working in a legal office and gain valueable experience. As a matter of fact, we have hired Houston School of Technology internship students. Obtaining this type of specific education and training, would put you on a fast track to a career in a legal office.

We really wish you the best of success in your job search and career.

ADA CARLTON, PERSONNEL MANGER

lw

Job 2 Proofread the following memo.

TO: All Nonattorney Staff

FROM: Managment Team

DATE: May 1, 20—

SUBJECT: Confidentiality Issues

Recently we experienced a situation in which attorney/client confidentiality was breached by a member of our staff. The staff member told a caller that one of our attorneys was in court and who the attorney was representing. While it is permissible to explain that an attorney is in court, it is a violation of confidentiality to state the matter and especially the clients' name.

Although you are all aware of confidentiality issues, we wanted to write and distribute this memo to review some principals about the level of confidentiality expected of all members of our staff.

Sharing Client Names. This is the mother of all rules: Never, ever, tell who or what we represent to anyone without an attorney's permission.

Discussing work. Do not discuss the work you do here at the firm with *anyone,* even if you do not mention names. Do not discuss your work with your spouse, your family, your friends, or other colleagues. Additionally, do not discuss the work you are doing for a particular attorney with other staff members of the firm if they, themselves, are not also working on the matter.

Answering the phone. Again, you may tell a caller than an attorney is in court or at a deposition or a meeting, but never divulge the client's name or the nature of the court appearance, deposition, or meeting. Use discretion when an attorney is taking a late lunch or will arrive at the office late or has left the office early. Without understanding the full circumstances, callers may get the wrong impression if they are told at 2:30 that an attorney is at lunch or at 4:30 that an attorney has all ready left for the day.

Leaving your desk. When you are away from your desk, be aware of the papers and flies left unattended and open on your desk. Also be conscience at all times of what you leave on your computer screen. Clients or others may happen by your desk and see or read confidential information. Your workstations are your responsability.

As a final matter of discussion, if you have any doubt about whether you should repeat a client's name or discuss an issue, don't. It is better to err on the side of not saying enough than saying to much. Also, don't be afraid to ask your attorney for his guidance if you have questions regarding confidentiality.

AC:lw

Job 3 Proofread the following e-mail message regarding continuing legal education (CLE).

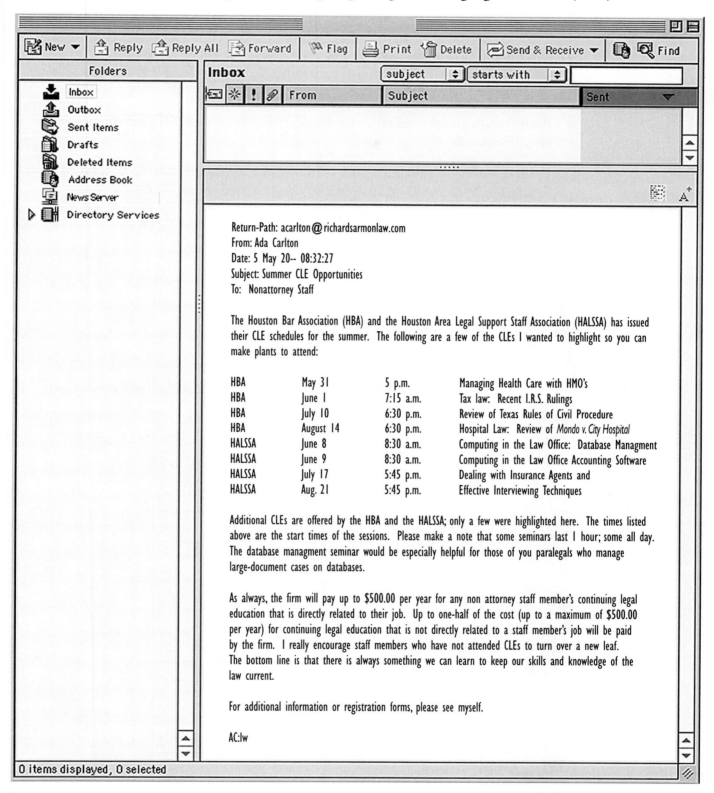

New ▾ | Reply Reply All Forward | Flag Print Delete | Send & Receive ▾ | Find

Folders

- Inbox
- Outbox
- Sent Items
- Drafts
- Deleted Items
- Address Book
- News Server
- ▷ Directory Services

Inbox   subject ◆ starts with ◆

| | From | Subject | Sent ▾ |

Return-Path: acarlton@richardsarmonlaw.com
From: Ada Carlton
Date: 5 May 20-- 08:32:27
Subject: Summer CLE Opportunities
To: Nonattorney Staff

The Houston Bar Association (HBA) and the Houston Area Legal Support Staff Association (HALSSA) has issued their CLE schedules for the summer. The following are a few of the CLEs I wanted to highlight so you can make plants to attend:

HBA	May 31	5 p.m.	Managing Health Care with HMO's
HBA	June 1	7:15 a.m.	Tax law: Recent I.R.S. Rulings
HBA	July 10	6:30 p.m.	Review of Texas Rules of Civil Procedure
HBA	August 14	6:30 p.m.	Hospital Law: Review of *Mondo v. City Hospital*
HALSSA	June 8	8:30 a.m.	Computing in the Law Office: Database Managment
HALSSA	June 9	8:30 a.m.	Computing in the Law Office Accounting Software
HALSSA	July 17	5:45 p.m.	Dealing with Insurance Agents and
HALSSA	Aug. 21	5:45 p.m.	Effective Interviewing Techniques

Additional CLEs are offered by the HBA and the HALSSA; only a few were highlighted here. The times listed above are the start times of the sessions. Please make a note that some seminars last 1 hour; some all day. The database managment seminar would be especially helpful for those of you paralegals who manage large-document cases on databases.

As always, the firm will pay up to $500.00 per year for any non attorney staff member's continuing legal education that is directly related to their job. Up to one-half of the cost (up to a maximum of $500.00 per year) for continuing legal education that is not directly related to a staff member's job will be paid by the firm. I really encourage staff members who have not attended CLEs to turn over a new leaf. The bottom line is that there is always something we can learn to keep our skills and knowledge of the law current.

For additional information or registration forms, please see myself.

AC:lw

0 items displayed, 0 selected

COMPUTERIZED PROOFREADING

Job 4 Prepare a letter.

1. Several staff members have expressed their desire to attend CLEs. You need to reserve a space for them and enclose payment. Load the file C14JOB4 from the template CD-ROM.

2. Proofread the letter, and make all necessary corrections. Refer to the handwritten notes for details.

3. Format the letter and address it to Mr. Nicho Estephan, Houston Area Legal Support Staff Association, P.O. Box 13948, Houston, Texas 77004-6591.

4. Save the document as C14JOB4R.

5. Produce the document by following the standard procedures.

Seminar	Name	Cost
interviewing	Janice McCarter	85 -M
	Alberto Jiminez	85 -M
	Arnel Jolly	125
computing/db	Alberto Jiminez	65 -m
	Zelda Ward	85
computing/acct.	Zelda Ward	85
	Kiyoko Corr	85
	Clay Metzgar	85

Writers usually know what they mean to say. Sometimes, however, their words get in the way. Consider this example:

Being shipped by overnight mail to Hong Kong, Mr. Lim was sure the documents would reach the meeting on time. Working furiously until the minute the meeting began, the documents arrived just in time to be distributed by the Hong Kong representative.

Was Mr. Lim shipped by overnight mail to Hong Kong? Did the documents work furiously until the minute the meeting began? Not only inexperienced writers make errors like these. Experienced business writers are just as likely to do so, especially when they write— or proofread—in haste. For business writers, lack of clarity may mean not getting a job, misleading a client, or simply confusing one's coworkers. Writers should pay careful attention, but proofreaders must also be able to recognize and improve text that lacks clarity.

EDITING FOR CLARITY

Good ideas must be expressed clearly to be communicated effectively. Ideas that are not clearly worded may amuse the reader and embarrass the writer, but more importantly, the message may be misunderstood. The writer must convey the message so that the reader can clearly understand it. The proofreader's job is to be aware of the errors that interfere with clarity and to eliminate them.

Three common errors that cause a message to be unclear are misplaced and dangling modifiers, lack of parallel construction, and use of complex rather than simple words.

MISPLACED AND DANGLING MODIFIERS

A modifier is a word or group of words that describes. Modifiers must be positioned in the sentence so that the intended meaning is clear to the reader. If a modifier is misplaced, who or what performed the action of

LEARNING OBJECTIVES

- Identify misplaced and dangling modifiers.
- Identify errors caused by lack of parallel construction.
- Use simple rather than less familiar words.
- Use strong verbs instead of noun phrases.
- Use appropriate proofreading symbols to indicate changes in text.
- Spell correctly a list of commonly misspelled words.

the sentence is unclear. If a modifier "dangles," it refers to the wrong word (or to no word) in the sentence. Incorrect modifiers destroy sentence clarity. To improve clarity, apply the following rules.

15-1 Place modifiers next to, or as close as possible to, the words they describe.

Incorrect: There should be no doubt about the intended message of the letter in the reader's mind.

Correct: There should be no doubt in the reader's mind about the intended message of the letter.

Check the position of words such as *only, at least,* or *merely* to be sure the intended meaning is clear.

Incorrect: These discount cards *only* are given to full-time employees.
(This sentence conveys that only discount cards, and nothing else, were given to full-time employees.)

Correct: These discount cards are given *only* to full-time employees.
(This sentence conveys that the discount cards were not given to any people other than full-time employees.)

The correct sentences above make sense because the misplaced modifiers were moved closer to the words they modify.

15-2 An introductory phrase or clause must be followed immediately by the word that it modifies. Correct dangling modifiers by inserting the noun or pronoun that the modifier describes, or change the dangling phrase to a complete clause. The phrase or clause is italicized in the examples. The word being modified is in bold.

Incorrect: *While walking along the beach*, the **sun** sank from view. (The *sun* was not *walking*.)

Correct: *While walking along the beach*, **Amy** watched the sun sink from view.

Incorrect: *Proofreading hurriedly*, **mistakes** were made by Hernando frequently.
(*Mistakes* did not *proofread hurriedly*, and *frequently* does not modify *Hernando*.)

Correct: *Proofreading hurriedly*, **Hernando** frequently made mistakes.

Correct: *When Hernando was proofreading hurriedly*, he frequently made mistakes.

A modifier must be close to the word or phrase it describes or explains.

WORKPLACE CONNECTIONS

In business communications a misplaced modifier can mean the difference between conveying your intended meaning and conveying a meaning you did not intend at all.

When you proofread, put yourself in the place of the recipient of the message. If you cannot comprehend the message or if you need to read it several times before you do understand it, the recipient of the message may have the same difficulty. Either edit the message or query the author.

Note: A few introductory phrases are permitted to dangle. Examples include *Generally speaking, Taking all things into consideration,* and *Confidentially speaking.*

> Taking all things into consideration, Duff's decision was the best one for everyone involved.

CHECKPOINT 15-1, 15-2

Proofread for misplaced and dangling modifiers. Keep the introductory phrase, but correct the rest of the sentence by rearranging or adding words to make the meaning clear.

a. After placing my order, my meal arrived promptly.

b. To open a savings account, a deposit of $100 is required.

c. Reading by the fire, my cat jumped into my lap.

d. Driving down the street, everything appeared to be in place to me.

e. Sasha only works during summer vacation. (Hint: Summer is the only time she works.)

PARALLEL CONSTRUCTION

Words, phrases, and clauses should be expressed in similar grammatical form when they are within a sentence and related in meaning. When similar elements are expressed in a similar structure, they are **parallel.** Parallel construction makes sentences, lists, and headings easy to read and understand.

Parallel constructions in sentences are logically connected by the coordinating conjunctions *and, but, nor,* and *or.* Make sure the sentence elements connected by these conjunctions are of the same grammatical form. That is, they are all words, phrases, or clauses. In lists and headings also be sure to apply this principle. For example, if one heading (major or subheading) appears in complete-sentence form, the others should also.

15–3 Within each sentence, balance a noun with a noun, an adjective with an adjective, a phrase with a phrase, and a clause with a clause.

> | *Incorrect:* | The manager's duties include *preparing the* payroll and *the depositing of the* money. |
> |---|---|
> | *Correct:* | The manager's duties include *preparing the* payroll and *depositing the* money. |
> | *Incorrect:* | The information was *not verified, not accurate,* and *was not very convincing either.* |
> | *Correct:* | The information was *not verified, not accurate,* and *not convincing* either. |

Be sure the items in lists are bulleted or numbered in the same manner, and balance the wording of the items with the same word, phrase, or clause construction.

Use the same phrase or clause structure for each bulleted or numbered item in a list. If the items in a list suggest a hierarchy, use numbers instead of bullets.

Incorrect: The responsibilities for the committee working on the summer outing are these:
- Plan a menu and order the catering.
- Organize activities for adults and children.
- The employees must be given at least a month's notice.

Correct: The responsibilities for the committee working on the summer outing are these:
- Plan a menu and order the catering.
- Organize activities for adults and children.
- Provide at least a month's notice to employees.

15-4 Conjunctions used in pairs (*both . . . and, either . . . or, neither . . . nor, not only . . . but also, whether . . . or*) should be followed by words in the same grammatical form. The conjunctions in the following sentences are indicated in bold.

Incorrect: The college offers **both** a degree in chemical engineering **and** civil engineering.
(The conjunction *both* is followed by a noun and a prepositional phrase; the conjunction *and* is followed by a noun.)

Correct: The college offers a degree in **both** chemical engineering **and** civil engineering.
(The conjunction *both* is followed by a noun; the conjunction *and* is followed by a noun.)

Incorrect: Devan **not only** is self-assured **but also** positive and upbeat.
(The conjunction *not only* is followed by a verb and an adjective; the conjunction *but also* is followed by adjectives.)

Correct: Devan is **not only** self-assured **but also** positive and upbeat.
(The conjunction *not only* is followed by an adjective; the conjunction *but also* is followed by adjectives.)

15-1, 15-2

a. After placing my order, I received my meal promptly.
b. To open a savings account, you need a $100 deposit.
c. Reading by the fire, I felt my cat jump into my lap.
d. Driving down the street, I noticed that everything appeared to be in place.
e. Sasha works only during summer vacation.

Proofread the following sentences, and correct the structure where it is not parallel. If a sentence is correct, write *C* to the right of the sentence.

a. Ike's summer plans include painting the house, refinishing some furniture, and to play golf.

b. Constentino's hobbies include collecting Civil War memorabilia, work in his garden, and hiking.

c. Either Steffi will accept the transfer to Minneapolis or remain in Louisville.

d. Mac not only won a trip to South America but also a car.

e. Chrissie is studying accounting, French, and how to keyboard.

SIMPLE WORDS

Business writers often use certain words and phrases because they *sound* right or businesslike. These words, which are usually longer and more complicated than needed, often sound dull and pompous to the reader. Word length and word difficulty are often related, but not always. Many people know words such as *fastidious* and *ergonomics* but do not know words such as *pi* and *id.*

In general, short, simple, familiar words are more likely to be understood. Familiar words allow the reader to concentrate on the message; complicated and unusual words may call attention to the words themselves. When a shorter, less complicated word is available, the writer should use it.

15–5 Edit for less familiar words by choosing short, simple words instead.

Less familiar:	Did you *utilize* our voice messaging system when you called?
Simple:	Did you *use* our voice messaging system when you called?
Less familiar:	Please *ascertain* whether Camilla is traveling to Turkey.
Simple:	Please *find out* whether Camilla is traveling to Turkey.

Following is a partial list of less familiar words with their shorter, simpler counterparts.

> **Good writers are those who keep the language efficient. That is to say, keep it accurate, keep it clear.**
> —Ezra Pound

a. painting the house, refinishing some furniture, and playing golf.

b. collecting Civil War memorabilia, working in his garden, and hiking.

c. Steffi will either accept the transfer to Minneapolis or remain in Louisville.

d. Mac won not only a trip . . . but also a car.

e. accounting, French, and keyboarding.

Less Familiar Words	Simple Words
ascertain	find out
cognizant	aware
commence	begin
compensate	pay
conceptualize	see
consummate	complete
encounter	meet
endeavor	try
expedite	rush, speed up
facilitate	help
hypothesize	guess
indicative	indicates, means
monitor	check
operational	working
perpetuate	continue
perplexing	confusing, puzzling
procure	get
reciprocate	return
sufficient	enough
terminate	end
transmit	send (or state how sent)
utilize	use

CHECKPOINT 15-5

Edit the following sentences by substituting simple words for more difficult words. If a sentence is correct, write *C* to the right of the sentence.

a. Cecil's lease on the building was terminated because he did not pay the rent.

b. We plan to compensate all 50 people who attended the rally at Quaker Square.

c. Your offer to host the conference is indicative of your desire to facilitate our newly formed organization.

d. Please ascertain who else is joining us on the tour.

e. After transmitting the details to the branch offices, the home office commenced the contest.

STRONG VERBS

Messages are clearer to the reader when the writer uses specific, descriptive verbs to convey the action in the message. Telling a reader that you will *contact* him or her is not as clear as telling him or her that you will write, call, or visit in person.

Additionally, do not change a strong verb into a verb and noun phrase combination. For example, do not change the verb *describe* into the verb and noun phrase *make a description*. The phrase will be wordier and will not be as direct or strong as the simple verb form.

15–6 Edit to change weak verbs to strong verbs. Edit to change verb phrases that include nouns to strong verbs.

Weak verb:	All vacations will be affected by the new production deadline.
Strong verb:	All vacations will be postponed until we have met the new production deadline.
Weak verb:	When she looked at us, we knew she was serious.
Strong verb:	When she glared at us, we knew she was serious.
Verb and noun phrase:	Fillippe will make a selection regarding the new phone system by the end of the month.
Strong verb:	Fillippe will select the new phone system by the end of the month.
Verb and noun phrase:	Moriah and Jake held a discussion concerning how the new tax laws will affect our retirement plans.
Strong verb:	Moriah and Jake discussed how the new tax laws will affect our retirement plans.

15–5

a. Cecil's lease on the building ended . . .

b. We plan to pay all 50 people . . .

c. Your offer to host the conference indicates your desire to help our newly formed organization.

d. Please find out who . . .

e. After [faxing] the details to the branch offices, the home office began the contest.

CHECKPOINT 15-6

Edit the following sentences by substituting strong verbs for weak verbs or verb and noun phrases. If a sentence is correct, write *C* to the right of the sentence.

a. Your new assignment will be the verification of all student transcript requests.

b. I hope to make the corrections to this brief by 5 p.m. today.

c. The court clerk gave us the new trial date.

d. Miss Wiesenthal wants to bring about a change in the delivery schedule.

e. Please make revisions to these letters and get them out today.

a. . . . will be to verify all . . .

b. I hope to correct this brief . . .

c. C

d. . . . wants to change the

e. Please revise these letters and [mail] them today.

SPELLING APPLICATIONS

15-7 Compare the words in Column A with the corresponding words in Column B. Use the appropriate proofreading symbols to correct the misspelled words. If both columns are correct, write **C** to the left of the number.

	Column A	Column B
1.	category	catagory
2.	conscientious	concientious
3.	curteous	courteous
4.	develop	develope
5.	enviroment	environment
6.	foreigner	foreignor
7.	reminisent	reminiscent
8.	symetrical	symmetrical
9.	technique	technique
10.	thoroughly	throughly

CHAPTER SUMMARY

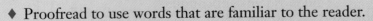

♦ Errors in misplaced modifiers and in parallelism usually disrupt the flow of a sentence. To detect such errors, listen carefully as you read the document to yourself.

♦ Proofread to use words that are familiar to the reader.

♦ Learn to recognize the problems that undermine clarity of writing, and know their remedies.

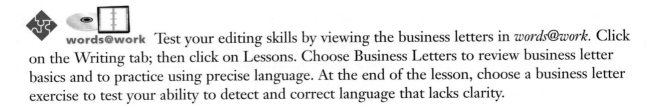

words@work Test your editing skills by viewing the business letters in *words@work*. Click on the Writing tab; then click on Lessons. Choose Business Letters to review business letter basics and to practice using precise language. At the end of the lesson, choose a business letter exercise to test your ability to detect and correct language that lacks clarity.

Proofread the following documents, checking particularly for errors in parallelism, misplaced and dangling modifiers, and complex words.

P-1

November 30, 20--

Ms. Greta Doesky
327 First Street
Great Bend, KS 67530-8247

Dear Ms. Doesky

We look forward to seeing you at your studio appointment next Friday, December 7, at 10:30 a.m. Please bring (1) two changes of clothing, (2) cosmetics and hair care products, and (3) you may bring a musical instrument or other prop of your choice. We will endeavor to complete the photo shoot within an hour.

Sincerely

P-2

TO: Elizabeth
FROM: Shigeki
DATE: November 14, 20--
SUBJECT: Planning Meeting

Please plan to meet in my office at 3:15 p.m. tomorrow to have a discussion on how we can encourage students to take technical courses.

Although not all graduates will continue their education, they will find they need marketable skills. This idea is predicated on research that shows that graduates who have had technical courses are coveted. Employers are cognizant that these students not only have marketable skills but also better attitudes toward change, better problem-solving skills, and will have an appreciation for technical work.

15-7
1. catagory — e
2. concientious — s
3. curteous — o
4. develope
5. enviroment — n
6. foreignor — e
7. reminisent — c
8. symetrical — m
9. C
10. throughly — o

P-1
1. Please bring . . . (3) a musical instrument or other prop . . .
2. We will try to . . .

P-2

1. . . . tomorrow to discuss how we can encourage . . .
2. This idea is based on research that shows that graduates who have had technical courses are in demand.
3. Employers know that these students have not only marketable skills but also better attitudes toward change, better problem-solving skills, and better appreciation for technical work.

P-3

1. 9-HOUR BATTERY
2. While recording, you can use the power zoom lens to film . . .
3. The autofocus system will automatically focus on any subject . . .
4. . . . you will enjoy not only the date display feature but also the time display feature.
5. To purchase your SDB Camcorder at this discount, [stop by our store] [by May 31].

CAMCORDER SALE

POWER ZOOM LENS
AUTOFOCUS SYSTEM
DATE/TIME DISPLAY
THE BATTERY LASTS 9 HOURS

These are only some of the features that you will like about our best-selling SDB Camcorder. You will also like the 25 percent off sale price! While recording, the power zoom lens can be used to film either close-up or distance shots. The autofocus system will focus on any subject that appears within a small circle on the lens automatically. Should you forget when you recorded your scenes, you will not only enjoy the date display feature but also the time display feature.

To make a purchase of an SDB Camcorder at this discount, contact us soon.

PROGRESSIVE PROOFREADING

You work as an assistant to Sylvia Guzman, owner-manager of Best Natural Products Co. One of your responsibilities is to proofread documents for mechanical errors and edit them for correctness, conciseness, and clarity. Your office uses modified block with indented paragraphs and mixed punctuation.

Job 1   Proofread the memo, and edit it for clarity and conciseness.

TO: All Personal   **Interoffice**
                                                              Communication
FROM: Sylvia

DATE: October 24, 20--

SUBJECT: Good Telephone Techniques

Because our voices are the first contacts that many individuals have with us outside the company, we should strive to make a good first impression when we answer the telephone. Please review the following suggestions for developing better telephone techniques:

TELEPHONE TECNIQUES

I.   INCOMING CALLS

    A.   Answer promptly.
    B.   Greet the caller pleasantly.
    C.   You should identify yourself and the company.
    D.   Be helpful to the caller.
    E.   Be curteous at all times.
    F.   Screen calls as directed by your manager or myself.
    H.   Write messages accurately and so they are legible.
    I.   Let the caller end the call.

2.   MAKING OUTGOING CALLS

    A.   Be sure of the number.
    B.   Plan your call.
       1.   Know what you are going to discuss.
       2.   You should gather any related materials before placing the call.
    C.   Let the phone ring several times before hanging up.
    D.   Identify yourself.
    E.   Time zone differences.
    F.   Be considerate.

Job 2 Proofread the two invoices against the telephone messages from which they were prepared. Use the price list to check the item numbers and prices. The terms are **2/10, n/30;** the sales tax is **6 percent;** shipment is via **UPS;** and the orders are numbered consecutively beginning with **BH090190.**

1402 Graham Road
Bryan, TX 77801-4128
Telephone: (409) 555-0136

Price List

Item Number	Product Description	Size	Price
AE-2349	Scouring Cleanser	9 oz	$ 4.75
LA-6180	Liquid Cleanser	16 oz	3.30
BD-7307	Automatic Dishwashing Concentrate	47 oz	8.95
BG-2294	Germicide	1 qt	11.85
BH-5568Q	Concentrated Cleaner	1 qt	6.40
BH-5561G		1 gal	22.35
BH-5565G		5 gal	97.20
NB-90010	Laundry Concentrate	10 lb	19.95
NB-90021		21 lb	39.95
LL-9751Q	Liquid Laundry Concentrate	1 qt	5.95
LL-9751G		1 gal	21.10
SS-73822	Dishwashing Liquid	22 oz	4.75
SS-6431G		1 gal	23.95
ST-8011Q	Concentrated Fabric Softener	1 qt	5.10
ST-8011G		1 gal	17.50

Chapter 15: Editing for Clarity

Best Natural Products Co.

1402 Graham Road
Bryan, TX 77801-4128
Telephone: (409) 555-0136

INVOICE

Mrs. Nancy Rosenbloom
219 Ortiz Drive
Groves, TX 77619-3120

Date: October 25, 20--

Order No.: BH090190
Date Shipped: October 25, 20--
Shipped Via: UPS
Terms: 2/10, n/30

Quantity	No.	Description	Unit Price	Total
2	LA-6180	Liquid Cleanser	3.30	6.60
1	NB-90010	Laundry Concentrate, 10 lb	19.95	19.95
2	ST-8011G	Concentrated Fabric Softener	5.10	10.20
		Total		36.75
		Sales Tax		2.21
		Total Amount		38.96

To _Sales Dept._
Time _9:20 a.m._ Date _10/25_

While You Were Out

M _rs. Nancy Rosenbloom_
of _219 Ortiz Drive, Groves TX 77619-3120_
Phone No. _555-0189_
☑ Telephoned   ☐ Please call back
☐ Returned your call ☐ Will call again
☐ Left the following message:
Send 2 liquid cleanser,
1 10-lb laundry conc, and
2 qt conc fab soft. Also
info about water purification
system.

By _js_

Best Natural Products Co.

1402 Graham Road
Bryan, TX 77801-4128
Telephone: (409) 555-0136

INVOICE

Kwai San Restaurant
427 Center Street
Lufkin, TX 75901-1200

Date: October 25, 20--

Order No.: BH090191
Date Shipped: October 25, 20--
Shipped Via: UPS
Terms: 2/10, n/30

Quantity	No.	Description	Unit Price	Total
10	BD-7307	Automatic Dishwashing Concentrate, 47 oz	8.95	89.50
1	BH-5565G	Concentrated Cleaner, 5 gal	97.20	97.20
5	BG-2249	Germicide	11.85	59.25
12	AE-2349	Scouring Cleanser	4.75	4.75
		Total		250.70
		Sales Tax		15.04
		Total Amount		265.74

To _Sales Dept._
Time _1:45 p.m._ Date _10/25_

While You Were Out

M _Kwai San Restaurant_
of _427 Center St., Lufkin, TX 75901-1200_
Phone No. _(409) 555-0191_

☑ Telephoned ☐ Please call back
☐ Returned your call ☐ Will call again
☐ Left the following message:

Send 10 47 oz a. d. w. conc.
1 conc. Cleaner (5 gal), 5 qt
germicide, 12 scouring
cleansers

By _js_

Best Natural Products Co.

1402 Graham Road
Bryan, TX 77801-4128
Telephone: (409) 555-0136
www.natural-products.com

October 25, 20--

Mrs. Nancy Rosenbloom
219 Ortiz Drive
Groves, TX 77619-3120

Dear Mrs. Rosenbloom

I am writing this letter to tell you that you telephone order of October 25 is being shipped by UPS today.

Thank you for your interest in our nonpolluting and biodegradable cleaning products and our water purification system. Our cleaning products are not only throughly effective and safe for cleaning but also safe for the enviornment.

The quality of water is one of the most important choice we have to make today. Our company is working on the development of a water purifying system that is economical, spacesaving, and will be easy to operate. The system should be available in about 6 months. A broshure will be sent to you under separate cover in the near future.

Mrs. Rosenblooom, we do appreciate your business. Any time you have questions about our products, please do not hesitate to call us using our toll-free number, 800-555-012.

Sincerely yours

Cyrus A. Gerhart
Customer Service

kr

COMPUTERIZED PROOFREADING

Job 4   Proofread and edit a letter.

1. Load the file C15JOB4 from the template CD-ROM.

2. Use the following statement for verifying the correctness of the information in the letter. Edit the letter carefully for errors in conciseness and clarity. Also, check for mechanical errors.

3. Save the revised document as C15JOB4R.

4. Produce the document by following the standard procedures.

Best Natural Products Co.

1402 Graham Road
Bryan, TX 77801-4128
Telephone: (409) 555-0136
www.natural-products.com

STATEMENT

Account of   Hank W. Loran
1735 North 16 Street
Lake Jackson, TX 77566-9800

Date	Charges	Credits	Balance
June 3	179.34		179.34
July 1		179.34	------
July 25	144.57		144.57
August 22	135.91		280.48

Minneapolis Financial Corp.
928 Irving Avenue S
Minneapolis, MN 55403-7640
Phone (800) 555-0100
Fax (612) 555-0101
minneapolisfinancial.com

January 16, 20--

Dear Friend and Financial Member

We would like to take this opportunity to thank you for your business last year. We were pleased you chose our company to provide solid financial services and advice to you. Our goal is to make our members completely satisfied with the services and products they receive from Minneapolis Financial Corp.

We are looking forward to a continued relationship with you in the coming year. The new changes in tax laws will affect how we manage our financial products. Our financial consultants are fully trained in the new laws and are ready to meet with you individually or speak with you by phone to answer your questions and analyze your financial needs.

Again this spring we will be offering several "Spring into Action" seminars in the Minneapolis area to help you better understand the products that could be of benefit to you. You will soon receive a brochure with an early notice and invitation to attend. Only after our valued members have the first opportunity to register will we publicize the seminars and open them to the public. We hope you will be able to join us.

To make contacting our financial consultants easier, we have expanded our customer service lines. Please call our toll-free number to speak to a financial consultant. We are here to serve you any day of the week from 10 p.m. to 8 p.m. You may also contact your financial consultant at any time by e-mail through a link at our web site at any time. As always, our commitment is to you, our valued member.

Sincerely yours

Craig Mason
Vice President, Member Services

Chapter 2, Job 1

BRENTWOOD COMPUTER CENTER
213 Rainbow Circle
Camden, NJ 08101-7650

PURCHASE ORDER

MINNEAPOLIS FINANCIAL CORP.
928 Irving Avenue S
Minneapolis, MN 55403-7640

Purchase Order No.: 4PS28510
Date: December 29, 20--
Date Shipped: December 29, 20--
Terms: 2/10, n/30
Shipped Via: CNC Lines

Quantity	Description/Stock No.	Unit Price	Total
3	Conversion Software, ASV1	$ 62.00	$ 186.00
3	Spelling Verification Pkg., 23S	175.00	525.00
1	Memory Expansion Board, 183M	345.45	345.45
1	Scanner, KC837	7,500.00	7,500.00
1	Sheet Feeder, 21TC	125.00	125.00
			$8,591.45 8,681.65

Chapter 2, Job 2

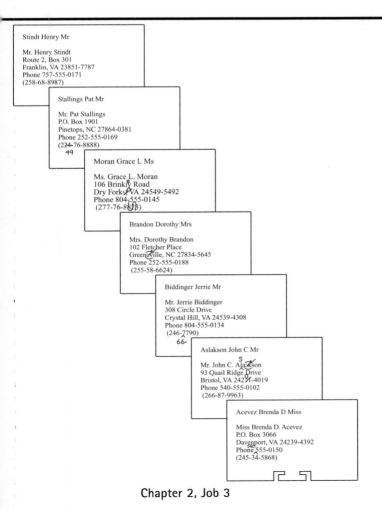

Stindt Henry Mr

Mr. Henry Stindt
Route 2, Box 301
Franklin, VA 23851-7787
Phone 757-555-0171
(258-68-8987)

Stallings Pat Mr

Mr. Pat Stallings
P.O. Box 1901
Pinetops, NC 27864-0381
Phone 252-555-0169
(224-76-8888)
49

Moran Grace L Ms

Ms. Grace L. Moran
106 Brinkly Road
Dry Forks, VA 24549-5492
Phone 804-555-0145
(277-76-8888)

Brandon Dorothy Mrs

Mrs. Dorothy Brandon
102 Fletcher Place
Greenville, NC 27834-5645
Phone 252-555-0188
(255-58-6624)

Biddinger Jerrie Mr

Mr. Jerrie Biddinger
308 Circle Drive
Crystal Hill, VA 24539-4308
Phone 804-555-0134
(246-7790)
66

Aslakson John C Mr

Mr. John C. Aslakson
93 Quail Ridge Drive
Bristol, VA 24271-4019
Phone 540-555-0102
(266-87-9963)

Acevez Brenda D Miss

Miss Brenda D. Acevez
P.O. Box 3066
Davenport, VA 24239-4392
Phone 555-0150
(245-34-5868)

Chapter 2, Job 3

Minneapolis Financial Corp. 401(k) Plan

The following is an example of the benefits that may be achieved for the plan year for a single employee with a salary of $20,000 (based on estimated 20-- tax rates).

Contributions	Amount
Employee salary deferral (5%)	$1,000
Employer matching contribution (25% of first 4% deferred)	200
Employer basic contribution (3%)	600
Total benefits	$1,800

	Tax Savings
Federal taxes (19% of salary deferral)	$190
State taxes (4%)	40
Tax savings to employee	$230
Net out-of-pocket cost	$770*

for a $1,000 salary deferral

Chapter 2, Job 4

Software Success Learning Center

INCORPORATING TECHNOLOGY INTO THE CLASSROOM
SUMMER SESSIONS FOR K-12 EDUCATORS

Software Success Learning Center (SSLC) is offering summer sessions that present the latest information and ideas about technology to educators. Conveniently held during June, July, and Aug, our classes are offered in three-week sessions designed to meet your scheduling and instructional needs. All SSLC courses are offered in our computer labs where hands-on training takes place.

Courses	*Sessions Offered*
Fundamentals of Classroom Tech	1B, 1C, and 2A
Incorporating Word Processing into Classroom Curriculum	1B, 2A, 2C, and 3A
Using Writing and Grammer Software	2A and 3C
The Internet for K-12 Educ	1C, 2C, and 3C
Development of Online Projects for Secondary Students	2A & 2B
Beginning Web Pages for Educators	2B
Beginning Desktop Publishing for Educators	1A, 2A, and 2B
Advanced Desktop Publishing for Educators	2B, 3A, 3B, and 3C

Schedule of Sessions

1	First three-week session	June 4-22	Mon-Friday	A	9 a.m. — noon
2	Second three-week session	July 9-27	Mon-Friday	B	1 p.m. — 4 p.m.
3	Third three-week session	Aug 6-24	Mon-Friday	C	6 p.m. — 9 p.m.

Faculty

Prof Paul Uhr Senior, M.B.A.
Miss Lillie Taylor, CPS, Office Manager, Quadrangle Products, Inc.
Dr William R. Joyner, Ph.D., Information Sciences Dept, State College of Tech
Ms Wanda Masterson, MOUS Certified Instructor

Registration is limited to 25 per classroom; enrollment is accepted until classes are full. All classes are $199 each; register for two or more classes and receive a 10% discount on each class.

Chapter 3, Job 1

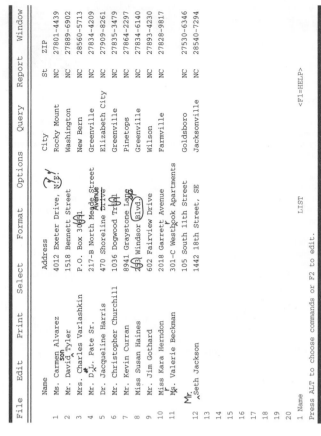

Chapter 3, Job 2

INTERNET USERS' GROUP

Organizational Meeting

You are invited to attend the initial meeting of a new group of our clients—Internet users who want to meet and share knowledge of research and other use practices. The Internet Users' Group will be held in the Prince Rm of the Tryon Hotel on Feb 20 at 7:30 PM. Dr Rachel A. Shaw, Ph.D., professor of Internet research at Texas A&M Univ, will be the guest speaker at this organizational meeting.

Anyone using or interested in using the Internet for research, for information searches, or for fun is encouraged to join. Therefore please pass this announcement along to your friends.

The Internet Users' Group will meet monthly to discuss research-related topics. Guest speakers from industry will share how they are using the Internet to achieve results. New browsers and valuable Internet sites will be demonstrated and discussed. Group members will be happy with the support and education they receive, including our plan to have an annual conference sponsored by competitive software developers.

The goals of the Internet Users' Group are to provide a network so that all members will be able to use the Internet most effectively and to keep software developers aware of consumer needs.

Members attending the first organizational meeting will determine the best time and location for the monthly meetings and will appoint representatives to board positions.

Chapter 3, Job 3

INTEROFFICE MEMORANDUM

TO: Department Managers and Supervisors

FROM: Garry Morrison, General Manager

DATE: September 26, 20--

SUBJECT: Expense Reduction

Please analyze your tentative budget carefully; then let me have your strategies for reducing our costs as soon as possible but no later than October 10.

As you review the budget, you will see that our utilities expense is almost double what it was four years ago. Advertising expense has increased about 30 percent. Taxes are up more than 20 percent. The cost of insurance rises every year. If we are to remain competitive in the business environment, we must reduce our expenses.

My goal is to incorporate your ideas into the management plan for the November 7 annual meeting.

dw

Chapter 3, Job 4

1. You have been an enthusiastic and dependable supporting member of Partners, Inc., for five years.

2. You have backed Partners with enthusiasm for a number of years—thank you!—and we want you to know your support has not gone unnoticed.

3. Because you have so generously contributed your time and other resources to Partners, the Advisory Board members invite you to be our guest at our annual gala dinner on March 30 at the City Center at 6:30 p.m. You may bring a guest.

4. We are already at the height of planning the annual Partners' Auction. This year the auction will be held on Feb. 15. As in the past, all proceeds will go to help the youth of our community. May we count on your continued support?

5. If your answer is YES, and we hope it will be, please notify us by January 20 using the enclosed reply card. You may also phone in to tell us of your support at 555-0123 during normal working hours.

6. As we prepare for this year's auction scheduled for February 15, may we once again count on your support? If your answer is YES, and we hope it will be, please let us know the items or service that you will provide for the auction by January 20.

7. If you will be able to attend, please return the enclosed reservation form by March 16 so that we can reserve a place for you.

8. Please be sure to mark your calendar for the big event—this is the one fundraising event you won't want to miss!

9. For further information about Partners, Inc., look us up on the Web at http://www.partners4u.org.

10. Enclosure

Chapter 4, Job 1

Partners, Inc.

January 10, 20—

Ms. Joan Daniels, Mgr.
WEXZ Newstalk 1530
517 North Ninth Street
Denver, CO 80204-7825

Dear Ms. Daniels

PUBLIC ANNOUNCEMENT

For the past four years, your station has very generously advertised the Partners' Auction as a public service announcement. The Partners' Auction is held annually to raise money to support projects for the youth in our community. Can we count on your continued enthusiasm and support this year?

If your response is YES, and we hope it will be, please read the enclosed news release on your Community Calendar program. We would like the announcement to begin on January 20 and have it run through February 5.

Sincerely yours

Joseph A. Ramirez
Executive Assistant

gg

Enclosure

Chapter 4, Job 2

Partners, Inc.

NEWS RELEASE

January 10, 20--
To release January 20, 20--

FIFTH ANNUAL PARTNERS' AUCTION

The Fifth Annual Partners' Auction will be telecast on WRAL-TV from noon to midnight on Sat., February 5. Local merchants and businesses have generously donated approximately fifteen hundred gifts, including merchandise, trips, and services. Viewers can bid on any of them by calling one of the numbers that will be listed on the television screen. The retail value of each item will be given, and each item will be sold to the highest bidder. Most of the items can be viewed prior to the auction by visiting Partner's web site at www.partners4u.org.

All people working with the auction donate their time with enthusiasm. That way every nickel, dime, and dollar goes directly to aid the youth of the community. Because of community involvement, last year's auction raised over $1.2 million. Remember, show your support for youth projects by marking your calendars to support Partners' Auction on Feb. 5.

Chapter 4, Job 3

Partners, Inc.

January 14, 20--

Mr. E. C. Troiano
AMS Electronics
5245 Trade St.
Denver, CO 80214-8275

Dear Mr. Troiano

Mark your calendar for the Fifth Annual Partners' Auction to be held on Saturday, February 5, in Scott Pavilion. The auction is sponsored by area businesses for the benefit of Partners, Inc., an organization devoted to helping the youth of the community. As a loyal supporter of Partners, you know how vital the auction is as a means of raising funds for the organization.

WRAL-TV will telecast the auction from noon to midnight. As each item is put up for bid, it will be displayed on television and its retail value will be given. You can place your bid for any item by calling the phone numbers listed on the television screen. Should your bid be for more than the retail value of the item, the difference between the two is deductible on your taxes.

Because the auction is staffed with volunteers, all proceeds go directly to Partners. We hope that you will participate in Partners' biggest fundraiser of the year. When Partners benefits, the entire community—not just one group—benefits.

Sincerely yours

Joseph Ramirez
Executive Assistant

Chapter 4, Job 4

March 1, 20--

Mr. Peter Wallace, Sales Manager
General TV and Appliance, Inc.
1927 Greeley Boulevard
Denver, CO 80208-1927

Dear Mr. Wallace

You have been an enthusiastic and dependable supporting member of Partners, Inc., for five years.

Because you have so generously contributed your time and other resources to Partners, the Advisory Board members invite you to be our guest at our annual gala dinner on March 30 at the City Center at 6:30 p.m. You may bring a guest.

If you will be able to attend, please return the enclosed reservation form by March 16 so that we can reserve a place for you.

For further information about Partners, Inc., look us up on the Web at http://www.partners4u.org.

Sincerely

Gary McDougald

rlm

Enclosure

Chapter 4, Job 5

PHELPS REAL ESTATE AGENCY

1125 Umstead Drive   Indianapolis, IN 46204-6142
Phone (317) 555-0142   Fax (317) 555-0182

January 20, 20--

Ms. Patsy Strum
1 Kildaire Farm Road
Indianapolis, IN 46205-9241

Dear Ms. Strum

Good news! The house you are interested in on ~~Thirty-third~~ 33d Street has been reduced $5,000. The price is now within the range you mentioned to me on the 4th. May I urge you to act quickly.

Because of the favorable mortgage rates that are now available, you can own this 2200-square- (or 2,200) foot house and still have mortgage payments of less than $900,00 per month. For a limited time the Indianapolis Federal Savings and Loan Association will approve your application for an adjustable rate loan within ten working days. If it is not approved, you will not be charged the 1 % discount rate.

Please call me at the office (555-0142) or on my cell phone (555-0110) to set up an appointment. My office hours are from 9;00 to 5 p.m. Mon through Sat, but as you know, I would be happy to meet with you at your convenience.

Sincerely

Terry B. Andrus
Agent

df

Chapter 5, Job 1

GREENWOOD SUBDIVISION. Spacious and convenient single-level for economy-conscious owner. While its main features are 3 bedrooms and a formal living room with fireplace, it also has a nearby park/playground, a semiwooded backyard, a 12 × 27 foot deck, and a 12 × 27 foot hot tub area. Check out the curb appeal!

For more details, call Chris at 555-01700.

260

Chapter 5, Job 2

PHELPS REAL ESTATE AGENCY

1125 Umstead Drive   Indianapolis, IN 46204-6142
Phone (317) 555-0142   Fax (317) 555-0182

January 25, 20--

Mr. Nicholas Toracelli
Delhi Association of Realtors
325 Alabama Street
Indianapolis, IN 46204-6154

Dear Mr. Toracelli

I have a new listing in the Greenwood subdivision that I would like to place on the weekly realtors' tour. The facts you need for the tour are as follows:

   a. Address: 4231 Charles Street
   b. Price: $129,900
   c. Bedrooms/Baths: 3/2
   d. Square Feet: ~~approx. 71 years~~ 1,723
   e. Age: ~~1,723~~ approximately 71 years
   f. Lot Size: 125 feet by 75 feet

This home sounds average by description, but it is actually a beautiful home that has been immaculately maintained. It is well worth the competitive asking price. I would like as many realtors as possible to tour it.

Please let me know when you can accommodate my request to place this home on the tour schedule. The only day not available on my calendar is the ~~fourth~~ of February. If you have any questions, you can reach me on my cell phone (555-0170).

Sincerely

Chris Rice
Agent

df

Chapter 5, Job 3

Delhi Association of Realtors
325 Alabama Street
Indianapolis, IN 46204-6154
(317) 555-0196

MINUTES OF MEETING
DELHI ASSOCIATION OF REALTORS

Place of Meeting

The Delhi Assoc. of Realtors held its monthly meeting on Tuesday, January 18, 20--, at The Heritage Restaurant. The social hour began at six o'clock, and dinner was served at 7. Seventy-eight of the 85 members were present in addition to four guests.

Call to Order

Immediately following dinner, J.R. Hawkins, president, called the meeting to order and welcomed the members and guests. She noted that the January attendance was 10% above the December attendance.

Approval of Minutes

The minutes were presented by Secretary Tom Phelps. James Miller noted that the state convention would be held on the 9th of March instead of on April 10, as stated in the minutes. The correction was made, and the minutes were approved.

Treasurer's Report

In the absence of Sabrina Peoples, Tom Phelps gave the treasurer's report. The Association has a balance of $1,210 in the treasury, and bills amounting to $76.10 ($35.10 to Rouse Printing Company and $41.00 to The Heritage Restaurant) are outstanding. An extension of 15 days has been granted to members who have not paid their dues.

Chapter 5, Job 4

2

Market Review

Rodney Blankenship was called on to give a summary of the developments that have taken place in the local real estate market. Phelps Real Estate Company has been selected as exclusive marketing agent for Breckenridge subdivision on Leesville Rd. The 79-lot single-family subdivision is a Drexter development. Northwoods Village, a 228-unit luxury apartment community developed by Dallas C. Pickford & Associates, will open on the 1st of August. The community is located at Ten Northwoods Village Drive, one-half mile south of Interstate 40.

Speaker

Following the business session, President Hawkins introduced Mrs. Mrs. Sally Dunbarton, president of Dunbarton Associates, as speaker for the meeting. Mrs. Dunbarton discussed the potential effects of recent tax legislation on the real estate market. She predicted that the prime rate will drop another 1/2 point before it hits bottom. In the local area an additional 12-15 apartment buildings should be on the market within the next 6 months.

Adjournment

Following the presentation, Tom Phelps drew the lucky number to determine who would win the centerpiece. 320 was the lucky number, and the winner was Midori Genda. He drew

The meeting was adjourned at 9:15 p.m. Members were reminded that that the next meeting would be on the 3d Tuesday of February.

Respectfully submitted,

Tom Phelps, Secretary

Chapter 5, Job 4 (cont'd)

DO YOU NEED A REAL ESTATE AGENT?

Do you need a real estate agent when you buy or sell a house? Your immediate response might be, "I can do this myself. How hard can it be?" Take it from someone who's been there--unless you have plenty of time and a lot of experience, you could be taking a large risk if you do not seek the help of a professional realtor.

A knowledgeable real estate agent provides home buyers with pertinent information to help them meet their needs in terms of location. The requirements of a family with a ten-year-old child are different from those of a couple with grown children. For one family, the proximity of a reputable school is important. For another family, easy access to services such as banking, grocery stores, and pharmacies is vital.

A professional agent also advises buyers on what they can afford. For example, should a buyer with an annual income of $35,000 be looking at homes in the $90,000 range? An experienced agent advises buyers to spend no more than 2 1/2 times their gross income. The agent also prepares prospective home buyers for the loan application process. Most first-time home buyers are not aware of the amount of paperwork involved.

Once a buyer finds a suitable house, the agent guides the buyer through the transaction by helping to negotiate a price and by putting the buyer in touch with mortgage lenders, contractors, appraisers, inspectors, and insurance agents.

A professional realtor can also save a seller time, money, and frustration. Too often a homeowner seeks the help of a professional only after encountering problems. One seller took 44 hours of unpaid vacation time and spent $350 on advertising, $78.25 on telephone calls, and $865 on maintenance while the house was on the market (a total of $1,293.25 in expenses alone). Additionally, the client experienced a great deal of frustration before engaging a professional realtor.

When enlisting the help of a real estate agent, keep the following points in mind:

1. Ask for references from clients who have recently purchased or sold property.
2. Investigate the community in which you are interested.
3. Deal with a professional agent who has a good reputation.
4. Find out if the company that the realtor represents belongs to the local real estate board.

Chapter 5, Job 5

2

By taking advantage of an agent's experience, access to properties, and knowledge of the local real estate market, home buyers and home sellers alike can avoid the pitfalls inherent in purchasing or marketing their homes.

Chapter 5, Job 5 (cont'd)

Chapter 6, Checkpoint 6-2

a.
Ms. Katrina Ann Dewar
8577 Estate Drive
West Palm Beach, FL 33411-9753

~~SALES PROMOTION~~

Dear ~~Madam~~ Ms. Dewar

b.
Please let me know when we can get together to discuss the property.

~~Very~~ Sincerely Yours,

Miss Donna Raynor

Enclosure

ah

c.
Sincerely
QS
Bradford Liang, Manager

dt

c Celina Walston
Hand Delivered

d.
Sincerely Yours

GLOBAL TRAVEL COMPANY

Mallory Duke

We will put your name in the hat for our monthly drawing.

Enclosures

e.
January 2, 20--
QS
Mr. Dean Sorensen, President
AcuSale Resources Inc.
One Broadway Avenue
Detroit, MI 48215-1842

f.
I am enclosing your copies of the contract with this letter.

Yours truly,

Marlene Sanchez-Dwyer
Director

DS
rim, Enclosures
c Peter Forsythe

g.
Acme Box Company
Attention Customer Service
P.O. Box 1610
Burleson, TX 76028

~~Dear Mr. Driver~~
Ladies and Gentlemen

h.
Offers like these do not happen
SS
every day, so please let us hear

from you soon.

Cordially,

Marsha Stallones
Sales and Marketing director

Chapter 6, Checkpoint 6-3

 June 16, 20--

Ms. Jennifer Elaine Carson
Route 2, Box 507B
Huntsville, AL 35807-8615

PURCHASE ORDER 471

Dear Ms. Carson

Thank you for your order for six reams of antique white stationery, Stock No. 331. The quality of the stationery you have selected will let your customers know that they are important to you.

Because of the recent shipping strike, we have encountered delays in receiving merchandise from the factory. We have been informed that the shipment has been sent, however, and we should receive it within a week. You can expect your order within ten days. We hope this delay will not inconvenience you.

We appreciate the business you have given us in the past, and we look forward to serving you in the future.

Sincerely,
QS
Audrey D. Leapley, Manager
Shipping Department

ec

c R. P. Michaels

Chapter 6, Checkpoint 6-5

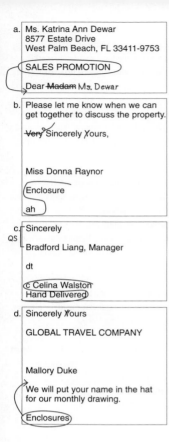

Martindale Publishing

TO:	Associate Editors	**Internal Memorandum**
FROM:	Denise Bright, Executive Editor *db*	
DATE:	April 10, 20--	
SUB:	Production Meetings	

On Monday, April 25, all associate editors should plan to meet in Conference Room C, third floor, at 10 a.m. The purpose of this meeting is to identify topics that are of concern to you as supervisors.

Each of you is a vital member of our editorial team, and your input is essential to keeping production running smoothly during this very heavy copyright year. I will use your input to establish agenda items for future meetings.

Chapter 6, Job 1

PERIN OFFICE SYSTEMS

March 17, 20--
QS
Miss Sandra Mendoza
Phillips and Solomon
31 N. Main St.
Champlain, NY 12919-4300
DS
Dear ~~Mr.~~ Miss Mendoza

Thank you for the opportunity to demonstrate our new DataPhone telephone system at the TeleCom Exhibition last week. As you make your decision on a new system, keep in mind that DataPhone offers the following features:

1. **Speed dialing.** This feature can bring as many as 25 often-called numbers together in one place on the desktop console. By pressing a preprogrammed button, you can place a call in less than 3 seconds. Speed dialing eliminates searching for phone numbers.

2. **Call pickup.** This feature helps to eliminate unanswered calls by allowing anyone to answer a ringing phone.

3. **Conferencing.** This feature provides an easy, convenient way to bring people together without having to travel or even leave their desks.

4. **Call forwarding.** This feature is particularly useful since it allows calls to be forwarded to another extension. A person who is away from his or her desk or in a meeting is never out of reach.

5. **Speaker.** An optional feature, this is an extremely convenient way to talk hands-free, to take notes, or to operate a computer.

Perin Office Systems provides installation and employee training free of charge to companies that purchase the DataPhone system. Call us today to discuss your phone needs.

Sincerely

Ms. Elena E. Suppan
Regional Manager

ri

PERIN OFFICE SYSTEMS

March 17, 20--

Eastman Brothers, Inc.
Attention Project Committee
7861 Monroe Street
Tallahassee, FL 32301-7654

Ladies and
Gentlemen

PRELIMINARY DESIGN REVIEW

Enclosed is a brief report reviewing the preliminary design factors that your project committee should consider when planning the 15,000-square-foot addition to Eastman Brothers' existing facilities.

Stacey Cosentino and her staff will provide complete documentation for these recommendations at the initial planning session on April 7. In the mean time, best wishes as you proceed with your project plans.

Sincerely yours,

Ms. Elena E. Suppan
Reg. Manager

jp

Enclosure

Chapter 6, Job 2

OFFICE DESIGN FACTORS

Eastman Brothers, Inc.

Because office design does affect job performance and job satisfaction, several factors must be considered in the preliminary stages of planning the construction or renovation of any facility. This report discusses these factors and gives recommendations that may decrease absenteeism and increase employees' productivity by as much as 30%.

Work Space

The area where workers spend most of their time is their work space. Factors affecting work-space design are discussed in the following paragraphs.

Enclosures. The open office plan with enclosures, or cubicles, gives workers the privacy they need, supports communication, and improves productivity more than either the fully open or fully closed office plan. To be effective, the partitions surrounding each work area should be higher than standing height on 3 sides.

Floor area. The amount of usable floor space a worker can call his or her own is based on job need and status. According to a survey conducted by Perin Office Systems, the recommended space requirements for various employees are as follows:

Top-level executives	425 square feet
Middle-level executives	305 square feet
Supervisors	200 square feet
Office employees	75–100 square feet

Layout. The physical arrangement (layout) of furniture and walls greatly affects job performance, comfort, status, and ease of communication. Workers should have two good work surfaces and a single entrance. The layout should be such that another worker's work space is not directly visible from any other worker's work space.

Chapter 6, Job 3

2

Lighting

Proper lighting is determined by the quality and quantity of light. Approximately 150 footcandles are recommended for workers who use computers. Most lighting problems are caused by too much light, resulting in glare on documents or reflections on monitors. Although most workers prefer to be near a window, windows do cause glare.

Ambient light fixtures, which illuminate the entire office area, combined with task lighting, which lights specific work surfaces, create the most effective lighting system.

Noise

Office conversations, ringing telephones, and outside noise account for most office noise. Sound-absorbent materials used throughout the building, acoustical enclosures on printers, and layout are effective means of reducing office noise. Office noise should be less than 65 decibels (Canada Safety Council, 1999).

Energy

Energy needs include lines for power, telephones, and data. To determine these needs, the following questions must be answered: Do you expect high growth in computer usage? Do you expect to rearrange workstations frequently? If so, how often?

Access floors raised of the structural slab provide an excellent solution for distributing heat, air conditioning, and wiring for data and telephone services. These floors have unlimited capacity and may be accessed at any point by service units without calling an electrician. Additionally, quality and speed of transmission will not be affected as your transmission needs grow.

Chapter 6, Job 3 (cont'd)

3

REFERENCES

Fishman, Charles. "We've Seen the Future of Work, and It Works, But Very Differently." *Fast Company,* Issue 4, August 1996.

"Noise and Acoustics." Office Health and Safety. 14 Jan. 2000. Canada Safety Council. 26 May 20--. <http://www.safety-council.org/info/OSH/noise.htm>.

Chapter 6, Job 3 (cont'd)

PERIN OFFICE SYSTEMS

March 17, 20--

Please check to be sure that I haven't missed any errors. Mr. Holms prefers the mod. block with indented paragraphs and mixed punct.

Thanks
tr

Mrs. Jessica shimer
2905 Sandcastle Dr.
Tallahassee, FL 32308-9625

Dear Mrs. Shimer:

Thank you for your interest in the Penn Laser Copier, Model 212. Enclosed is a brochure detailing its unique features, particularly its specifications and cost.

The Penn Laser Copier is the most technologically sophisticated copier on the market today. This laser-driven copier uses a scanner to digitize originals. Text (including columns) can be manipulated before printing begins. Because it is digital, the laser copier can transmit images to other printers and produce high-resolution copies in seconds.

After you have had an oportunity to review this brochure, I will give you a call to provide you with additional product or price information or to set up a demonstration. In the meantime, please call me at the number listed below if you have any questions.

Sincerely Yours,

Robin C. Holms, District Sales Representative

tr

Enclosure

Chapter 6, Job 4

TO: All Perin Managers

FROM: Dale Ericson

DATE: (current date)

SUBJECT: Computer Maintenance

Because more and more managers are using computers, each person should establish safe practices for operating and maintaining computers and peripherals. Please review these procedures to keep your equipment in good working order:

1. Keep equipment away from direct sunlight, heat vents, and open windows. Extreme temperatures can damage chips and other components.

2. Keep food and beverages away from equipment and diskettes.

3. Handle CDs with care. Improper use can impair their performance.

4. Keep paper clips that have been stored in a magnetic container away from diskettes. Keep diskettes away from magnets or any electronic equipment. These items contain magnetic fields that can cause portions of data to be erased.

5. Use antistatic mats under your desk area. Static electricity can cause memory loss in your computer.

6. Never oil your printer or any part of your system. Oil will clog the machine.

7. Check that you have sufficient power to run your equipment.

8. Do not take anything apart, even if, in your judgment, you can fix it. Call Helen Mathys (Ext. 278), and she will contact our service representative.

Chapter 6, Job 5

Civic Plaza Building
701 West Jefferson Street
Louisville, KY 40202-4161
502.555.0120
www.louisvillechamber.org

Louisville Chamber of Commerce

WELCOME, ROSE SOCIETY MEMBERS

A gracious welcome awaits you and the other 2,500 (or 2500) Rose Society members and guests who will be attending the Society's convention in Louisville. This meeting is the second Society meeting to be held here. the Society first met in Louisville 16 (or sixteen) years ago. Both the organization and the city were was a bit younger and smaller then.

Louisville, one of Kentucky's fun-filled vacation cities, is located right on the northern edge of Southern hospitality. You'll find Louisville has a lot of things going for it—attractions such as the Kentucky Center for the Arts on the riverfront; turn-of-the-century neighborhoods offering boutiques and restaurants; and Churchill Downs, home of the Ky. Derby. In addition, great food and shopping are around every corner. Everyone who comes to Louisville finds something interesting.

No ital
Maps and brochures high lighting points of interest are included in your registration packet. We hope that your stay in Louisville will be enjoyable and that you will visit our city again.

Chapter 7, Job 1

To: June Fejes <jfejes@netline.com>
From: Alexis McQuillan <mcquillan@louisvillechamber.com>
Subject: Louisville Zoo
cc   :x-Attachment: LZG_map.jpg   LZG_rate.doc

Dear Ms. Fejes:

We are delighted to send you the information you requested about the Louisville Zoological Garden.

From the map on the attached document, you can see that the zoo is divided into 5 areas. Each of the areas offers a unique and rewarding natural experience. Something is available for every member of the family to enjoy. This month two Komodo dragons and a baby giraffe are the special attractions.

On the attached rate list, you will note that preschool children and senior citizens are admitted free. Note, too, there are always group rates available.

The zoo operates on a daily schedule throughout the year. The zoo staff maintains an informative web site, updated daily, that you might also like to visit. Log on to www. louisvillechamber.org.

Stop by our office to pick up a pamplet that describes the zoo and contains a coupon good for a $5.00 discount on one adult day pass. We hope you will be able to use it soon.

Sincerely,
Alexis J. McQuillan
Louisville Chamber of Commerce
Department of Tourism

Chapter 7, Job 2

Civic Plaza Building
701 West Jefferson Street
Louisville, KY 40202-4161
502.555.0120
www.louisvillechamber.org

Louisville Chamber of Commerce

February 10, 20--

Mrs. Alita Guitterez, President
National Sales Company, Inc.
3910 Trade Street
Louisville, KY 40206-5133

Dear Mrs. Guitterez:

Welcome to Louisville! We don't think we exagerate when we say that Louisville is a *great* place to do business.

As a member of the business community, you are eligible for membership in the Louisville Chamber of Commerce. On the first Tuesday of each month, we have a breakfast meeting to which each new businessman and businesswoman are invited. This meeting provides an opportunity for us to get to know one another. Each 3d Tuesday we have a dinner and a and a business meeting at the Arbor Inn.

We hope your schedule will permit you to attend the next dinner meeting, which will be at Timmon's Restarant on the 6th at 7:30 p.m. The Hospitality Committee are in in charge of this function if you can attend, please call 555-0120.

To welcome you as a new member of the business community, we plan to include a feature about your company in the next issue of our newsletter. Since you are more knowledgeable about your company than we are, we would like you to submit an article of about 500 (or five hundred) words giving an explanation of your company's services and/or products. To meet our printing deadline. We need the material by March 25th.

Again, welcome to our city!

Very truly yours,

Clyde Shepherd
Director of Public Relations

tr

Chapter 7, Job 3

June 11, 20--

Miss Ruth Niemer, Director
Convention Housing Bureau
U.S. Chamber of Commerce
P.O. Box 54321
Des Moines, IA 50318-4126

Dear Miss Niemer:

Don Jenkins, our president, and I are planning to attend the U.S. Chamber of Commerce Convention in your city, August 20-25.

Since the number of rooms reserved for this convention is limited, we want to make our reservations now. Both of us need single rooms. We would like to have adjoining rooms, if possible. We would prefer to stay at the convention hotel; however, if it is not available, either the Plaza or the Palmer Hotel is all right.

There are a number of Louisville Chamber members planning to attend. We plan to arrange a breakfast gathering on Wednesday morning, the 23rd. Can you forward information from the convention hotel on catering options? Don Jenkins or I hope to begin making those arrangements early next week.

Thank you for your help.

Sincerely yours,

Allen Keen
Director of Economic Development

xx

Chapter 7, Job 4

Virginia State College

989 Johnstown Road
Chesapeake, VA 23320-4961

January 10, 20--

Mr. Greg Washington
4572 East Ninth Street
Chesapeake, Va 23320-4572

Dear Mr. Washington

Your request for readmission to Virginia State College as a psycology major has been reviewed by members of the Admissions Committee and I at our January 8 meeting.

After the 3d semester a a student must have earned 36 hours, and he must have a grade point average (GPA) of 1.80 to remain in school.

You was enrolled for three semesters 2 years ago. During that time you earned 27 hours with a gpa of 1.67. Consequently, readmission is not possible at this time.

We recommend that you attend summer school as a nonmatriculated student. If you do so, you must take 2 3-hour courses that are relevant to your major area of study. If you receive a grade of C or better in each of these courses, the committee and I will be happy to reconsider you petition for readmission as an psycology major.

Sincerely yours

Douglas W. Wrenn
Associate Dean

rv

Chapter 8, Job 1

Virginia State College

MEMO

TO: All Faculty

FROM: Brianne Layman, Dean

DATE: January 10, 20--

SUBJECT: Computer Requirements for Incoming Students

Associate Dean Douglas Wrenn and I have undertaken a study of computer use on campus. Our findings, which you can read in full at www.virginiastatecollege.edu/deansoffice/, leads us to recommend that all incoming, full-time students be required to own a computer. We recognize the potential burden this may place on some students. However, we feel responsible for acknowledging the permanent position technology plays in our lives and in the lives of our students.

Several other schools in the state have already instituted this requirement for incoming students. Our neighbors, Lafayette College and St. Martin's, began requiring students to have computers 2 years ago. Administrators at both schools, who I have consulted, said the plan met with very little criticism. Faculty, in particular, appreciates the fact that students no longer have to rely on campus computer labs and their hours.

A task force is being formed to address the minimum requirements of the computer systems and to study options for offering computer systems to students at a discount. Both Lafayette and St. Martin's has agreements with local vendors that allow a 10-20% student discount. The only requirement is that they have the ability to communicate with the college network.

Your feedback is welcome. You may direct it to Douglas Wrenn or myself. In addition, we would like one faculty member from each discipline to serve on the task force. You taking the time to offer your input will be time well spent on an issue that will help place our students in the forefront of their educational fields.

rv

Chapter 8, Job 2

Virginia State College

MEMO

TO: Department Chairmen~~s~~

FROM: Brianne Layman, Dean

DATE: January 10, 20--

SUBJECT: Parking Regulations

In an effort to improve staff parking conditions, the Campus Traffic Committee ~~have~~ has developed the following parking regulations. Please see that all members of your department receives this information regarding the new regulations.

1. All of the current campus parking permits expire on August 14. As of August ~~15~~ 15 staff members are required to have a valid parking permit for the new school year.

2. Staff parking is allowed only in designated areas. Staff ~~is~~ are not allowed to park in areas designated for student parking.

~~3.~~ Permanant~~e~~ permits must be displayed in the rear window of all vehicles.

~~4.~~ Any staff member in possession of more than 5 unpaid parking tickets will forfeit ~~his or her~~ ~~their~~ right to park on campus.
(or staff members ... their rights)

My thanks go especially to Officer Gonzalez, who has been keenly aware of the numerous parking problems and whom played a significant role on the Campus Traffic Committee. In fact, it was ~~him~~ he who suggested that the committee be formed. Officer Gonzalez will continue to monitor parking conditions on campus.

rv

Chapter 8, Job 3

Return-Path: BLayman@virginiastatecollege.edu
From: BLayman@virginiastatecollege.edu
Date: Wed, 12 January 20-- 09:14:06 EDT
Subject: RE: Internship Program
To: rschindler@virginiastatecollege.edu

Rosemary,

I was talking with my friend Stuart Steinman last week, and he gave me an idea. What if the college developed an internship program with several area businesses? It would give our students real, practical experience in their chosen fields. At the same time, the businesses would benefit from the services our students provide, as well as from the students' ideas and enthusiasm.

Areas that might lend themselves to internship programs include information management systems, software development, graphic design, and CAD/CAM. Can you think of others?

Here are three people who want to help.
Stuart Steinman, Learning Design Co.
Manny Santos, OTC Systems
Constance Clark-Powers, City Concepts
Also, the Board of Directors would be a good source of contacts.

Following are some questions we would need to answer, probably with the help of the businesspeople involved:
1. What time requirements do businesses have? Is six months long enough? Do internships need to be a year?
2. How many hours per week are feasible for students?
3. Should internships be offered only to seniors?

I'm sure there are a dozen other questions, Rosemary, but these are the ones that popped into my head. Let's sit down and talk about this next week. Let me know when you're available.

Thank you.
Brianne

Chapter 8, Job 4

Return-Path: Marcos Ortez <ortezm@ridgehillsre.com>
From: hartsell@ridgehillsre.com
Date: 12 February 20-- 09:27:50 EDT
Subject: Newton Township new Listing
To: roberts@ridgehillsre.com, hodge@ridgehillsre.com, landaverde@ridgehillsre.com
CC:

Asad, Carla, and Maribel,

I wanted to let you know we got the Cheney property in Newton Township. I assured Mr. Cheney that my best agents would handle his property. He is ~~anxious~~ eager to sell but wants to hold out on his asking price for at least six months before he considers lowering it. I counseled him to be more willing to bargain, but he insists his temperment~~a~~ is such that he would rather wait for the right price than to sell to~~o~~ soon. He says he knows what the land is worth, and that's the amount he wants.

I advise~~s~~ each of you to walk Mr. Cheney's property. It's 50 acres, so wear your hiking shoes. Get a map of the lot divisions from ~~myself~~ me before you go. If you can envision where the best home ~~sights~~ sites are on each lot, it will be easier to help ~~perspective~~ prospective buyers see the possibilities.

Mr. Cheney is our fi~~r~~st client in this section of the county. Marketing his property open~~s~~ the door to other clients in the area. Let's make a good showing since this is a valua~~e~~ble opportunity. Jake will be putting the signs up this afternoon. All three of your telephone numbers are on the signs. You might want to walk the property yet this week, before you start rec~~ei~~ving calls. I expect this property to move fairly quickly.

Good luck.

Marcos

Chapter 9, Job 1

3168 NORTHWOOD DRIVE
RUSTON, LA 71270-6653
318-555-0190
www.ridgehillsre.com

Feb~~u~~ruary 19, 20--

Miss Bethany Whitley
Plant Manager
Toggs Manufacturing Co.
P.O. Box 7022
Indianapolis, IN 46208-9865

Dear Miss Whitley:

The ~~one hundred~~ 100-acre site on Five Mile R~~d~~d. you considered for your new plant is still available. The owners have al~~l~~ready rejected some offers, but new circumstances have made the owners ~~anxious~~ eager to sell. I believe they are prepared to ~~except~~ accept the offer that you and ~~me~~ I discussed.

If you still wish to obtain this property, I suggest that you submit a~~n~~ offer immediat~~e~~ly. Interest rates are not likely to decrease any more this year. In fact, ~~it is~~ they are likely to increase.

Remember, the owners are insisting on a cash transaction. As a prerequisit~~e~~, I would suggest that you obtain advi~~c~~se from legal ~~council~~ counsel regau~~r~~ding ~~about~~ the best way to finance the ~~principle~~ principal loan and to handle the transfer. Please call me to discuss your plans about this matter.

Sincerely yours,

Marcos Ortez
General Manager

yn

Chapter 9, Job 2

RIDGE HILLS REAL ESTATE

3168 NORTHWOOD DRIVE
RUSTON, LA 71270-6653
318-555-0190
www.ridgehillsre.com

INTEROFFICE MEMORANDUM

DS

TO: All Personnel
FROM: Marcos Ortez
DATE: July 14, 20--
SUBJECT: Congratulations

Please join me in congratulating Maribel Landaverde, who has received the Louisiana Realtors' Association salesperson-of-the-Year award. Maribel's performance this passed year has certainly been deserving of recognition. I am proud that the Association choose her for the award.

Maribel has been with Ridge Hills Real Estate for nine years. During that time she has increased her sales by at least 14 percent each year. The year Maribel started, she broke the company's sales records for a first-year agent. Taking a wider perspective, Maribel's performance has a positive affect on the whole company. Her drive and enthuziasm inspire all of us. In addition, her award brings attention to the company from all over the state.

Thank you, Maribel, for your outstanding work. We are proud to be your colleagues.

yn

Chapter 9, Job 3

TO: Jill Carmichael, Advertising Manager

FROM: Marcos Ortez, General Manager

DATE: February 27, 20--

SUBJECT: Review of Advertising Costs from 2002 to 2004

The attached table shows a comparison of our advertising costs for the past three years. Will you please look at the costs to see where we can reduce expenses without adversely affecting our business. Regardless, I am all ready to shave the budget wherever possible.

Please consider which of our advertising methods is the most effective. The costs for all accounts except television and newspapers appear to have increased 50 percent or more during this time. Is there one among them that really is not producing very well? Should we consider spending fewer dollars in one area and more dollars in another? If so, please recommend which ones need to be omitted and which, if any, need to be increased.

I always appreciate your perspective on our budget. May I have your comments by March 20. Thanks.

xx

Attachment

ADVERTISING COSTS 2002 through 2004			
	2002	**2003**	**2004**
Television	$14,795.72	$15,947.50	$19,588.52
Radio	870.08	1,180.12	1,409.61
Newspapers	11,096.79	12,785.63	14,589.70
Homebuyer's Guide	2,292.18	2,933.88	3,885.12
Circulars	3,597.28	4,672.30	5,047.90
Miscellaneous	641.20	769.44	961.80
Total	**$33,293.25**	**$38,288.87**	**$45,482.65**

Chapter 9, Job 4

Mercado Travel Agency

November 5, 20--

Mrs. Nyela Weiss
1166 Norwood Street
Cleveland, OH 44197-8032

Dear Mrs. Weiss

Thank you for your letter requesting brochures, price lists and information sheets about cruises leaving from Miami, FL. Your inquiry comes at a time when a number of interesting exotic cruises are available at fabulously low prices.

You should receive up-to-date information within the next few days from three cruise lines about their winter cruises. When you are making a choice, consider each line's total cost the cost of air travel to the point of departure, and the itinerary. As you will see prices for a seven-day cruise range from $1195 to $3,150 per person.

The enclosed brochure provides helpful information about choosing a cruise. After you make your decision about the cruise, fill out and return the data sheet. You can then leave everything in our hands and rest assured that satisfactory arrangements will be made.

We look forward to serving as you laison to the cruise line of your choice.

Sincerely

Miss Cassandra E. Spellman
Marketing Manager

dp

Enclosures

Chapter 10, Job 1

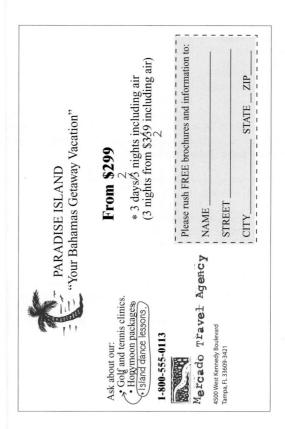

Chapter 10, Job 2

CHOOSING THE RIGHT CRUISE FOR YOU

As the winter cruise season approaches, discounts on ship fares are plentiful. Smart consumers are taking advantage of the special bargains. Now is the time to consider taking a leisurely cruise. It may fulfill a lifetime dream for you? If you have never pictured yourself as a passenger on a cruise ship, consider the following facts:

Passenger Profile

Once cruises were a pastime for the rich and the retired. Today cruises are taken by individuals from all walks of life and all income levels. Forty-eight percent of cruise passengers now earn less than $40,000 a year. Nearly half are under forty-five years of age, and ten percent are under twenty-five.

More than a million and a half people will take cruises on about one hundred cruise ships this year and cruise lines are competitively vying for this business. Two qualities of the cruise experience are being stressed: value and convenience. Now is a great time to participate in what some refer to as the "cruise revolution."

Cost and Convenience

Consider the price of the average cruise. The price that you pay includes accomodations, baggage handling, meals, entertainment (including first-run movies and live performances), room service, daily activities ranging from computer lessons to aerobics classes, travel to any number of ports and reduced round-trip airfare to and from the port city.

Convenience is another factor that you must consider as you contemplate taking a cruise. In what other way can you travel from one country to another without having to unpack and repack your bags? Where else can you spend days or weeks without having to open your wallet or purse constantly? And you don't have to worry about arranging travel schedules, making plane reservations, or waiting long hours in airports.

Activities on Board

So that a cruise meets your expectations, you should take time to find out what various cruise lines offers and to who they cater. For example, some cruise lines cater to families with children and make special provisions for them. Other lines cater only to adults. Some provide for academic pursuits, while others provide primarily entertainment and recreation.

Give some thought to the types of activities that you enjoy. Do you want entertainment? Do you want physical fitness programs? Do you want to learn something? At least one cruise ship regularly doubles as a floating university. There is no pressure to participate in any of the activities provided by the cruise line. If you wish, you can relax on deck with a book or watch television in your own cabin. You can choose your own recreation.

Some passengers desire the traditional dining room experience where guests dress in formal attire. Others prefer a more relaxed dining atmosphere where casual dress is all right. Both tastes can be accomodated on today's cruises.

Cruise Itinerary

Another important criterion that will affect your selection of a cruise is the planned itinerary of the ship. Consider the number of stops the ship will make and the ports you can visit. Are there particular cities you have always wanted to tour? Your travel agent can provide you with a detailed list of port choices and itinerary options to help you decide on the best cruise.

How to Get Started

After you have made some of the major decisions regarding your preferences in a cruise see your travel agent. The agent can help determine which cruise suits your specific needs and provide answers to any other questions that you might have. In other words, your travel agent is the liaison between you and the cruise line. Contact your travel agent today and take the worry out of traveling.

From: cspellman@mercadotravel.com
Date: 20 November 20--
Subject: Group Travel to Orlando
To: pzhon@linderschools_k12.edu
CC:

Dear Ms. Zhon,

Yes we can help you and your students arrange a trip to Orlando for the Business Professionals of America convention in May. We will be able to book flight arrangements and hotel accommodations with special group discounts. We can also arrange for car or van rental during your stay or provide you with information regarding Orlando's mass transit system.

As soon as I receive answers to the following questions I will be able to plan your trip, giving you accurate and helpful information.

1. Date of trip (departing date and returning date)
2. Number of adults and number of students who need air travel
3. Number of adults and number of students per room
4. Preferred mode of transportation in Orlando

Remember airline tickets will cost more if your itinerary needs to be changable. The more definite we can make the plans, the less money you and your students will need to spend.

I look forward to working with you to plan this fun trip to a very friendly, fun city.

Cassandra E. Spellman
Marketing Manager

TO:	Mercado Agents
FROM:	Cassandra Spellman
DATE:	November 8, 20--
SUBJECT:	The Cruise Season

Welcome to Cruise Season! This promises to be our busiest season yet. Is everyone geared up for a couple of busy months?

As the cruise season nears we will receive more and more inquiries from prospective clients. To help you relate to these callers, I have posted a national weather map in the office. I will update it daily. Please check it each morning to see what is happening in the rest of the world. In particular check Michigan, Ohio, Indiana, Illinois and Wisconsin, where we've done our heaviest marketing.

Remember, there is an extra 10 percent discount for the Bahamian cruises. Be sure to present this as extra incentive but do not neglect the other cruise packages. Those discounted cruises have fewer frills than the others, so make sure callers understand the differences.

Finally, as a special incentive just for our agents, Mrs. Mercado has reserved a deluxe two-person cabin on a ten-day cruise to Tahiti. The reservation will be transferred to the agent who books the most cruise clients between December 1 and February 27. Wouldn't you look good in that cabin? Good luck!

DISCOVER YOUR PLACE IN THE GARDENS

If you haven't seen Colonial Gardens yet you are in for a treat. Discover the natural wonder of 10,000 acres of lakes, woodlands, gardens, and wildlife. Enjoy golf on our 18-hole, par-73 championship course. Take advantage of all the extras Colonial has to offer: tennis, swimming, nature trails, riverboat rides, and fishing.

All 210 of our rooms at the Colonial Inn have waterfront or forest views, private balconies, and comfortable furnishings. If you're planning a meeting, put us in your plans. We have more than 11,000 square feet of meeting space. You also can enjoy our charming cottages or romantic villas.

Colonial. It's for families, couples, and friends. It's for people who appreciate nature's beauty.

Call 1-800-555-0107 for reservations or information.

Chapter 11, Job 1

State of Georgia
Department of Tourism

7653 Peachtree Road, NE
Atlanta, GA 30308-9873
www.state_of_georgia.com

20-- CALENDAR OF EVENTS
SOUTHEAST GEORGIA

March

| 10–17 | St. Patrick's Day Celebration Dublin Bobbie Whitehead | 478/555-0197 |

April

| 26–27 | Harness Festival Hawkinsville Dana Morrow | 478/555-0130 |
| 14–28 | Dogwood Festival Jessup Kita Hagino | 912/555-0192 |

May

| 10–24 | Vidalia Onion Festival Vidalia Lewis Green | 912/555-0111 |

June

| 14–28 | Blueberry Festival Alma Deweese Arnold | 912/555-0158 |

July

| 4 | Fantastic Fireworks Extravaganza 4th Dublin Andre Southern | 478/555-0144 |

October

| 6 | Great Pumpkin Festival Cochran Joann Keena | 478/555-0163 |
| 27 | Georgia Sweet Potato Festival Ocila Gail Madigan-Boggs | 229/555-0185 |

Chapter 11, Job 2

State of Georgia
Department of Tourism

7653 Peachtree Road, NE
Atlanta, GA 30308-9873
www.state_of_georgia.com

August 4, 20--

Ms. Gladys McCoy, Director
Macon Tourism and Trade
410 Riverside Drive
Macon, GA 31204-3798

Dear Ms. McCoy:

(or We are)
We're getting ready to publish next year's addition of *Georgia—A Peach of a State*. You undoubtedly will want to provide updated copy for our article on central Georgia.

Please provide current information (avoid repetition of last year's material) on planned activities, festivals, and so on, on the enclosed form by September 30th so that we can incorporate your ideas into next year's publication and calendar of events.

Will Macon participate as usual in "Georgia Days," which will be held at Cumberland Square in Atlanta from June 17–21 of next year? Please use the enclosed form to submit your registration and exhibit needs so that we can reserve appropriate space for you.

I understand you had record attendance at the Cherry Jubilee Street Party last month. Congratulations on the excellent job you do in organizing and motivating your volunteers.

Sincerely

Carter B. Tamara
Associate Commissioner for Tourism
State of Georgia

sj

Enclosures

Chapter 11, Job 3

COASTAL GEORGIA

The coastal area of the state holds charms that will entice the visitor to return. Savannah, with its combination of European architecture, historic sights, meandering streets, and lush foliage, is the beginning of Georgia's 100 miles of coastline. A busy port city on the Savannah River, Savannah was founded 257 years ago as England's last colony in the New World.

An hour's drive south of Savannah is the port city of Brunswick and the more southern resort islands. First laid out in 1771, Brunswick is now a modern port handling sea tonnage from the world over. Fascinating (and beautiful) Victorian architecture is represented in all its glory here. Roads from Brunswick lead to four islands known as "golden" for their sunny skies and warm sands nearly year-round.

St. Simons Island has lush resorts, vacation condos, horse stables, marinas, tennis courts, golf courses, boutiques, art galleries, and interesting restaurants. The quaint village boasts a community park and fishing pier. The view of Jekyll Island—not to mention the Atlantic Ocean—is well worth the climb up the historic 1872 lighthouse.

Sea Island lies across a thin strip of marsh; its fame is rooted in the easy affluence and elegance of the Gilded Age. A focal point is The Cloister, one of the country's enduring grand resort hotels.

Jekyll Island, formerly the vacation spot for some of America's wealthiest families, evokes the quiet feeling that time has stopped and history has been preserved. Leisure-time pursuits include biking and jogging, pier and deep-sea fishing, tennis, and water skiing.

Cumberland Island, 16 miles long, is one of the world's largest barrier islands. With outstanding scenic qualities, Cumberland offers natural wildlife, backpacking, and camping.

Chapter 11, Job 4

Chapter 12, Job 1

Date: Thur, 11 Jan 20-- 08:32:27
Subject: Feedback
To: Elaina Gooding <egooding@sfanet.com>
CC: eugene@dhscc.netlinx.com

Mrs. Gooding:

Thank you so much for your feedback on the programs you attended here at Diamond Hills Senior Community Center. Our aim is to please.

With regard to your question about continuing Computer Education, I am glad to report that there will be several opportunities starting in April. Though we are still working on the schedule, we are sure we will be offering the following courses:

Computing 237: I'm Finally on the Internet—Now What do I do?
Computing 242: Family research on the Internet
Computing 243: Advanced Family Research on The Internet

Finally, your comment about access to the building is well taken. I have spoken to the facilities manager, who has agreed to keep the Diamond Street Entrance open. This entrance, which has no stairs and provides easier access to the Elevator, will be accessible during all day and evening classes. I have posted a notice on the front door to inform all DHSCC members of this alternate entrance. I apologize for your trouble with the Addison street entrance.

Thank you for your interest in our Programs and for helping us make DHSCC a better place.

Sameera Dharia, Director
Diamond Hills Senior Community Center

Chapter 12, Job 1

Chapter 12, Job 2

397 ADDISON STREET
SAN FRANCISCO, CA 94131-3507
415-555-0126
WWW.DHSCC.COM

January 13, 20--

VOLUNTEER OPPORTUNITIES

Volunteerism is an important part of our community, especially for seniors. Therefore, many of our Diamond Hills Seniors are very active in volunteer activities. Their involvement ranges from a few hours a month to a few hours a day. If you haven't yet found your volunteering niche, consider these opportunities. See Micki in the main office for telephone nos and other contact information for each of these Organizations:

Organization	Types Of Volunteer Duties Or Tasks
American Red Cross—Local Chapters	Assist with blood drives in the Bloodmobile; fill out paperwork; answer phones; oversee general office duties.
Community Partners For Youth	Meet with a local youth whose interests are matched to yours to provide companionship, mentoring, and friendship.
Children's hospital	Read to or play games with children; hold and/or feed babies; run errands for parents of hospitalized children; entertain siblings of hospitalized children.
San Francisco Bay National Wildlife Refuge	Greet visitors; conduct tours of the Andersen nature center; perform general office work (computer knowledge required).
Elder Abuse Prevention	Answer Crisis lines; provide counseling (training provided); assemble mailings; perform general office duties.
Literacy Alliance—South Bay	Tutor illiterate adults (training and materials provided).
Meals On Wheels of San Francisco	Deliver midday and/or evening meals to shut-ins (every effort is made to match volunteers with clients in the same neighborhood).
San Francisco Bay Girl Scouts Council	Support a Brownie or Girl Scout troop by conducting a special class, chaperoning outings, or assisting with arts and crafts projects.

Chapter 12, Job 2

Chapter 12, Job 3

397 ADDISON STREET
SAN FRANCISCO, CA 94131-3507
415-555-0126
WWW.DHSCC.COM

January 20, 20--

Ms. Julia Gorham
San Francisco Bay Girl Scouts
538 North 152d Avenue
San Francisco, CA 94188-6242

Dear Ms. Gorham:

As you and I thought would happen, we had many Diamond Hills seniors respond to our call for volunteers, which we posted a week ago. About a dozen senior women wish to volunteer with the San Francisco Bay girl scouts. I would like to invite you to come to Diamond Hills to speak to this group of volunteers.

In particular, these women have questions about how to chaperoning outings. They need to feel comfortable with the rules and guidelines of the Girl Scouts Organization. The arts and crafts will be a pleasure for these women, as most of them spend a great deal of time working on crafts. In fact, several of the women recently constructed a miniature dollhouse and are now working on its furnishing. They thought the girls might be interested in a project such as this.

Many of the women who are interested in volunteering were once Girl Scouts themselves, and they expressed gratitude for the role the Girl Scouts played in their lives. I am happy that Diamond Hills can coordinate a volunteer effort between our seniors and the San Francisco Bay Girl Scouts.

Would you be able to speak to our volunteers next Tuesday or thursday? If not, we will do our best to accommodate your schedule. I look forward to hearing from you.

Sincerely Yours,
Sameera Dharia

QS

Chapter 12, Job 3

Chapter 12, Job 4

Winter Schedule

DHSCC Course Offerings

January 3—March 30

(All classes last for two hours unless otherwise noted. All classes are held at DHSCC unless otherwise noted. Meeting rooms may change. call to confirm.)

Course	Time	Fee (if any)	Room
Arts 277: Flower Arranging	Wednesday 10:30	$12.00	134
Arts 427: Hand Papermaking	Wednesday 3–6	$15	130
Arts 428: Advanced Papermaking	Wednesday 6–9	$22	130 ~~122~~
Computing 101: Why Do I Need A Computer?	Tuesday 8:00 Wednesday 12:00 Friday 2:00	--	222
Computing 102: Buying a Computer	Tuesday 10:30 Wednesday 2	--	222
Computing 103: Setting up and Hooking up	by appointment		
Computing 210: Why Do I Need the Internet?	Tuesday 12 Thursday 4	--	216
Cooking 111: Cooking For One	Monday 10:30 Thursday 6	$35	DHSCC kitchen
Cooking 118: Recipes to Freeze and Eat Later	Monday 10:03	$35	DHSC kitchen
Cooking 208: Canning and Preserving—Modern and Simple	Tuesday 2	$40	DHSCC kitchen

Chapter 12, Job 4

Andy Breyer's
Mountain Dulcimer Instruction

Arts 510: Beginning Mountain Dulcimer I

Have you ever wondered if the mountain dulcimer is the instrument for you? In
this eight-week course, you will learn the fundamentals of tuning and playing this
sweet-sounding instrument. Through folk songs and lively fiddle tunes, you will
be introduced to many different types of playing techniques. If you do not already
own an instrument, a limited number of rentals are available through J. C. at
Rockwell Music by calling 415-555-0139. Please bring a cassette recorder and
blank audiotape to the first class.

Cost: $70

Time: Wednesday, 7–9 p.m.

Duration: Eight weeks, January 4 through February 22

Location: Room 170, Diamond Hills Senior Community Center, 397 Addison Street, San
Francisco, CA 94131

Arts 511: Beginning Mountain Dulcimer II

Expand your horizons and continue your exploration of the mountain dulcimer.
Learn to play ballads and other haunting melodies in a variety of different keys.
Beginning Mountain Dulcimer I or some other background in playing the
dulcimer is recommended. See above for rental information.

Cost: $70

Time: Tuesday, 7–9 p.m.

Duration: Eight weeks, January 4 through February 22

Location: Room 170, Diamond Hills Senior Community Center, 397 Addison
Street, San Francisco, CA 94131

Chapter 12, Job 5

B&B Supply Company
P.O. Box 5314
Phoenix, AZ 20721-8011

INVOICE

TOPS
909 South 35th Street, NW
Seattle, Washington 98121-1974
Phone (564)555-0191   Fax (564)555-0141

Date: August 15, 20--

Order No.: LA19284

Shipped By: UPS

3

Terms: 2/10, n/20

Quantity		Description	Unit Price	Total
1		Print cartridge	26.50 ~~24.95~~	26.50 ~~24.95~~
5	boxes	3½-inch ~~Zip~~ diskettes	68.00 ~~41.95~~	340.00 ~~209.75~~
6	boxes	T-III manila file folders	8.79	52.74
12	reams	G-P dual-purpose paper, 20 lb	5.25	63.00
12	reams	G-P copier paper, 20 lb	6.65	79.80
12	rolls	Magnetic tape, 1/2 inch	1.89	22.68
5	doz	Express pens, violet ink	9.12	45.60
1		Tape dispenser	5.45	5.45 ~~583.97~~ 635.77

Chapter 13, Job 1

TRAVEL EXPENSE REPORT

Travel Authorization No.

239407

Employee Name							I.D. Number				
Rebecca D. Chou							T6103				

Destination							Date(s)				
Portland, Oregon							8/25/-- to 8/27/--				

Purpose of Trip

AMS meeting; meeting with managers of TOPS

Date	From To	Miles	Transportation Amount	Air	Taxi	Meals	Lodging	Total
8/25	Seattle/ Portland	129	45 15	--	--	22 50	80 00	147 65
8/26	Travel within Portland	165	57 65 ~~7~~	--	--	53 20 ~~7~~	80 00	191 45 ~~190 85~~
8/27	Portland/ Seattle	129	45 15	--	--	16 55 ~~25~~	--	61 70
Totals			148 05 ~~147 95~~			92 75 ~~82 95~~	160 00	400 80 ~~390 98~~

Signature _____

Date   8/29/--

Total Expenses
(Attach Receipts) $~~390.98~~ 400 80

Chapter 13, Job 2

TOPSTOPS

(Temporary Office Personnel Services)
909 South 35th Street, NW
Seattle, Washington 98121-1974
Phone (564)555-0191   Fax (564)555-0141

August 21, 20--

Mrs. Mazie Dunstan
2001 King Alfred Drive
Tacoma, WA 98411-0045

Dear Mazie

At last week's meeting you stated that your goal was to make sure that our temporary office personnel
stand out above all the rest. You said that you wanted the hallmark of TOPS personnel to be their
excellent communication skills. Think about the following idea for how we can accomplish this goal.

We should provide training in proofreading and editing for our temps. As you know, 93% of the temps
we place in offices produce letters, memos, and reports while out on assignment. Marketing our temps
as "trained in proofreading" would be a terrific angle. I made a few calls and found that none of the other
temp agencies in the Seattle area provide training in proofreading.

For training material, I suggest we use a book from South-Western Educational Publishing entitled The
Basics of Proofreading. The text contains 15 chapters and is written for either classroom instruction or
individualized training. I found Chapter 9 dealing with format issues to be especially useful.

We could offer the class as an independent study or we could coordinate classes at one of the branch
offices in the evenings. If this recommendation is implemented, the payoff in our temps' productivity
and accuracy would well worth the cost of the books and training. After all, 90 percent is a large number
of temps who need these skills.   ? 90 or 93 ?

I am eager to hear what you think; please contact me when you have time to discuss this idea.

Sincerely

Hugh Ireland
Seattle Branch Manager

plp

Chapter 13, Job 3

TELEWORK: MYTH AND REALITY

Television commercials depict them—"successful-looking" 30-somethings in spotless, sun-filled urban homes working at computers while their youngsters play contentedly in the next room. That is someone's version of a teleworker. But is it a realistic version? And could this be the life for you?

Telework: A Definition

Teleworking, as opposed to telecommuting, means "using telecommunications to work wherever you need to in order to satisfy client needs." This distinction is made by the International Telework Association & Council (ITAC). The organization's mission is to educate employers and employees alike about the benefits of telework.

Myths Debunked

Teleworking is not about answering the phone in your pajamas. Nor is it about being a full-time parent *and* a full-time employee at the same time. Teleworking does not mean that someone is less ambitious, devoted, or dedicated to his or her job. It just means that he or she chooses, with employer support, to put in some productive work time away from the office.

Realities of Telework

Teleworking does allow full-time employees greater flexibility in their work schedules, which appeals to many parents. In fact, a research study titled "Telework America 2000" revealed that the average home teleworker is in his or her early forties. Those who choose to telework—and who apply the concept appropriately (see myths, above)—find that their productivity increases sharply. One local fire chief recorded an increase of 20 percent when he decided to stay home, away from interruptions, to write his incident reports. In other words he cut his report-writing time by 20 percent. When ITAC preaches telework, "productivity" is its main campaign slogan.

Is Telework Right for Any Employee and Any Company?

No. Some jobs require interaction—they require workers to be in the same room with each other. Those same workers might do other tasks, though, that require concentration and uninterrupted work time. Such tasks are ideal for telework.

Chapter 13, Job 4

Not every person is right for telework either. An employee must have adequate job skills and be self-motivated. An employee must also have a home setting that allows him or her to perform any and all necessary tasks. That usually means having a computer, a modem, an Internet connection, and other basic office supplies.

Is Telework Right for You?

If you crave human contact or if you thrive on personal interaction at work, whether for social or professional reasons, then teleworking might not be for you. On the other hand, if you long for a few hours when the phone does not interrupt you, then teleworking might be just what you need.

REFERENCES

"Telecommuting (or Telework): Alive and Well or Fading Away?" *International Telework Association & Council*. 1 Aug. 2001 <http://www.telecommute.org/aboutitac/alive.shtm>.

"Telework America (TWA) 2000: Research Results." *International Telework Association & Council*. 1 Aug. 2001 <http://www.telecommute.org/twa2000/research_results_summary.shtml>.

Chapter 13, Job 4 (cont'd)

RICHARDS & ARMON
Attorneys at Law
One Radisson Square, Suite 1500
Houston, Texas 77022-3626   richardsarmonlaw.com
Telephone (713)555-0103   Fax (713)555-0151

[insert date]

[insert applicant's name and address]

Thank you for your interest in a position at Richards & Armon.

[paragraph A]
We have reviewed your résumé and are impressed with your credentials. Although you are ~~Despite the fact that~~ very well qualified for an administrative assistant position with our firm, ~~at this point in time~~ (or at this time) we are completely staffed. We will keep your application in our current files for the next three months. If a position opens within that time, we will contact you to arrange an interview. If you do not hear from us, you may apply with us again after the three-month period.

[paragraph B]
We have reviewed your résumé and note that while you have [insert number of years] years of [insert specific type of experience or just say "office"] experience, you lack training or education specific to a legal office. We highly recommend the legal office training program at the Houston School of Technology (HST). HST offers day and evening classes in legal terminology, transcription, and legal office technology. The legal office program at HST also coordinates internships for its students so they can begin working in a legal office and gain valuable experience. ~~As a matter of fact,~~ we have hired ~~Houston School of Technology~~ HST internship students. Obtaining this type of specific education and training would help you begin your ~~put you on a fast track to~~ a career in a legal office.

We ~~really~~ wish you ~~the best of~~ success in your job search and career.

ADA CARLTON, PERSONNEL MANAGER

lw

Chapter 14, Job 1

TO: All Nonattorney Staff

FROM: Management Team

DATE: May 1, 20—

SUBJECT: Confidentiality Issues

Recently we experienced a situation in which attorney/client confidentiality was breached by a member of our staff. The staff member told a caller that one of our attorneys was in court and who the attorney was representing. While you may explain that an attorney is in court, it is a violation of confidentiality to state the matter and especially the client's name.

Although you are all aware of confidentiality issues, we wanted to review some principles about the level of confidentiality expected of all members of our staff.

Sharing Client Names. This is a critical rule. Never tell who or what we represent to anyone without an attorney's permission.

Discussing work. Do not discuss the work you do here at the firm with *anyone*, even if you do not mention names. Do not discuss your work with your spouse, your family, your friends, or other colleagues. Additionally, do not discuss the work you are doing for a particular attorney with other staff members of the firm if they, themselves, are not also working on the matter.

Answering the phone. Again, you may tell a caller that an attorney is in court or at a deposition or a meeting, but never divulge the client's name or the nature of the court appearance, deposition, or meeting. Use discretion when an attorney is taking a late lunch or will arrive at the office late or has left the office early. Without understanding the full circumstances, callers may get the wrong impression if they are told at 2:30 that an attorney is at lunch or at 4:30 that an attorney has already left for the day.

Leaving your desk. When you are away from your desk, be aware of the papers and files left unattended and open on your desk. Also be conscientious at all times of what you leave on your computer screen. Clients or others may happen by your desk and see or read confidential information. Your workstations are your responsibility.

Finally, ~~As a final matter of discussion,~~ if you have any doubt about whether you should repeat a client's name or discuss an issue, don't. It is better to err on the side of not saying enough than saying too much. Also, ~~don't be afraid to~~ ask your attorney for guidance if you have questions regarding confidentiality.

AC:lw

Chapter 14, Job 2

Chapter 14, Job 3 (top-left)

Return-Path: acarlton@richardsarmonlaw.com
From: Ada Carlton
Date: 5 May 20-- 08:32:27
Subject: Summer CLE Opportunities
To: Nonattorney Staff

The Houston Bar Association (HBA) and the Houston Area Legal Support Staff Association (HALSSA) have issued their CLE schedules for the summer. The following are a few of the CLEs I wanted to highlight so you can make plans to attend:

HBA	May 31	5 p.m.	Managing Health Care with HMO's
HBA	June 1	7:15 a.m.	Tax law: Recent I.R.S. Rulings
HBA	July 10	6:30 p.m.	Review of Texas Rules of Civil Procedure
HBA	August 14	6:30 p.m.	Hospital Law: Review of Mondo v. City Hospital
HALSSA	June 8	8:30 a.m.	Computing in the Law Office: Database Managment
HALSSA	June 9	8:30 a.m.	Computing in the Law Office Accounting Software
HALSSA	July 17	5:45 p.m.	Dealing with Insurance Agents and ?
HALSSA	Aug. 21	5:45 p.m.	Effective Interviewing Techniques

Additional CLEs are offered by the HBA and the HALSSA; only a few were highlighted here. The times listed above are the start times of the sessions. Please make a note that some seminars last 1 hour; some all day. The database managment seminar would be especially helpful for those of you paralegals who manage large-document cases on databases. (or for those paralegals who)

As always, the firm will pay up to $500.00 per year for any non-attorney staff member's continuing legal education that is directly related to their job. Up to one-half of the cost (up to a maximum of $500.00 per year) for continuing legal education that is not directly related to a staff member's job will be paid by the firm. I really encourage staff members who have not attended CLEs to turn over a new leaf. The bottom line is that there is always something we can learn to keep our skills and knowledge of the law current.

For additional information or registration forms, please see myself.

AC:lw

consider furthering
their legal education

Chapter 14, Job 3

Chapter 14, Job 4 (top-right)

May 22 , 20—

Mr. Nicho Estephan
Houston Area Legal Support Staff Association
P.O. Box 13948
Houston, TX 77004-6591

Please reserve a seat at the upcoming CLEs for the following staff members of our firm. I have noted the members of your organization because they are entitled to receive a discount on the seminar fee.

June 8, Computing in the Law Office: Database Management

Names	Cost
Alberto Jiminez, member	$ 65
Zelda Ward	85

June 9, Computing in the Law Office: Accounting Software

Names	
Kiyoko Corr	85
Clay Metzgar	85
Zelda Ward	85

August 21, Effective Interviewing Techniques

Names	
Alberto Jiminez, member	85
Arnel Jolly	125
Janice McCarter, member	85
Total due	$700

Enclosed is our firm's check for $700. Please send a confirmation letter to my attention. Since the first seminar is only two weeks away, please send the confirmation by June 1.

ADA CARLTON, PERSONNEL MANAGER

lw

Enclosure

Chapter 14, Job 4

Chapter 15, Job 1 (bottom-left)

Best Natural Products Co.

Interoffice Communication

TO: All Personal (Personnel)

FROM: Sylvia

DATE: October 24, 20--

SUBJECT: Good Telephone Techniques

Because our voices are the first contacts that many individuals have with us outside the company, we should strive to make a good first impression when we answer the telephone. Please review the following suggestions for developing better telephone techniques:

TELEPHONE TECNIQUES (TECHNIQUES)

I. INCOMING CALLS

 A. Answer promptly.
 B. Greet the caller pleasantly.
 C. You should identify yourself and the company.
 D. Be helpful to the caller.
 E. Be curteous at all times.
 F. Screen calls as directed by your manager or myself.
 G. Write messages accurately and so they are legible.
 H. Let the caller end the call.

II. MAKING OUTGOING CALLS (OR I. MAKING INCOMING CALLS
   II. MAKING OUTGOING CALLS)

 A. Be sure of the number.
 B. Plan your call.
  1. Know what you are going to discuss.
  2. You should gather any related materials before placing the call.
 C. Let the phone ring several times before hanging up.
 D. Identify yourself.
 E. Be aware of Time zone differences. (or Recognize)
 F. Be considerate.

Chapter 15, Job 1

Chapter 15, Job 2 (bottom-right)

Best Natural Products Co.

1402 Graham Road
Bryan, TX 77801-4128
Telephone: (409) 555-0136

INVOICE

Mrs. Nancy Rosenbloom
219 Ortiz Drive
Groves, TX 77619-3120

Date: October 25, 20--

Order No.: BH090190
Date Shipped: October 25, 20--
Shipped Via: UPS
Terms: 2/10, n/30

Quantity	No.	Description	Unit Price	Total
2	LA-6180	Liquid Cleanser	3.30	6.60
1	NB-90010	Laundry Concentrate, 10 lb	19.95	19.95
2	ST-8011G	Concentrated Fabric Softener	5.10	10.20
		Total		36.75
		Sales Tax		2.21
		Total Amount		38.96

Chapter 15, Job 2

1402 Graham Road
Bryan, TX 77801-4128
Telephone: (409) 555-0136

INVOICE

Kwai San Restaurant
427 Center Street
Lufkin, TX 75901-1200

Date: October 25, 20--

Order No.: BH090191
Date Shipped: October 25, 20--
Shipped Via: UPS
Terms: 2/10, n/30

Quantity	No.	Description	Unit Price	Total
10	BD-7307	Automatic Dishwashing Concentrate, 47 oz	8.95	89.50
1	BH-5565G	Concentrated Cleaner, 5 gal	97.20	97.20
5	BG-2240	Germicide	11.85	59.25
12	AE-2349	Scouring Cleanser	4.75	~~57.00~~ 4.75
		Total		~~250.70~~ 302.95
		Sales Tax		~~15.04~~ 18.18
		Total Amount		~~265.74~~ 321.13

Chapter 15, Job 2 (cont'd)

October 25, 20--

Mrs. Nancy Rosenbloom
219 Ortiz Drive
Groves, TX 77619-3120

Dear Mrs. Rosenbloom

~~I am writing this letter to tell you that~~ your telephone order of October 25 is being shipped by UPS today.

Thank you for your interest in our nonpolluting and biodegradable cleaning products and our water purification system. Our cleaning products are not only throughly effective and safe for cleaning but also safe for the environment.

The quality of water is one of the most important choices we have to make today. Our company is working on the development of a water purifying system that is economical, spacesaving, and will be easy to operate. The system should be available in about 6 months. ~~A brochure will be sent to you under separate cover in the near future.~~ We will send a brochure to you this week.

Mrs. Rosenbloom, we do appreciate your business. Any time you have questions about our products, please ~~do not hesitate to~~ call us using our toll-free number, 800-555-012?

Sincerely yours,

Cyrus A. Gerhart
Customer Service

kr   ## Chapter 15, Job 3

October 25, 20--

Mr. Hank W. Loran
1735 North 16 Street
Lake Jackson, TX 77566-9800

Dear Hank:

You are both my friend and my valued customer. That is why I find it embarrassing to have to write to you about your overdue account.

When you applied for credit, I extended it to you on the basis of your credit report. The history on your account reflects that until recently it has been classified as "prompt pay." Now it is in jeopardy of being placed in the "slow pay" category.

Why you have not paid is puzzling to me. You must have a good reason, and I want to find out what that reason is. Please use this opportunity to explain and to let me help you work something out. Otherwise, your "prompt pay" rating will be in danger.

To retain your good credit reputation, you must send a check today for $280.48, the amount that is now more than 60 days overdue.

Sincerely yours,

Carl Barr
Credit Manager

Chapter 15, Job 4

Appendix

Frequently Misspelled Words

absence	congratulations	extension	miniature	recommend
accidentally	conscientious	familiar	miscellaneous	reference
accommodate	conscious	fascinate	mortgage	regard
accumulate	consensus	February	nickel	relevant
achievement	convenience	fluctuating	ninth	reminiscent
acknowledgment	coordinate	foreign	noticeable	repetition
advantageous	copyright	foreigner	occasionally	representative
amateur	courteous	forty	occurrence	responsible
analysis	criticism	fulfill	omitted	restaurant
analyst	debtor	grammar	opportunity	rhythm
analyze	definitely	gratitude	optional	schedule
announcement	dependable	height	pamphlet	separate
annual	develop	immediately	parallel	similar
apologize	development	implemented	particularly	sponsored
arrangement	dominant	independent	permanent	strictly
bankruptcy	efficiency	ingredient	permissible	sufficient
beginning	eligible	insistent	perseverance	surprise
benefited	eliminate	insurance	persuade	symmetrical
brochure	embarrass	integral	precede	technique
bulletin	emphasize	itinerary	prerequisite	temperament
calendar	employee	judgment	privilege	therefore
category	enthusiasm	knowledgeable	procedure	thoroughly
changeable	entrepreneur	leisure	productivity	transferred
commitment	environment	liaison	programmer	unanimous
committee	equipped	license	psychology	undoubtedly
compatible	exaggerate	management	pursuit	usable
competitive	experience	managing	receiving	valuable
concession	explanation	merchandise	recognize	waive

Two-Letter State Abbreviations

Alabama, AL	Illinois, IL	Nebraska, NE	South Carolina, SC
Alaska, AK	Indiana, IN	Nevada, NV	South Dakota, SD
Arizona, AZ	Iowa, IA	New Hampshire, NH	Tennessee, TN
Arkansas, AR	Kansas, KS	New Jersey, NJ	Texas, TX
California, CA	Kentucky, KY	New Mexico, NM	Utah, UT
Colorado, CO	Louisiana, LA	New York, NY	Vermont, VT
Connecticut, CT	Maine, ME	North Carolina, NC	Virgin Islands, VI
Delaware, DE	Maryland, MD	North Dakota, ND	Virginia, VA
District of Columbia, DC	Massachusetts, MA	Ohio, OH	Washington, WA
Florida, FL	Michigan, MI	Oklahoma, OK	West Virginia, WV
Georgia, GA	Minnesota, MN	Oregon, OR	Wisconsin, WI
Guam, GU	Mississippi, MS	Pennsylvania, PA	Wyoming, WY
Hawaii, HI	Missouri, MO	Puerto Rico, PR	
Idaho, ID	Montana, MT	Rhode Island, RI	

Common Prepositions

about	but	near	than
above	by	next	through
across			throughout
after	concerning	of	to
against	considering	off	toward (s)
along		on	
among	despite	onto	under
around	down	opposite	underneath
as	during	out	unlike
at		outside	until
	except	over	unto
before			up
behind	for	past	upon
below	from	per	
beneath		plus	
beside	in		with
besides	inside	regarding	within
between	into	respecting	without
beyond			
	like	since	

INDEX

Bold numbers reference key terms in the text. *Italic* entries refer to words discussed as words.

run-in headings and, 83
   styles for correspondence, 74
parallel construction, **243**–245
parentheses, 58, 149, 183
participial phrases, 156
passive voice, **231**–232
percents, 57
periods, 147–**148**
   in abbreviations, 21, 23, 26
   with quotation marks, 178–179
personal names. *See also* names
   abbreviations for, 22
   capitalization of, 196
   in correspondence, 74–75
   spelling of, 214
personal titles, 22. *See also* titles
   capitalization of, 196–197
   for correspondence, 73–75
   word division and, 41
phrases, clauses *vs.*, 154
place names. *See* addresses
plagiarism, 178
possessive case nouns, 176–178
possessive case pronouns, 115, **117**–118,
   176–178
postscript, 76
predicate, **97**–98
prefixes, 40, 198
prepositions, **116**, 198
   of, 129
   lists following, 174
   with numbers, 59
   phrases, 156
product names, 199
professional titles, 22–23, 196–197.
     See also titles
pronouns, **97**
   agreement with antecedents,
     113–115
   appositives used for, 160
   cases of, **115**–119
   complements as, 98
   dangling modifiers and, 242
   gender-neutral, 120
   indefinite, **103**, 114–115
proofreading, defined, **1**
proofreading symbols, **1**, 10–11
   for abbreviations, 22
   for capitalization, 195
   for commas, 149
   for errors of addition, 6
   for format errors, 70
   methods of, 3–4, 6
   for numerical expression, 51
   for punctuation, 148, 171

to query authors, 113
   for word division, 38
proper adjectives, 197–198
proper nouns, 41, 197–201
P.S. (postscript), 76
punctuation, 149
   abbreviations with, 26
   apostrophes, 176–178
   brackets, 183–184
   for clarification, 171–172
   colons, 173–175, 182
   commas, 58, 150–160, 178–179
   dashes, 40, 181
   exclamation points, 147–**149,**
     178–179
   italics, 180–181
   pairs of symbols, 183
   parentheses, 58, 183
   periods, 21, 23, 26, 147–**148,**
     178–179
   question marks, 147– **148**, 178–179
   quotation marks, 178–179
   semicolons, 153, 172–173, 182
   styles, for business letters, 77–78
   terminal, 147–149, 178–179
   underscore, 180–181

Q

quadruple space (QS), 72
quantities, verbs and, 102
querying authors, 214, 216
question marks, 147– **148**, 178–179
quotation marks, 149, 178–179
quotations, 153
   brackets within, 184
   capitalization for, 195
   colons for, 174
   dashes for, 182
   ethical use of, 178

R

reading aloud, 6
redundant expressions, 229–230
reference initials, 75, 175
reference line, 74
references, 83–84
reflexive pronouns, **118**
regardless, 138
regular hyphens, **37**
reports, format for, 82–87
restrictive elements. *See* essential
   elements
retroactive to, 138
rough drafts, 10–11
round numbers, 52. *See also* numbers

run-in enumeration, 183
run-in headings, 83
run-on sentences, **104**–105

S

salutation, 73, 175
season names, 200
semicolons, 172–173
   dashes *vs.*, 182
   to separate elements in a series, 153
sentence fragments, **104**
sentences
   beginning with numbers, 52
   capitalization in, 195–198
   structure of, 97–98, 104–105,
     154–158, 172–173
serial numbers, 58
series, elements in a, 153
shortened word forms, 25
sic, 184
side headings, 83, 180
similar words, distinguishing between,
   129–137
simple sentences, **154**–155
simple subject, **97**
simplified style, for correspondence,
   77–78
smart quote style, 179
soft hyphens, **37**
source document, **3**
spacing
   abbreviations with, 21, 26
   in correspondence, 79
   following terminal punctuation, 148
   hard spaces, **38**
spelling errors, 4, 12
state names, 24, 152
stet, 10
style sheets, **86**
subjective case pronouns, 115–116
subject lines, for correspondence, 74
subjects, **97**
   clauses, 157
   compound, **99**–100
   implied, 156
   normal *vs.* inverted order of, 101
   verb agreement, 99–104
suffixes, 40, 198
syllables, word division between, 37–39
symbols, 25, 57. *See also* punctuation

T

table of contents, 84
team proofreading, 3, 52
technical material, 56